Contents

Introduction   iv

GNVQ Foundation Health and Social Care: Summary of units   ix

Core skills: Summary of units at Level 1   x

Chapter 1   Understanding Health and Well-being   1

Chapter 2   Understanding Personal Development and Relationships   37

Chapter 3   Investigating Working in Health and Social Care   75

Chapter 4   Contributing to a Team Activity   111

Chapter 5   Investigating Common Health Emergencies   137

Chapter 6   Planning Diets   177

Chapter 7   Exploring Health and Recreational Activities   211

Chapter 8   Exploring Physical Care   239

Chapter 9   Investigating Health and Care Service Provision   269

Appendix A: Glossary   299

Appendix B: Bibliography   303

Appendix C: Answers to Test Yourself questions   304

Index   307

Introduction

What is a GNVQ?

A General National Vocational Qualification (GNVQ) is an alternative to A-levels or GCSEs. There are three levels:

- **Foundation GNVQ** – equivalent to four GCSEs at grades D-G, normally one year of full-time study
- **Intermediate GNVQ** – equivalent to four GCSEs at grades A-C, normally one year of full-time study
- **Advanced GNVQ** – equivalent to two A-levels, normally two years of full-time study.

How is a GNVQ structured?

All GNVQ courses are made up of **units**:

- **mandatory vocational units** – those you **must** study
- **optional vocational units** – those you **choose** to study
- **mandatory core skills units** in **Communication**, **Information Technology** and **Application of Number** – not studied as separate units, but taught and tested in the activities and assignments on the vocational units.

What is in a unit?
Let us take Unit 1 of the Foundation GNVQ in Health and Social Care as an example in the diagram below.

1 Unit title

Unit 1 Understanding health and well-being

2 Each unit is divided into **elements** (usually two or three) – this is the first element in this unit

Element 1.1: Plan how to improve health and well-being

A student must:
1 describe the main factors which contribute to good health and well-being
2 identify reasons for improving own health and well-being
3 suggest ways to improve own health and well-being
4 prepare a plan for improving own health and well-being
5 present the plan clearly

3 Each element is divided into **performance criteria.** These describe all the things for which you must be able to provide **evidence** that you can do.

4 The **range** explains the areas you will need to cover for each performance criterion. For example, the areas listed under 'Main factors' relate to performance criterion 1 above

RANGE
Main factors: diet (nutritional content, balanced), exercise (frequency, types), recreational activities (intellectual, physical, social)
Reasons: increased mobility, increased self-esteem, reduced risks to health and well-being
Ways to improve health and well-being: balanced diet, improved level of fitness, increased participation in recreational activities
Plan to include: diet, recreational activities, fitness/exercise; identifying present habits, setting of targets for improvements, ways to improve

5 The **evidence indicators** describe the minimum **evidence** that you will need to supply to satisfy all the requirements of this element. Your tutor will advise you about other evidence you can include

EVIDENCE INDICATORS
A plan for improving own health and well-being covering one week. The plan should be presented clearly and should identify reasons for improvements and describe the main factors which contribute to good health and well-being.

What is the Foundation GNVQ in Health and Social Care?

It is made up of:
- **three mandatory vocational units**
  Unit 1: Understanding Health and Well-being
  Unit 2: Understanding Personal Development and Relationships
  Unit 3: Investigating Working in Health and Social Care
- **six optional vocational units**
  Unit 4: Contributing to a Team Activity
  Unit 5: Investigating Common Health Emergencies
  Unit 6: Planning Diets
  Unit 7: Exploring Health and Recreational Activities
  Unit 8: Exploring Physical Care
  Unit 9: Investigating Health and Care Service Provision

At Foundation level you should choose **three** optional units to study. You can choose these from any of the vocational units from any Foundation GNVQ course offered at your school or college. You may only choose a maximum of two units entitled 'Unit 3: Investigating working in ...' and you may not choose two units with identical titles.

What do the units cover?

- **Unit 1: Understanding Health and Well-being**
  – The main factors that contribute to good health
  – Risks to good health and how to reduce them
  – Your own health and how to improve it
- **Unit 2: Understanding Personal Development and Relationships**
  – The main stages of personal development
  – The influence of personal relationships
  – Relationships between clients and carers
- **Unit 3: Investigating Working in Health and Social Care**
  – Employment opportunities, the skills and qualifications required
  – A study of two jobs
  – Finding and applying for a job
- **Unit 4: Contributing to a Team Activity**
  – Developing skills in team work: planning an activity, carrying it out and reviewing it
  – The role of the individual in a team, including one-to-one reviewing between individual students and tutors
  Any team activity undertaken for any of the other vocational units will provide evidence for this unit.
- **Unit 5: Investigating Common Health Emergencies**
  – Hazards in care settings and how to reduce them
  – How to deal with common health emergencies
- **Unit 6: Planning Diets**
  – The importance of a balanced diet
  – Special diets
  – Planning diets to meet the needs of different people
- **Unit 7: Exploring Health and Recreational Activities**
  – The importance of recreational activities to health
  – A survey of local recreational facilities
  – How recreational activities meet the needs of different people

- **Unit 8: Exploring Physical Care**
  - How physical assistance is provided
  - The types of physical aid available
  - The importance of maintaining a client's independence and dignity while providing physical assistance
- **Unit 9: Investigating Health and Social Care Provision**
  - The organisation of health and social care services, locally and nationally
  - How clients gain access to services
  - How information is communicated to clients

How is a GNVQ assessed?

External assessment

Written tests on the three mandatory units are set by either BTEC, RSA or City & Guilds. They are either multiple-choice or short-answer questions. Each test lasts for about one hour and the pass mark is 70 per cent.

Internal assessment

This will take place at your school or college. Your **assessors** will probably be your teachers. Their assessments are checked by **verifiers** (internal and external) to ensure that the assessments agree with national standards.

Assessment is based on showing the assessor what you have achieved. You will need to compile a **portfolio** of relevent **evidence** of your achievements. Your assessor will advise whether you have provided enough evidence to pass a unit, and how to provide any missing evidence.

You may complete the units one by one. There is no time limit on gaining your GNVQ – you can resit external tests and resubmit your portfolio as often as you like to reach the required standard.

What grades are there?

For each unit completed, you will obtain a **pass**.

To obtain the GNVQ, you must pass all the required units and written tests, including the core skills. The grades for the GNVQ are: **pass**, **merit** or **distinction**. These depend on the quality of your evidence, particularly evidence of:
- **planning**
- **information-seeking and information-handling**
- **evaluation**
- **quality of outcomes.**

Your tutors will explain these skills.

What if I don't agree with an assessment?

You may appeal against an assessment. Every school and college **must** have an appeals procedure to deal with this. You are entitled to a copy of this at the beginning of your course.

Creating your portfolio

A portfolio is a record of your achievements during your course. It will demonstrate to your assessors that you have achieved the relevant skills, knowledge and understanding to gain your GNVQ.

Store your written evidence in an A4 ring-binder divided into sections for each unit you are studying. The portfolio should include forms to be completed by your assessor relating to your evidence.

It will need an **index** as a single piece of evidence may be useful for more than one unit or element. Devise a coding system so that you can cross-reference evidence to more than one unit in the index. The index should include evidence that is not in the ring-binder, such as video or audio tapes, large drawings, maps, etc., which you will need to keep separately.

Types of evidence

- **Performance** or **direct evidence**, for example, reports, assignments, an assessor's written report or a written observation of something you have done.
- **Supplementary** or **indirect evidence**, for example, photographs, videos, audio tapes, evidence of written or oral questioning and practical tests, references from workplace supervisors.

All evidence should arise from the work you have agreed to complete during discussions with your assessor. How much and what sort of evidence will also be discussed and should form the basis of your **individual action plan** (see pages 126-8) for an activity or assignment.

> **Remember**
> - When planning any activity, think carefully about which **vocational** and **core skills** units, elements, performance criteria and range statements you can cover. **Remember that a piece of work can provide evidence for more than one element or unit.** For example, a leaflet on healthy eating would be far better produced using a computer, than handwritten.
> - Present your portfolio in a professional way.
> - The evidence should be **sufficient** (enough), **authentic** (your own work) and **relevant** (test what the performance criteria asks to be tested).
> - The assessor and verifiers should find the portfolio easy to read, understand and access. The index should identify what the evidence refers to.
> - The documentation should be easy to read.
> - You should know exactly what is in your portfolio as you will be asked questions about it by the assessor and the verifiers.

How to use this book

Each of the nine chapters in this book deals with one of the nine vocational units of the Foundation GNVQ in Health and Social Care.

There are activities thoughout the chapters and assignments at the end of each chapter. The chart on page ix lists the unit and element titles, and the activities and assignments which relate to them. The activities and assignments offer opportunities to provide evidence for the core skills (see page x).

Test yourself questions

These are at the end of each chapter. They will check your understanding of what you have read. The answers are in Appendix C.

Key words

Some key words and phrases are printed in CAPITALS. They are listed at the end of each chapter and explained in Appendix A.

GNVQ Foundation Health and Social Care: Summary of units and elements

This summary shows how the activities and assignments relate to the units and elements. By keeping a record of your work, many of these exercises will generate useful evidence for your portfolio.

MANDATORY UNITS	Activities	Assignments
1 Understanding health and well-being		
1.1 Plan how to improve health and well-being	1.1–1.4	A1.1
1.2 Investigate risks to health	1.5–1.11	A1.2
2 Understanding personal development and relationships		
2.1 Investigate personal development	2.1–2.15	A2.1
2.2 Explore personal relationships	2.16–2.19	A2.2
2.3 Explore relationships between clients and carers	2.20	A2.3
3 Investigating working in health and social care		
3.1 Investigate working in health and social care services in the UK	3.1–3.5	A3.1
3.2 Investigate jobs in health and social care	3.6–3.8	A3.2
3.3 Plan for employment in health and social care	3.10–3.11	A3.3
OPTIONAL UNITS		
4 Contributing to a team activity		
4.1 Plan an activity with a team	4.1–4.7, 7.8	A6.1, A7.1, A9.1
4.2 Undertake a role in a team activity	4.8, 4.9, 7.8	
4.3 Review the activity	4.10–4.13	
5 Investigating common health emergencies		
5.1 Investigate key health and safety factors in care settings	5.1–5.12	A5.1
5.2 Explore common health emergencies in care settings	5.13–5.26	A5.2
5.3 Investigate emergency care procedures		
6 Planning diets		
6.1 Explore the main features of a healthy diet	6.1, 6.2	A6.1
6.2 Investigate balanced diets for clients with different needs	6.3–6.5	A6.2
6.3 Plan and cost diets	6.6	A6.3
7 Exploring health and recreational activities		
7.1 Investigate health and recreational activities	7.1–7.7	A7.1
7.2 Survey the use of local recreational activities	7.8	
7.3 Suggest recreational activities for clients with specific needs	7.9	
8 Exploring physical care		
8.1 Investigate the provision of physical assistance	8.1–8.12	A8.1
8.2 Investigate the use of aids to physical care	8.13	A8.2
8.3 Investigate how aids to physical care help maintain independence	8.14–8.17	A8.3
9 Investigating health and social care provision		
9.1 Investigate the organisation of health and care services	9.1–9.3	A9.1
9.2 Investigate access to health and care services	9.4–9.7	A9.2
9.3 Investigate communicating information in health and care	9.8–9.10	A9.1, A9.3

Core skills: Summary of units at level 1

This summary shows how the activities and assignments provide opportunities for evidence of the core skills.

Core skills	Activities	Assignments
Communication		
1.1 Take part in discussions	1.1, 1.4, 1.7, 2.1, 2.2, 2.3, 2.6, 2.8, 2.11, 2.15, 2.17, 3.5, 3.8, 3.11, 4.1, 4.3, 4.6, 4.7, 6.6, 7.7, 7.9, 8.8, 8.13, 8.17, 9.2, 9.3, 9.4, 9.6, 9.7	A2.1, A3.1, A5.1, A7.1, A8.2, A9.1, A9.2, A9.3
1.2 Produce written material	1.2, 1.3, 2.1, 2.2, 2.3, 2.11, 2.15, 3.3, 3.5, 3.8, 3.11, 4.1, 4.3, 4.4, 4.6, 4.7, 4.9, 5.3, 6.5, 6.6, 7.1, 7.3, 7.4, 7.5, 7.9, 8.3, 8.4, 8.17	A1.1, A2.1, A2.2, A2.3, A3.1, A3.2, A3.3, A5.1, A5.2, A6.1, A7.1, A8.1, A8.2, A8.3, A9.1, A9.2, A9.3
1.3 Use images	2.1, 2.2, 2.3, 3.11, 4.3, 4.7, 4.9, 5.9, 7.8, 7.9, 8.4, 8.17	A1.1, A3.1, A6.1, A7.1, A9.3
1.4 Read and respond to written materials	2.2, 2.3, 3.2, 3.8, 3.11, 4.1, 4.3, 4.4, 4.7, 4.9, 5.3, 5.9, 7.3, 7.7, 7.8, 8.3, 8.4, 8.8, 8.13, 8.17, 9.1, 9.3, 9.5, 9.9	A1.1, A1.2, A2.3, A3.1, A6.1, A7.1, A8.1, A8.3
Information technology		
1.1 Prepare information	1.5, 2.2, 3.11, 4.3, 4.6, 4.7, 4.9, 4.12, 6.1, 6.6, 8.17	A1.1, A1.2, A2.1, A2.3, A3.1, A3.3, A5.1, A7.1, A9.1, A9.3
1.2 Process information	1.5, 3.11, 4.3, 4.6, 4.7, 4.9, 4.12, 6.1, 6.6, 8.17	A1.1, A1.2, A2.1, A2.3, A3.1, A3.3, A5.1, A7.1, A9.1, A9.3
1.3 Present information	1.5, 2.2, 3.11, 4.3, 4.6, 4.7, 4.9, 4.12, 6.1, 6.6, 8.17	A1.1, A1.2, A2.1, A2.3, A3.1, A3.3, A5.1, A7.1, A9.1, A9.3
1.4 Evaluate the use of information technology	4.7, 4.9, 6.1, 6.6	A3.1, A3.3, A7.1, A9.1
Application of number		
1.1 Collect and record data	1.3, 1.4, 1.5, 2.1, 2.5, 4.3, 4.7, 4.8, 4.12, 6.1, 6.6, 7.4, 7.7, 8.3	A3.1, A6.3
1.2 Tackle problems	1.4, 4.3, 4.7, 4.8, 4.12, 6.1, 6.2, 6.6, 8.3, 9.8	A6.3
1.3 Interpret and present data	1.5, 2.2, 2.5, 4.3, 4.7, 4.8, 4.12, 6.1, 6.2, 6.3, 6.6, 8.3	

CHAPTER 1

Understanding Health and Well-being

What is covered in this chapter

- Planning how to improve health and well-being
- Investigating risks to health

These are the resources that you will need for your Understanding Health and Well-being portfolio:
- your written answers to the activities in this chapter
- your written answers to the Test Yourself questions at the end of this chapter
- your completed assignments: A1.1 and A1.2.

Introduction

The first part of this chapter focuses on the factors which contribute to good health. You will look at your own health and well-being, the food you eat, the exercise you take, and the recreational activities you enjoy. You will then present a plan of how to improve your health and well-being.

The second half of the chapter looks at:
- basic health needs
- the main risks to health and how to reduce them
- the effect that major changes may have on health and well-being and how people cope with these changes.

Planning how to improve health and well-being

People in the UK are living longer but, if you look at the numbers of people who die from preventable causes, it is clear that the situation could be better.

What contributes to good health and well-being?

The World Health Organisation describes health as:

'A state of complete physical, mental and social well-being and not merely the absence of disease or infirmity.'

In other words, health is not just being free of illness or disability (physical health). It also includes mental and social well-being.

But what is well-being? It is not easy to define. It describes how you feel about yourself. It includes your relationships with other people that contribute to your own 'feel good' factor.

Activity 1.1

a Spend a few minutes with colleagues trying to define what health and well-being mean to you.

1

b Check how your ideas match up to the World Health Organisation's description of health above.

We will consider the following three main factors that contribute to health and well-being:

Recreational activities

Diet → **Health and well-being** ← Exercise

Activity 1.2

Make a list of ways that you think diet, exercise and recreational activity affect both physical and mental well-being.

Come back to this activity after reading the chapter and decide whether you need to alter your list.

Which of these people is not healthy?

All the people above could be healthy. There is nothing in the pictures to prove that they are not. It is important for you to realise that health and well-being is not about being super-fit, never eating junk food or never drinking alcohol. It is about maintaining a **balance** to meet your **individual needs**.

But why do I need to think about it now?
Most of you reading this will be teenagers and may not be too worried now about ill-health that shows up later, in middle age. However, it is important to consider all aspects of your health now in order to prevent later problems.

Diet

One of the commonest problems in the UK is a poor diet. This can be from over-eating and not getting the balance of nutrients right. You should monitor your diet now because:

- The damage caused by a poor diet may not be obvious, but it accumulates to cause ill-health in later years.
- Your current eating habits are just that – habits. You have a pattern of eating that may or may not be a good one. If you educate yourself into good eating habits now, they should stay with you into middle age.

A good diet now can be very beneficial in your later life.

Good diet is not just about physical dangers. There are also risks to a person's **self-image** (how they see themselves). People who are overweight, under-weight, anaemic or have rotten teeth may well feel unhappy about themselves and the way they look. This may affect their behaviour and also their general health.

Chapter 6 provides more information about the role of diet in health and well-being.

Exercise

Does exercise really matter?

Watch any international athletics meeting and you will see some people who look very muscular and fit. Others are thin and appear to have little muscle yet they are able to run long distance races. In both cases the athletes are very fit and exercise regularly. The types of exercise they do depend on their choice of sport: for example, the training that a shot-putter does is quite different to that of a distance runner.

Most of us will never become international athletes and we will never have to exercise as much as they do. But even if we do not want to be extremely fit, it is still important to exercise. If you exercise regularly, it helps to keep your body in efficient working order.

How to exercise

It is important to consider the best way to exercise. The first thing to recognise is that the type and pattern of exercise needs to fit in with your lifestyle. Most people fail to maintain an exercise programme because they are not prepared to make a major change in their lifestyle.

To be really useful, exercise has to be taken **regularly**. This is very important because:

- Increased fitness takes time to develop.
- Exercising only occasionally puts an unfair strain on your body and does not give it time to adapt to the increased activity.

Exercise has to be **planned** so that there is a build-up to a maximum level. To attempt to jog five miles on the first day is asking for failure. To build up to five miles over several weeks causes less physical and mental strain.

The mental strain is something that we all face when starting any new routine. By exercising regularly you fall into a pattern where you are mentally ready for the activity. It becomes a pleasurable activity as you increase fitness. This is where it is easier to plan exercise that fits into your lifestyle.

It is often easier for people to plan to exercise together as each person can support the others with encouragement to continue. It is also more enjoyable to exercise with friends.

The 'quick fix' exercise routine
It seems that every year there is a new trend in exercise routines. A new, miracle method of exercising is developed that will get you fit in half the time! Often the adverts will be endorsed by people who say the routine or equipment worked for them. These systems all prey on our own desires to get fit without having to work at it.

There are **no** ways of exercising that do not involve effort from you. Every new system is likely to work for some people who find the routine acceptable and can adapt their lifestyles to the activity. For others, who want the cure without the work, the new routine is a failure.

Activity 1.3

a There are more exercise bikes stored in cupboards and cellars than are ever used regularly. Why do you think this is?

b Aerobics groups have been very successful in helping people to maintain regular exercise. Why do you think aerobics have been so successful?

c Devise a simple questionnaire to find out:
- what exercise 'gadgets' people have bought
- how successful they were
- what exercise routines have been successful.

Look at the results. Are there any common features with successful regular exercise routines? Displaying your results in the form of a table or charts will help here. Use a computer if you can.

Types of exercise

There are many exercise programmes and equipment advertised. But exercise does not necessarily require specific equipment. What exercise does involve is increasing muscle activity with the associated improvements in the respiratory and circulatory systems (lungs and heart).

There are two basic types of exercise:
- **Aerobic exercise** Aerobic means 'with oxygen'. This type of exercise works the heart, lungs and muscles in such a way that there is sufficient oxygen supplied to meet the needs of the muscles. The aim is to work at 90 per cent efficiency. In other words, the exercise should not go to a stage where muscles are not receiving enough oxygen. Aerobic exercise includes:
  – swimming
  – running
  – cycling
  and, of course, aerobics.
- **Anaerobic exercise** Anaerobic means 'without oxygen'. This involves stretching and contracting muscles in a slow, controlled way. When a muscle

is being held in a contracted form, the blood supply is temporarily reduced. In such situations energy is generated without using oxygen. As soon as the blood supply returns oxygen is again available. Anaerobic exercise include:
– yoga
– general stretch work
– isometric routines (contracting muscles without causing movement).

Anaerobic situations also occur during aerobic exercise when the activity continues beyond the ability of the heart and lungs to supply oxygen. Being out of breath and needing to breath deeply for several minutes after stopping exercise is an indication that anaerobic conditions have occurred.

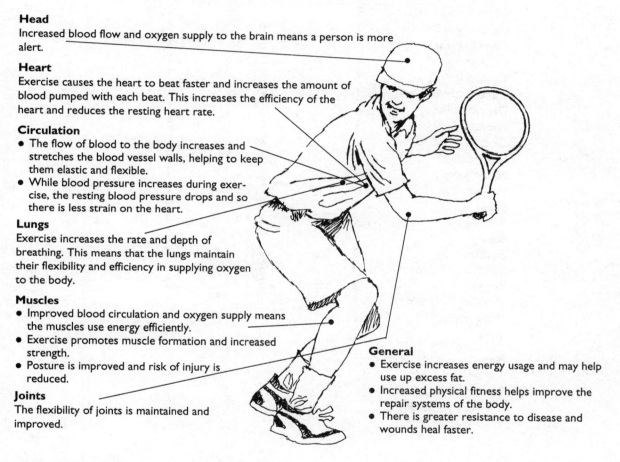

Head
Increased blood flow and oxygen supply to the brain means a person is more alert.

Heart
Exercise causes the heart to beat faster and increases the amount of blood pumped with each beat. This increases the efficiency of the heart and reduces the resting heart rate.

Circulation
• The flow of blood to the body increases and stretches the blood vessel walls, helping to keep them elastic and flexible.
• While blood pressure increases during exercise, the resting blood pressure drops and so there is less strain on the heart.

Lungs
Exercise increases the rate and depth of breathing. This means that the lungs maintain their flexibility and efficiency in supplying oxygen to the body.

Muscles
• Improved blood circulation and oxygen supply means the muscles use energy efficiently.
• Exercise promotes muscle formation and increased strength.
• Posture is improved and risk of injury is reduced.

Joints
The flexibility of joints is maintained and improved.

General
• Exercise increases energy usage and may help use up excess fat.
• Increased physical fitness helps improve the repair systems of the body.
• There is greater resistance to disease and wounds heal faster.

The benefits of exercise

Different exercise strategies
International athletes provide good models for the benefits of different exercise strategies. A weight-lifter, for example, needs great strength, while a marathon runner needs stamina and a gymnast needs suppleness. Each needs to exercise regularly but in a different way.

If you want to become fitter without concentrating on any particular sport, it is useful to exercise to develop:

- stamina
- strength
- suppleness.

The table below lists some activities and their importance in developing stamina, strength and suppleness.

The benefits of various physical activities

Activity	Stamina rating	Suppleness rating	Strength rating
Badminton	2	3	2
Canoeing	3	2	3
Climbing stairs	3	1	2
Cricket	1	2	1
Cycling (hard)	4	2	3
Dancing (ballroom)	1	3	1
Dancing (disco)	3	4	1
Football	3	3	3
Golf	1	2	1
Gymnastics	2	4	3
Hillwalking	3	1	2
Jogging	4	2	2
Judo	2	4	2
Rowing	4	2	4
Sailing	1	2	2
Squash	3	3	2
Swimming (hard)	4	4	4
Tennis	2	3	2
Walking (briskly)	2	1	1
Weightlifting	1	1	4
Yoga	1	4	1

Key
1 = no real effect
2 = beneficial effect
3 = very good effect
4 = excellent effect

Starting an exercise regime
It is best to start exercising slowly. This helps to:
- ensure that the exercise is aerobic
- reduce the risk of any strain injuries.

Aim to exercise for 20 minutes, three or four times a week. The exercise should be enough to increase the heart rate, but not so much that it does not return to its resting rate within about five minutes of stopping exercise.

Remember

When starting to exercise:

- warm up thoroughly
- start with gentle stretching to ensure that the muscles to be used are ready for the exercise
- avoid sudden changes of direction or jerky movements
- avoid exercises that put a strain on the lower back, such as sit-ups and double-leg raises. These may form part of a stricter exercise regime.

Whatever you do, try to make it enjoyable and to fit in with your lifestyle. For example, you could make it part of your routine to get off the bus to school or college two stops earlier than necessary and walk briskly. It is easy to do and helps to build-up stamina.

Activity 1.4

There are many tests that have been devised to determine physical fitness. Many involve detailed measurements and calculations. This activity will give you some idea of the level of exercise that will help you to improve your health.

Warning Do not attempt to carry out this activity if you know you have any breathing difficulties or heart disease. The activities are not dangerous, but it would be best to get medical advice about exercise routines.

a Work with a partner so that you can measure each other's pulse rate. You will need a watch with a second hand.

Together decide what you consider to be gentle exercise. (This may be as simple as walking steadily up stairs.)

b Before you start, measure your resting heart-beat by counting the heart-beats for 15 seconds using the pulse found in your wrist. Multiply the answer by four to get the beats per minute. Record this figure as resting pulse.

c Carry out your gentle exercise for 1 minute. Then record your heart-beat at 1-minute intervals until it gets back to the resting rate.

d Repeat the activity for longer periods of 2, 5 and 10 minutes (or possibly longer) until it takes more than 5 minutes for your pulse to return to its resting rate.

The last but one exercise level is the amount of exercise you should start off doing. The heart rate achieved is a guide as to the level you should work to.

e Using the result as a guide, start a programme of exercises three or four times a week. At the end of each exercise session, measure your maximum heart rate and the time taken to return to the resting rate.

Increase the amount of exercise to reach your maximum pulse that still returns to normal after 5 minutes rest. You should find that you are able to exercise more as you get fitter.

Exercise is good for you

Note The maximum heart rate that you should not exceed is calculated by subtracting your age from 220:

$$220 - \text{your age} = \text{maximum heart beats per minute.}$$

It is unlikely that you will approach this with the gentle exercises, but you should try to double your heart-beat during exercise.

Recreational activities

What you do as a break from work is important to your health and well-being. Recreational activities can be classified as those involving:
- **physical** exercise (see above)
- other people in a **social** setting
- **intellectual** activity.

Some activities may fall into more than one of these groups. For example:
- Dancing is a physical activity in a social setting.
- A quiz night is an intellectual activity in a social setting.

Recreation can overlap different classes of activity. Dancing involves exercise as well as being a social activity

The activities are all linked because they involve the development and maintenance of **physical**, **social** and **intellectual** well-being.

We have spent some time looking at physical activities. It is also important to consider social and intellectual activities. All three have an effect on reducing stress and increasing your mental well-being. The role of recreational activities is covered in greater detail in Chapter 7.

Relaxation and sleep
Whether these can be considered as recreational activities may be open to debate. However, they are both vital to health and well-being:
- During sleep and deep relaxation the body repairs itself.

- It is a time for growth to occur.
- Sleep involves dreaming. Even if you cannot remember your dreams, you do dream. This is a time when your brain appears to be processing information, and possibly supporting memory and learning. This is not really well understood. However, it is known that people deprived of dreaming sleep become physically and mentally ill.
- Sleep and relaxation also enable your muscles to be resupplied with nutrients to enable them to take on further exercise.
- Relaxation also helps to reduce stress. Stress is exhausting. It is important to deal with this exhaustion by making sure you get enough sleep and undertaking relaxing activities. For more about stress, see page 28.

What is enough sleep?
There is no precise answer to this question. Everyone's needs are different. Your need for sleep is determined by:
- your internal body clock
- your emotional state
- your level of stress
- your general well-being.

It is easier to say how much sleep is too little. This can be shown by the effect that lack of sleep has on you. It affects your ability to concentrate and, as a result, your ability to cope with the demands of the day.

Often you may find yourself in the situation where you feel physically tired, but cannot sleep because you are mentally alert. This is often an indication of your level of stress. To correct this you should try to reduce your stress levels and re-establish your correct sleep patterns.

Sleep patterns vary throughout life:
- Babies and young children need a lot of sleep but do so for short periods at a time and then wake.

Parents have to adapt to a new baby's sleep patterns

- As children grow up into adulthood, they need less sleep and soon a regular sleep pattern is established – they sleep for an average of about 8 hours at night, and remain awake during the day. However, some adults still have a sleep pattern of 'cat napping' during the day, and need little sleep at night.
- In old age, the pattern of early childhood can return – short periods of sleep followed by periods of being awake. This is normal and should be recognised by those working in caring sitations.

Developing a plan to improve health and well-being

If you have worked through the chapter this far, you will already have started to look at your own health and well-being. You will also have thought about some of the ways in which you can improve your current health.

Before you undertake any HEALTH PLAN, you should understand the benefits of improving it. These can be summarised as:

- **increased mobility** as a result of increased exercise and an improved diet. Weight loss may improve your flexibility and mobility, while weight gain (if you are underweight) may increase your general energy level and again improve your mobility.
- **improved SELF-ESTEEM** If you do something about the phrase: 'I'm too . . . (fat/thin/unfit/etc.)' you will feel better about yourself.
- **reduced risks to health,** particularly those that show up in later life. The big killers of middle age – heart disease and smoking-related diseases – often come from poor habits in earlier years. Changes to your diet, exercise routines and other habits now will be beneficial to you in later life.

Monitoring your recreational activities may help you to identify possible dangers to your well-being that can be addressed now. Habits are easier to establish than they are to get rid of. Assignment A1.1 is designed to help you plan to improve your health (see page 33).

Investigating RISKS TO HEALTH

So far you have studied yourself and some of the factors that help promote your health and well-being. We now need to look at risks to the health of people in general. By identifying the risks we hope you will be able to avoid them and also help people you work with avoid the dangers.

Basic health needs of individuals

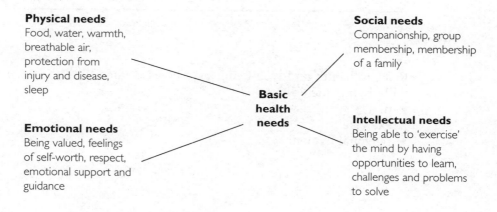

Physical needs
Food, water, warmth, breathable air, protection from injury and disease, sleep

Emotional needs
Being valued, feelings of self-worth, respect, emotional support and guidance

Basic health needs

Social needs
Companionship, group membership, membership of a family

Intellectual needs
Being able to 'exercise' the mind by having opportunities to learn, challenges and problems to solve

How are these needs are expressed and met in different groups of people? The table opposite explains.

Basic needs do not change. The differences are in the **ability** of an individual to provide for him or her own needs. Put another way, people need different amounts and types of support to meet their needs throughout life.

Different needs also have differing importance:
- The need for food and shelter and water are essential to stay alive.
- The next important need is for safety.
- Having achieved the first two, a person is in need of emotional and social support.
- Only when all these needs have been met is it realistic to consider needs for self-respect and self-esteem and, finally, personal fulfilment.

For example, if you consider people who are starving, they may take risks or degrade themselves by things that they would not do if they were fully-fed. Their primary need is for food and only later can they consider their own self-respect. This 'hierarchy of needs' was described by a researcher called Abraham Maslow (see Chapter 2, page 64)

Main risks to health

Health need	Risks
Physical	Risk of accidents
	Risks associated with poor diet
	Risks associated with poor exercise
	Risks associated with personal abuse, e.g. alcohol, drug abuse
	Risks associated with ill-health and disease
Social	Risks associated with loss and bereavement
	Risks associated with divorce
	Risks associated with changes in circumstances: employment, moving house, changing schools
Emotional	Risks associated with loss and bereavement, divorce, changing jobs, moving house or changing school
Intellectual	Risks associated with change and allied to all other areas

Risks to health and well-being may be associated with the normal activities of daily living, including:
- diet
- exercise
- personal hygiene.

How basic health needs are expressed and met

Life stage	Basic health need	How the need is expressed and met
Infant 0–2	Physical	Food, warmth, water from parents. Medical support/vaccination for long-term protection.
	Social	Very solitary relying on carers, brothers and sisters for social roles.
	Emotional	Very reliant on primary carers for emotional support.
	Intellectual	Learning to play and learn from new situation.
Child 2–10	Physical	Walking gives access to a range of areas. Food and warmth and protection from carers.
	Social	Developing circle of friends. Greater range of social contacts.
	Emotional	Very reliant on primary carers for emotional support and as models for beliefs.
	Intellectual	Learning through play. Formal education.
Adolescent 10–18	Physical	Rapid growth at puberty linked to taking more personal control of supplying physical needs.
	Social	Peer group (people of same age and interests) becomes very important. Group membership provides support beyond the family.
	Emotional	A time of mixed emotions needing careful support. Starts to move away from parents to peers for support.
	Intellectual	Formal education. More learning from experience as new situations are met in peer groups.
Adult 18–65	Physical	Becoming self-reliant and a provider of physical support for others (becoming a parent).
	Social	Develops through a variety of stages including marriage, starting a family and children leaving home.
	Emotional	Developing strong attachments to a partner. Being a model for and supplying support for others in family.
	Intellectual	Formal education reduces. Challenges come from work roles.
Older adult 65+	Physical	Senses become less efficient. General wear and tear means support from others or artificial aids (e.g. spectacles) may be needed.
	Social	Family will have left home. One partner may die before the other. Movement difficulties increase isolation. Organised activities support social well-being.
	Emotional	Friends and relatives get older and die. Children become independent, emotional support needs to come from other people. Often a time where reduced ability means self-esteem and self-worth are at a low ebb. Carers need to promote these.
	Intellectual	Mental activity often outstrips physical ability lending to some frustration. Intellectual stimuli are very important.

There are also risks associated with activities that people choose to undertake. These include:
- drug abuse (including alcohol and tobacco)
- unsafe sexual practices.

We all need to eat, exercise and practise good hygiene. But it is not essential to smoke, drink, take drugs or practise unsafe sex. However, in your group you will find people who risk their health with one or more of these activities.

Risk and diet

Chapter 6 describes what constitutes a balanced diet. It also describes some of the effects (the risks) of an unbalanced diet.

We will consider the following two questions about diet here:
- Who controls the food a person eats?
- What are the effects of the amount of money available to spend on food?

Who controls the food a person eats?
The answer to this question varies for different groups of people.

Babies
A baby is totally reliant on others for its food. Both breast milk and formula foods supply dietary needs. Even at this stage the diet can become unbalanced if formula food is not made up correctly.

Children
With children the control is still mainly with parents and carers. Children have access to a wider range of foods. For many, this will include sweets and biscuits. Eating these in excess can lead to tooth decay and becoming overweight. There is also a temptation to eat foods containing a lot of fat (chips, pizzas, crisps) that again leads to increased risks from overweight and heart disease in later life. Habits set up in childhood often last into later life.

Adolescents
Adolescents have even more control over their food intake. Most schools run cafeterias with a range of foods, and tuck shops selling sweets and snacks. This can also be a time of major changes in food intake as individuals choose new dietary patterns. Many people choose to become vegetarian during their teenage years. In itself this is not a problem, but there is a risk of an unbalanced diet if meals are not carefully planned. (This is particularly so if only one member of a group is vegetarian.)

Many adolescent people develop poor eating habits that can be encouraged in schools and colleges

Adults

Adults tend to be in charge of their own nutrition. They have access to more money, and diets change. There is a wide range of food available in ready-prepared forms. Lifestyles often dictate regular consumption of 'fast' foods. These are often high in fat and carbohydrate. Care needs to be taken to avoid obesity. Many adults reduce their physical activity without reducing their energy intake. This again leads to overweight.

Older adults

Older adults have lower energy requirements and need to reduce their food intake. They also tend to take less exercise. The cost of food can also be an issue and so there are greater risks of an unbalanced diet.

What are the effects of the amount of money available?

For many people living on a limited budget, planning meals becomes difficult. It is possible to provide a well-balanced diet on a limited income, but there is a risk that the types of food will become boring.

Lentils and brown rice followed by fresh fruit may well be nutritious, but they may not be appetising on a regular basis. Easier to prepare foods are normally more expensive. Lack of money can, therefore, often mean that more time has to be taken to prepare meals. Fillet steak and shin beef may be equally nutritious, but the fillet can be cooked in minutes, while the shin takes longer. The style of cooking is also limited by income.

Other risks linked to diet

Different groups of people can be exposed to other dangers from diet. In particular, two are worth considering. Both of them are common, even with people who have otherwise eaten a balanced diet:

- anaemia in adolescent women
- calcium and vitamin D imbalance in older women.

Anaemia in adolescent women

Many adolescent women suffer from anaemia. This is linked to the start of menstruation and its associated blood loss. The iron lost needs to be replaced by iron in food, but often the diet does not supply this.

While before puberty there was sufficient iron, the demands for iron caused by rapid growth and menstruation are often not met. Awareness of this potential problem, and action, will help stop anaemia in this group of people.

Calcium and vitamin D imbalance in older women

Women going through the menopause (see page 49) have a greater need for calcium than they did before that time. Changes in hormones during the menopause mean that bone regrowth is not efficient and calcium is lost. This leads to a bone weakening disorder called osteoporosis.

Vitamin D is needed to assist the absorption of calcium in the diet. It is important for women to ensure they have a diet containing both vitamin D and calcium in order to reduce the risks during the menopause.

Mrs L. has the typical 'stoop' of osteoporosis. She has lost 6 inches in height

Risk and exercise

Children

Young children are always exploring their surroundings. Their work is play and by 'working' they take plenty of exercise.

However, children can also be at risk where exercise is not encouraged by their parents/carers. Some circumstances, particularly at school, may discourage a child from taking part in physical activities. There is always the child who is last to be chosen for team games or who is never chosen. The child then becomes isolated from organised exercise and has low self-esteem because of rejection. The desire to be part of a group activity is denied and any exercise has to be solitary.

Rejection from team games is often as a result of poor fitness. The failure to exercise makes later rejection more likely and a vicious cycle starts. As individuals it is important that we value and encourage colleagues. There should be a commitment to assist friends to join in activities that support their health.

Adults

As people get older they have a greater choice of activities and work. There is a risk that exercise levels do not match needs. This is particularly important with adults.

The change in lifestyle brought about by starting work often means that exercise levels drop. Therefore levels of fitness drop and the risk of heart disease increases.

People at risk from lack of exercise tend to be those whose work roles involve minimal exercise and who choose not to undertake any exercise routine. Such people may also be at risk from a poor diet and overweight. It should be possible, however, for them to develop an exercise routine to fit with their lifestyle (see page 3).

Older adults

Many elderly people do not feel able to exercise. They may have been fit in earlier years but are unable to continue their activity. Exercise routines can be developed to meet their individual lifestyle needs.

Risk and personal hygiene

Poor personal hygiene causes the spread of more diseases that anything else. The common cold and influenza (flu) are spread by droplets coughed or sneezed out by an infected person. They are also breathed out but do not spread as far. Failure to use handkerchiefs (preferably disposable) increases the spread.

It often appears to be acceptable, even applauded, to continue working or attending school when there is a risk of spreading these diseases. This is largely because in mild doses the diseases cause little harm. However, if you work with people who at risk from the infection, such babies, children and people who are ill or elderly, then to spread colds and flu would be unreasonable!

Personal hygiene is important and is a way of maintaining good health. Use of soap and hot water in washing removes many bacteria from skin. It also removes dead skin cells and oils that provide a food source for bacteria and fungi. We are sure you are fully aware of your own responsibilities regarding personal hygiene.

However, if we consider different groups of people, hygiene issues become more important:

- Young babies are less resistant to disease and may suffer more damage from even mild doses of food poisoning. Older adults are in a similar situation. In both cases hygiene levels need to be higher than you might have in your own home.
- For older people who are reliant on others for care, other issues of personal hygiene are important. Ensuring that they are clean is not sufficient. Carers must look after other aspects of grooming such as hair and nail care. Shaving is important for men without beards. By paying attention to personal hygiene for these people, and supporting its achievement, you not only maintain physical health but you also promote emotional well-being.

It is important to keep babies' feeding bottles clean. Babies may suffer damage from even mild doses of food poisoning

Risk and the breakdown in normal daily activities

So far we have looked at health risks to people who, to a large extent, have their health under their own control. We have been talking about stereotypes of 'average' people. For most of these people diet, exercise and hygiene are a matter of **choice**.

However, some people in society have little choice about what they eat or what exercise they take. Personal hygiene may also be affected. People in this situation include:

- those who are physically or mentally unable to look after themselves, such as elderly people (see below)
- those who do not have a regular access to resources to meet their basic needs – this includes people who are unable to obtain social security benefits (such as homeless people, see below) and also many who do receive benefits, but who have difficulty meeting all their family's needs.

People unable to care for themselves, for whatever reason, are often cared for by others. The carers are responsible for helping the individuals to obtain food and exercise (and in many cases exercise is not seen as a priority) and ensuring that they have access to the things they need. Such people include:

- those who for mental reasons cannot support themselves
- those with physical disabilities that mean they need support.

The support required can vary from guidance in carrying out the activities to total dependence on the carer.

Elderly people

The number of elderly people in the UK is increasing. People are living longer and more people develop some form of dementia (such as Alzheimer's disease). In the later stages of dementia the person becomes totally dependent on others. (Dementia can occur in younger people but the incidence is greatest in elders.) In fact they return to the situation of babies in their requirement for total support.

Homeless people

It is unfortunate that many people in the UK today are living rough. Most of these people have no choice about the situation. Some, because of disability, may be ill-equipped to look after themselves.

These people have little access to money and cannot plan their diet. Their primary concerns are for the basics of food and shelter. The poor diet and lack of shelter exposes them to increased risk of illness. Tuberculosis is increasing in the UK because of this rising number of people living below the 'poverty line' (see page 59). They are also at risk of deficiency diseases – diseases which occur because particular nutrients are missing from the diet (see Chapter 6).

Activity 1.5

Imagine you have no home to go back to and no regular income. Everything you need has to be carried around.

a How would you get food, and what food might you get?

b How would you ensure that the food was 'hygienic' and safe to eat?

c How might you cope with food poisoning?

d How might you cope without easy access to clean toilets or washing facilities?

e How much would you be able to exercise, if you had barely enough food to survive?

Some people in society have little real choice about diet, exercise and sleep

Risk and smoking

Activity 1.6

a Conduct a small survey asking people the following questions:
  • Do you smoke?
  • Why do you (or do you not) smoke?
  • Do you know of any dangers from smoking?

b Present the results of your survey as pie charts. Use a computer if you can.

The results of such a survey are predictable. Many people smoke even though they know some of the risks. Almost everybody will know that smoking causes lung cancer and also that it is a cause of heart disease. The reasons why people smoke varies but, for whatever reason, they started and are now addicted.

Nicotine (from tobacco) is an addictive drug. People who smoke, while they may give all sorts of reasons, do so because they are drug addicts.

The risks of smoking
The risks that have been identified with smoking include:
• Chemicals in tobacco are known to cause cancer (particularly lung cancer).
• Lung tissues are damaged irreversibly by smoking. (Ninety per cent of emphysema cases have smoking as one of the causes.)
• Smoking leads to an increased risk of heart disease.
• Smoking leads to an increased risk of chest and throat infections.
• Bronchitis, the inflammation of the lungs and tubes to the lungs, is caused by smoking.
• Carbon monoxide in tobacco smoke reduces the ability of the blood to carry oxygen.
• Pregnant women may miscarry.
• There is a greater risk if premature birth, stillbirth and low birth-weight.

- The risks are not just to the smoker, but also to people nearby who inhale the smoke (passive smoking).

In hygiene terms, smoking literally stinks. Clothing, hair and skin become impregnated with the smell of smoke.

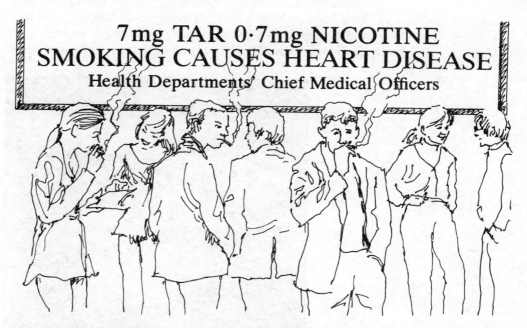

7mg TAR 0·7mg NICOTINE
SMOKING CAUSES HEART DISEASE
Health Departments' Chief Medical Officers

Group pressure often leads people to become addicted to drugs like tobacco, even though they know the dangers

Risk and alcohol

The situation with alcohol is more complex than tobacco. While it is addictive and can kill, it can also have a beneficial effect – in moderate quantities it can help prevent heart disease.

However, alcohol is a drug. In moderate amounts, it can make a person feel good about themselves (like a tranquilliser). But when it is taken in large amounts it can make the drinker depressed. This can eventually lead to alcoholism (addiction to alcohol).

Alcohol also has the effect of removing inhibitions. People who have had a drink often say or do things that they would not normally do and that they later regret. It's easy to say 'sorry' to someone you may have insulted when you were drunk. However, it's not so easy to say 'sorry' to a person killed by a driver who has been drinking.

Some of the consequences of drinking alcohol
- Reaction times become slower leading to increased risk of road accidents.
- Removal of inhibitions:
  - you may do things that you would not normally do, such as having sex with a friend (more likely unprotected)
  - you may say things you later wish you hadn't
  - you may generally do things without thinking.

- Damage to your stomach lining and liver:
  - Moderate to heavy drinking damages the stomach lining.
  - There is an increased risk of stomach ulcers.
  - The liver becomes damaged leading to cirrhosis.
- Overweight/poor diet:
  - Alcoholic drinks have high energy values and so lead to obesity.
  - Your diet can be affected. Heavy drinkers often spend money on alcohol and not food. As a consequence they suffer from malnutrition.
- In moderate quantities alcohol can help prevent heart disease.

How much alcohol is safe?

The answer to this question varies. If you are driving then the answer should be that no alcohol is safe (although the law allows 80 mg/100 ml blood = 4 units). If you are at home, in a relatively safe environment, it is not unreasonable to drink several units of alcohol. For an alcoholic (who is addicted to alcohol), any alcohol can be positively dangerous.

The Health Education Authority has produced guidelines on alcohol consumption. These indicate maximum recommended amounts and recognise the importance of not drinking every day (see the table opposite).

The risks of other drug abuse

Tobacco and alcohol are legal drugs. However, there are several drugs that are illegal to own, sell or use. These range from so-called 'soft' drugs, such as

Recommended alcohol consumption

	Maximum recommended	Increased risk	Harmful	Recommended number of alcohol-free
	(units per week)			
Men	21	50	50+	2–3
Women	14	35	35+	2–3
Pregnant women	Ideally no alcohol, at most 4 units			5–6

What is a unit?

1 unit = ½ pint of beer or lager

        1 small glass of wine

        1 small glass of sherry

        1 measure of vermouth or aperitif

        1 standard measure of spirits (UK)

Note 1 pint of extra strong beer or lager = 5 units

cannabis, to the 'hard', addictive drugs, such as crack cocaine. The table on page 24 describes some of the drugs and their dangers.

There are some dangers that are general to all or some drugs:

- **Criminal conviction** The use or sale of all of the materials in the table is controlled by law. A criminal record will reduce employment opportunities. Also, many abusers steal to get the money for drugs (see Cost below).
- **Diseases** Most drugs are taken by people in groups. They share the required materials. Where drugs are injected, shared needles will transmit the Human Immunodeficiency Virus (HIV).
- **Cost** The cost of drugs means that there is less money for other things, such as food. This means that many drug abusers suffer from malnutrition.
- **Relationships** There are knock-on effects to families and friends as a result of an drug abuser's mood changes, lack of money, crime, illness.
- **Increased risks** It is thought may drug abusers go on to try different, 'harder' drugs with the increased risk to health.
- **Death** Drug abuse exposes users to hazards which increase the risk of death. This may be increased risk of lung cancer for cannabis users or risk of HIV infection and AIDS for people injecting drugs.

Risk and sexual practice

Each of us may be involved in, or looking forward to, loving relationships that involve sexual intercourse. Some people may only ever have one sexual partner, while others may have many. Whoever your partner is, it is important to recognise the risks involved in sexual activity.

Pregnancy

At its basic level, sexual intercourse has evolved as a way of men and women producing more men and women. The sex act has the purpose of enabling sperm and an ovum (egg cell) to get together to start the process of producing other human beings. This is fine, so long as both people involved want the responsibility for a third person.

Illegal drugs: their effects and dangers

Drug	Form	How taken	Effects	Dangers
Cannabis	Resin (hash) or leaf	Smoked, often with tobacco in a pipe or cigarette	Relaxation, talkativeness, increase intensity or colour or sound	As for smoking tobacco. Using machinery or driving whilst under the influence is dangerous.
Amphetamine	Powder or tablets	Inhaled or swallowed	Stimulates the nervous system, produces feelings of alertness	Developing tolerance and need for larger doses. Loss of sleep, loss of appetite, anxiety attacks.
Cocaine and crack cocaine	Powder (cocaine), crystals (crack)	Powder is usually sniffed, but can be injected. Crack is smoked or heated and vapours inhaled	As for amphetamines	May cause respiratory problems, damage to nasal bones. Otherwise as for amphetamines.
Ecstasy	Tablets (various types)	Swallowed	Calming, heightened awareness of colour and sound, co-ordination may be affected	Similar to amphetamines. Damage to kidneys can occur if used without drinking plenty of water. (Particular problem at raves where overheating and sweating are a problem.)
LSD	Impregnated onto blotting paper	Dissolved on the tongue	Powerful hallucinogen — visions vary from joy and beauty to nightmares	May trigger psychotic responses. Actions during a 'trip' may put individual in danger.
Heroin	Powder	Injected, sniffed or smoked	Produces 'pleasant' drowsiness, nausea and vomiting depending on user. Addictive	Constipation, disrupted menstrual cycle. Dangers associated with method of use (HIV from shared needles).
Anabolic steroids	Tablets or injectable solution	Swallowed or injected	Promotes muscle growth	Drugs stimulate aggression. Growth restriction in young people. Reduced sex drive in men. Masculinisation of women. Many effects not reversible.
Organic solvents	Liquids, as a component of some glues and aerosols	Inhaled, often rebreathing exhaled air	Similar to drunkenness, including hallucinations	Serious brain damage, suffocation related to method of use, liver damage.

Many people, for whatever reason, do not wish to start a pregnancy but do want to have sex. The answer in this case is to practise some form of contraception. The safest form for stopping a pregnancy is the contraceptive pill, closely followed by using a condom with a spermicidal cream. The safest form for reducing the risks of catching diseases is the use of a condom (rubber, johnny, Durex).

Other risks associated with sex

There are several diseases specifically associated with sexual activity. All of them present dangers varying from:

- infertility (gonorrhoea)
- cervical cancer (genital warts)
- death (HIV/AIDS).

These diseases are known as sexually-transmitted diseases, or STDs.

The spread of these diseases is preventable by using safe sexual practice. All of the disease-causing organisms can be trapped by using a condom. If either partner is infected, the condom provides a barrier and stops the infection spreading. However, for condoms to work they must be used before any sexual contact has been made.

Activity 1.7

In the early 1980s there was a big campaign advising people to use condoms to prevent the spread of HIV and AIDS. The success of the campaign can be seen in the reduced number of cases of gonorrhoea and syphilis. The table below gives some statistics.

a Plot a graph of the total of these figures. Put the years on the *x* axis (bottom) and the total cases for gonorrhoea on the *y* axis (side). You could do this using a computer, if you have access to one.

New cases of STDs reported in England, 1980–90

| Year | Gonorrhoea | | | Syphilis | | |
	Men	Women	Total	Men	Women	Total
1980	34 087	20 346	54 433	3134	925	4059
1981	33 454	18 746	52 200	2963	847	3810
1982	33 058	19 098	52 156	2739	825	3564
1983	30 464	17 929	48 393	2662	665	3327
1984	29 791	17 871	47 662	2315	618	2933
1985	28 759	17 555	46 314	1819	585	2404
1986	24 450	16 255	40 705	1387	545	1932
1987	14 888	10 377	25 265	1029	509	1538
1988	10 487	7 891	18 378	846	396	1242
1989	11 346	8 415	19 761	923	488	1411
1990	11 757	7 329	19 086	810	495	1305

b Do the same for syphilis.

c What happens to the number of cases between 1980 and 1988?

d What happens in 1989 and 1990?

e Why do you think that there are the changes?

f Use more recent figures to see if the 1989 and 1990 results are the start of a trend.

The results of the activity should show that the 'safe sex' message got across. They will also show that some people may now be ignoring the message.

The message for you must be that barrier methods (condoms) help prevent disease transmission but they only work if they are used. It is each individual's responsibility to make sure that any sexual activity is safe. Gonorrhoea is curable; HIV/AIDS is not – it kills! Treat all sexual partners as potentially infected.

How to reduce risks to health

It is easy to say don't smoke, drink, do drugs or practise unsafe sex. We can also advise on appropriate diets and levels of exercise. In all of these cases, you have choices. You can choose to follow guidance or to ignore it. What is important is for you to make informed decisions and think about them before you do anything.

If we consider where you might be exposed to risk, we can identify ways of dealing with situations:

- **At home** you are subject to pressures from members of your family to conform to their ways of doing things. You may have no control over your diet, or over other people smoking.
- Away from home you are subject to different pressures. **At school or college** your teachers will impose rules and provide pressure for their ideas about risks. You will be influenced by your friends and colleagues.
- When you are away from both home and school participating in **leisure activities or at parties**, different pressures will be on you again. Drinking alcohol may reduce your inhibitions and you may be tempted to do things that are unsafe or that you would not normally do. At such times, you need to have thought about issues beforehand and stick to any decisions you have made.

Activity 1.8

a As a group, think of situations where you may be pressured to do things that you don't want to do or would not normally do. How might you deal with the situations? What might you feel like if you gave in to the pressure?

b Act out some situations where you are being pressured to do things. Follow this by acting out what your feelings might be the next day.

Some ideas for role-play:
- You know that a friend is trying to get you drunk at a party.
- Someone is asking you to try some drugs at school or college.
- The possible danger to a friend at a party who is drunk or high on drugs.

In all these situations it is for you to make an informed choice. This book only provides an outline in terms of guidance. You need to develop your own strategies for dealing with risks to your own health.

The effects of MAJOR CHANGES in circumstances on health

Throughout life we all have to face up to changes. Sometimes the changes are planned, while others are unexpected. The types of change we need to consider are:

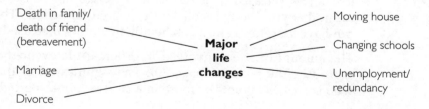

These all have similar effects. They are all a source of **stress** and all involve **loss**. This may be:
- loss of a partner, family member or friend
- loss of a lifestyle.

With loss comes a need to grieve and it is this process that is important.

Activity 1.9

Reflect upon changes in your own life. For some of you there may have been major upheavals, such as a divorce in your family or a death. For all of you there will have been changes of school.

a What things changed?

b How did you feel about the change?

c What effect did the change have on your health?

Your answer to the last question may be 'I don't know' or 'I don't think it did'. Let's now look at some of the things that can happen.

Grieving

Grieving is your response to loss. The process may involve:

- tiredness
- anxiety
- loss of appetite or change in eating habits
- becoming withdrawn
- depression
- guilt
- change in sleep patterns.

It can also include:

- suicidal thoughts
- panic
- increased risk of physical illness.

If you now look back at your response to change, you may be able to identify some of the indicators of your grieving processes.

Stress

In physical terms many of the responses to change are related to stress. Stress occurs when a person is unable to respond to all the demands made upon him or her.

Stress involves the release of adrenaline. This is the same hormone that causes the 'butterflies in the stomach' feelings when you are frightened. The purpose of adrenaline is to prepare your body for fighting or running from danger. The low levels released as a result of stress do not cause the 'butterflies' but do mean that your body is constantly 'geared for action'. The release of adrenaline can have long-term effects on health, including increased risk of heart attacks.

The amount of stress involved in different life events has been given a points score (see the table on page 30). The significance of this table is that anyone who scores 300 points or more in a twelve-month period is at risk of becoming ill.

Social effects of change

When your life goes through a change it is likely that your social activities will change. Moving school means that you lose contact with some friends. Getting married means that your activities are more likely to focus around you 'as a couple' than previously. The death of a partner means that the survivor can no longer do things as a couple. Friends may find it difficult to cope with the grief and so the survivor becomes isolated.

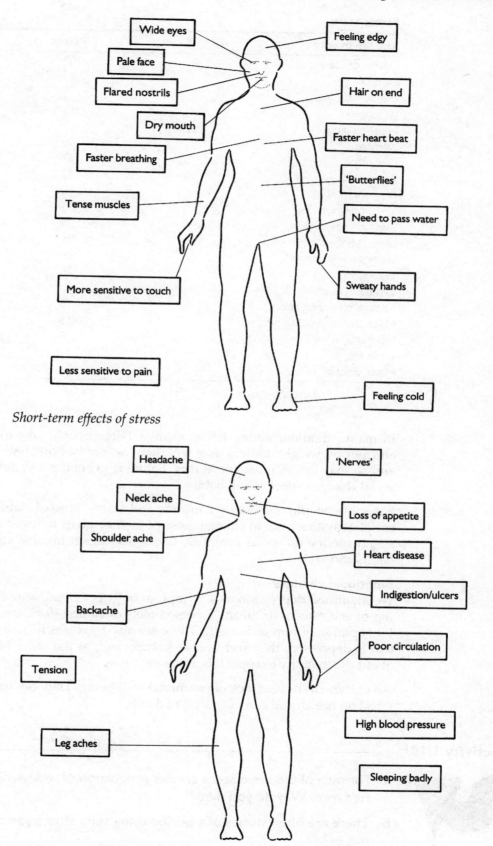

Wide eyes

Feeling edgy

Pale face

Flared nostrils

Hair on end

Dry mouth

Faster heart beat

Faster breathing

'Butterflies'

Tense muscles

Need to pass water

More sensitive to touch

Sweaty hands

Less sensitive to pain

Feeling cold

Short-term effects of stress

Headache

'Nerves'

Neck ache

Loss of appetite

Shoulder ache

Heart disease

Indigestion/ulcers

Backache

Poor circulation

Tension

High blood pressure

Leg aches

Sleeping badly

Long-term effects of stress

Stress scale

Key life events	Points
Death of husband or wife	100
Divorce	73
Marital separation	65
Jail sentence	63
Illness or injury	53
Marriage	50
Loss of job	47
Retirement	45
Pregnancy	40
Sex problem	39
Major change of work	39
Large mortgage taken on	31
Starting a new school	26
Leaving school	26
Change in residence	20
Change in sleeping habits	16
Major change in eating pattern	15
Holiday	13
Christmas	12
Minor violation of law	11

In many situations eating habits change. Some people take to comfort eating and put on weight. Others may feel they 'cannot be bothered' to prepare food and so may eat an unbalanced diet. Eating is generally a social activity and so social changes affect eating habits.

For some people the loss is of income and status. Loss of status can mean that social activities have to change. Loss of income gives reduced opportunities to spend money on social activities. It can also again involve changes in eating habits and style.

Emotional changes

We identified depression as a 'symptom of grief'. Depression leads to a lowering of self-esteem. It means a person feels devalued (feels unimportant, has a low opinion of him or herself). There are also increases in anxiety. When a person is depressed, they feel unable to cope and, at the same time, feel anxious about the inability to cope. It is a vicious circle.

All of these indicate a lack of emotional well-being. They can have a cumulative effect on health and can even lead to death.

Activity 1.10

a   For men of the same age, a greater proportion of widowers die than married men. Why do you think?

b   There are often stories of a person dying soon after a partner. Why might this be?

Coping with major changes

Some of the resistance to change is caused by fear of the unknown and a feeling of security in what has happened in the past. Knowing this helps us to face change ourselves or help others to cope with change.

Relaxation

The physical effects of change in lifestyle can be minimised by learning to relax. This is easy to say, but difficult to do. It is often best done by setting aside a time to do something not associated with the cause of the change. It could be reading a favourite book or sitting listening to music. It can even be carrying out specific techniques designed to assist relaxation. Yoga, for example, encourages controlled deep breathing to help relaxation.

Diet

A second way of dealing with the physical effects of change is to be aware of changes in dietary habits and to try to control or avoid them. This may not be easy for an individual but groups of people (families) can be supportive.

Exercise and hygiene

It is also important to maintain physical health by maintaining exercise and hygiene levels. Taking care about how you look increases your self-esteem and reduces the effects on emotional development.

Support

A final, but possibly most important, way of coping with change is to acknowledge any problems and seek support. This can be from friends, family or from trained professionals.

When helping a person pass through a change in life events it is important to recognise the three phases of response to change:

- **denial** that anything has happened, trying to carry on as if nothing has happened
- **shock** – feeling the pain of the change. People may cry, be angry or guilty. They may also feel rejected by others because of the change
- **acceptance** – a stage where the change is acknowledged and the individual starts to live his or her own life again. It often involves learning new skills and making new friends.

Don't forget that key life events include planned happy experiences as well as unplanned sad ones. If we consider a couple getting married the phases could be expressed as:

- denial – some marriages never happen because one partner fails to turn up or calls it off
- shock – many couples argue very soon after getting married. This may be an expression of the anger associated with the change
- acceptance – settling down to married life and learning the skills of living with another person.

Activity 1.11

a How did you cope with starting this Foundation GNVQ? Can you recognise some of the stages of adapting to change in your behaviour?

b How do you plan to move on when you have gained your GNVQ? What can you do to help you cope with the change?

Test yourself

1 What are the three main factors that contribute to good health and well-being?

2 Give three reasons for improving health and well-being.

3 List three ways in which smoking can damage a smoker.

4 Who besides a smoker is at risk from smoking?

5 How might setting targets help a person planning to improve his or her health?

6 What are the four basic health needs of all individuals?

7 How do the basic health needs change as a child gets older?

8 How many units of alcohol can be drunk before it is illegal to drive? How many units is it safest to have consumed before driving?

9 List two major life changes that are predictable and two that are unpredictable.

10 Give two effects that major life changes may have on a person's health.

Assignment A1.1
Personal planning

This assignment is designed to help you with your own plan for improving your health and well-being. You will need to make use of Chapter 6 on Planning Diets and Chapter 7 on Exploring Health and Recreational Activities.

Your tasks

1 Spend time checking out your current state of health and well-being.

   a Look up your height and weight on the graph (page 188) to see your weight status.

   b Review your diet to see if you are eating a well-balanced diet. (Remember to consider the snacks as well as the main meals.)

   c Record your current exercise activities and check your fitness.

   d Note down your leisure and recreational activities.

2 a Draw a picture of yourself like the one below. Label one side 'Me now' and the other 'Future me'.

b Use the information about your current state of health (from Task 1) to complete the 'now' part of the picture.

We have given you some examples on this picture to show you what we mean.

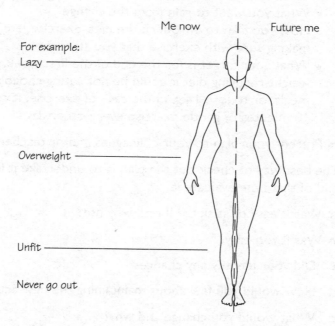

Me now | Future me

For example:
Lazy ————————

Overweight ————

Unfit ————————

Never go out

3 Study the 'now' diagram and think carefully about any areas that you may want to change. These may be because of either your current state of health and well-being or possible future issues.

a Make a list of the things that you wish to change.

b Identify which change is the most important to you and which is least important.

c For each area of change fill in a table like this (use a computer if you can):

Aspect to change	Long-term target	How will I know I've got there?	Short-term target	Medium-term target
Reward for reaching target				

4 Fill in the second half of the diagram with details of the 'future me'.

5 You now need to think about how you will check that your plan is working and how you will reward yourself when you reach any intermediate and final targets.

a Prepare a detailed plan for one week. This should include:
- What you have identified as needing changes/improving
- What you want to gain from the change
- How you plan to introduce the diet, exercise, etc. in the first week, making sure with exercise that you start slowly.
- What your target is for the end of the first week, for example, for a weight-reducing diet it could be not eating chocolate biscuits between meals, or to lose 1 kg. In the case of exercise, it could be to have done 10 minutes of gentle exercise every other day.

b Present your plan to your colleagues and/or teacher.

6 The best way to check out the plan is to undertake it for a week. At the end of that time evaluate it.

a Was it easy to stick to? If not, why not?

b Was it too easy?

c Did your identify any changes?

d How would you feel about maintaining the new activity?

e What would you change and why?

Evaluation is an important skill that you will need to develop.

Assignment A1.2
Risks to health

You have been working in a youth club for a few weeks. The leader realises that you know something about health needs and health risks.

Your tasks

1 As part of your work you have been asked to prepare a short report that describes the needs of all people. You are not expected to go into great detail, but you should prepare a short report with the following headings:
- Physical needs
- Emotional needs
- Social needs
- Intellectual needs.

As the youth club is involved in a lot of community work give examples of the way each of the needs are met for:

- infants
- children
- adolescents
- adults
- elders.

You may find it easiest to produce this part as a table. Use a word processor to write your report and produce your table, if you can.

2 a For two of the groups, list what you consider to be their main health risks. You should consider situations where a person may feel pressured to take a health risk. This may be in the home or somewhere where other people can have a big influence.

b Describe how the individuals might plan to avoid the risks.

3 The youth club leader has noticed that there is a lot of anger shown by people who are about to leave school and go to college. Many of the sixteen-year-old members seem to change their behaviour in the last weeks of their final summer term.

Prepare a list of ways that may help the members face major changes in their lives. At the same time, give other examples of changes and say what their effects might be on an individual and how the person might cope with the changes.

Key words

After reading this chapter you should be able to understand the following words and phrases. If you do not, go back through the chapter and find out, or look them up in the Glossary.

Diet	*Risks to health*
Health plans	*Major life changes*
Basic health needs	*Self-esteem*

CHAPTER 2

Understanding Personal Development and Relationships

What is covered in this chapter

- Personal development
- Personal relationships
- Relationships between clients and carers

These are the resources you will need for your Understanding Personal Development and Relationships portfolio:
- your written answers to each of the activities in this chapter
- your written answers to Test Yourself questions at the end of this chapter
- your completed assignments A2.1, A2.2 and A2.3.

Introduction

This chapter will focus on:
- how people develop during their lifetime and the things that influence how they develop, such as the size of family they were brought up in, the groups they have belonged to or the type of housing or neighbourhoods they have lived in
- the personal relationships (friendships, working relationships, parents) which people form at various times in their lives and how these affect how people behave.
- the kinds of relationship that may build up between clients (the people we help) and their carers or helpers.

Personal development

One useful way to study human development is to use the following headings:

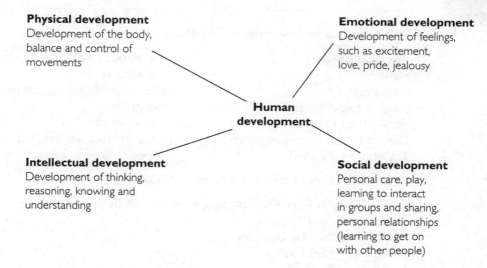

Physical development
Development of the body, balance and control of movements

Emotional development
Development of feelings, such as excitement, love, pride, jealousy

Human development

Intellectual development
Development of thinking, reasoning, knowing and understanding

Social development
Personal care, play, learning to interact in groups and sharing, personal relationships (learning to get on with other people)

Remember that 'growth' and 'development' are different things:
- Growth refers to an increase in actual size.
- Development means an increase in complexity.

For example, becoming taller is an obvious growth, while a baby's ability to reach for objects or transfer them from one hand to another shows a development of complex skills.

Growth is an increase in size   *Development is an increase in complexity of skills*

When looking at personal development we must also consider certain basic needs, which are both **physical** and **emotional**.

Activity 2.1

Discuss within your class group and make a list of things you consider to be basic human needs.

Does your list look something like this?

Physical needs	**Emotional needs**
Shelter	Affection
Protection	Continuous individual care
Fresh air and sunlight	Security
Activity and rest	Personal identity
Prevention of illness or injury	Dignity and self-respect
Training in life skills	Opportunity to learn from experience

You will find more about needs on pages 64–7.

We will look at the following stages of human development:
- children – 0–10 years
- adolescents – 11–18 years
- adults — 19–64 years
- elders – 65+ years.

Children

Birth to three years

Personal development begins at birth. The *sequence* of development is roughly the same for all children, but the *rate* of development will vary from child to child. Parts of the body near the brain develop first. For example, active use of the mouth, the eyes and hearing come before sitting, walking and the use of fingers.

Knowing what the *average* baby or child might be expected to do helps the family and carers to recognise possible problems. If necessary, suitable care or activities can be planned to correct these problems.

When a baby is born, one of the first questions a mother may well ask is 'Is my baby normal?' To check that all is well, a number of tests are carried on the baby:

- The airway, palate and colour are examined.
- A test, called the Apgar score is carried out. This test assesses the baby's heart rate, breathing, reflexes and colour.
- The baby's hips are checked to see that they are not dislocated.
- Head size and birth weight are recorded.
- Skin colour is observed – new babies may be jaundiced and they appear yellow.

Features of a new-born baby

Average weight	3.5 kg
Average length	50 cm
Head size	33–35 cm

Compared with other animals, the human baby is the most helpless and its growth is very slow. The new baby cries to attract its mother's attention and after a few weeks will smile and show pleasure when its mother or father appears. The table on pages 40–1 summarises human development in the first three years.

Children are generally referred to as infants in their first year and as toddlers in their second and third years.

Activity 2.2

Read the list of actions below and on page 42.

a Arrange to interview a parent of a child under the age of 4 to find out when the child was first observed carrying out these actions.

b Make your own chart displaying:

- the actions
- the average age when the actions would be accomplished
- the age when the child was actually observed carrying out the actions.

Use a computer to produce the chart, if you have access to one.

List of actions

Eyes followed a moving light	Reached for a toy
Smiled	Slept throughout night

Development: Birth to 3 years

Age	Physical development	Intellectual development	Emotional development	Socal development
1 month	Holds head erect for a few seconds. Eyes follow a moving light.	Interested in sounds.	Cries in response to pain, hunger and thirst	May sleep up to 20 hours in a 24-hour period. Stops crying when picked up and spoken to.
3 months	Eyes follow a person moving. Kicks vigorously.	Recognises carer's face. Shows excitement. Listens, smiles, holds rattle.	Enjoys being cuddled and played with. Misses carer and cries for him/her to return.	Responds happily to carer. Becomes excited at prospect of a feed or bath.
6 months	Able to lift head and chest up supported by wrists. Turns to a person who is speaking.	Responds to speech. Vocalises. Uses eyes a lot. Holds toys. Explores using hands. Listens to sound.	Can be anxious in presence of strangers. Can show anger and frustration. Shows a clear preference for mother's company.	Puts everything in mouth. Plays with hands and feet. Tries to hold bottle when feeding.
9 months	Stands when supported. May crawl. Gazes at self in mirror. Tries to hold drinking cup. Sits without support	Tries to talk, babbling. May say 'Mama' and 'Dada'. Shouts for attention. Understands 'No'.	Can recognise individuals – mother, father, siblings. Still anxious about strangers. Sometimes irritable if routine is altered.	Plays 'Peek a boo'. Imitates hand clapping. Puts hands round cup when feeding.
12 months	Pulls self up to standing position. Uses pincer grip. Feeds self using fingers. May walk without assistance.	Knows own name. Obeys simple instructions. Says about three words.	Shows affection. Gives kisses and cuddles. Likes to see familiar faces but less worried by strangers.	Drinks from a cup without assistance. Holds a spoon but cannot feed him/herself. Plays 'Pat-a-Cake'. Quickly finds hidden toys.
1.5 years	Walks well, feet apart. Runs carefully. Pushes and pulls large toys. Walks upstairs. Creeps backwards downstairs.	Uses 6–20 recognisable words. Repeats last word of short sentences. Enjoys and tries to join in with nursery rhymes Picks up named toys. Enjoying looking at simple picture books. Builds a tower of 3–4 bricks. Scribbles and makes dots. Preference for right or left hand shown.	Affectionate, but may still be reserved with strangers. Likes to see familiar faces.	Able to hold spoon and to get food into mouth. Holds drinking cup and hands it back when finished. Can take off shoes and socks. Bowel control may have been achieved. Remembers where objects belong.

Continued

Development: Birth to 3 years continued

Age	Physical Development	Intellectual development	Emotional development	Social development
2 years	Runs on whole foot. Squats steadily. Climbs on furniture. Throws a small ball. Sits on a small tricycle and moves vehicle with feet.	Uses 50 or more recognisable words; understands many more words; puts two or three words together to form simple sentences. Refers to self by name. Asks names of objects and people. Scribbles in circles. Can build a tower of six or seven cubes. Hand preference is obvious.	Can display negative behaviour and resistance. May have temper tantrums if thwarted. Plays contentedly beside other children but not with them. Constantly demands mother's attention.	Asks for food and drink. Spoon feeds without spilling. Puts on shoes.
2.5 years	All locomotive skills now improving. Runs and climbs. Able to jump from a low step with feet together. Kicks a large ball.	May use 200 or more words. Knows full name. Continually asking questions, likes stories and recognises details in picture books. Recognises self in photographs. Builds a tower of seven or more cubes.	Usually active and restless. Emotionally still very dependent on adults. Tends not to want to share playthings	Eats skilfully with a spoon and may sometimes use a fork. Active and restless. Often dry through the day.
3 years	Sits with feet crossed at ankles. Walks upstairs using alternating feet.	Able to state full name, sex and sometimes age. Carries on simple conversations and constantly questioning. Demands favourite story over and over again. Can count to 10 by rote. Can thread wooden beads on string. Can copy a circle and a cross. Names colours. Cuts with scissors. Paints with a large brush.	Becomes less prone to temper tantrums. Affectionate and confiding, showing affection for younger siblings. Begins to understand sharing.	Eats with a fork and spoon. May be dry through the night.

Sat without support	Crawled
Spoke first word	Put two or three words together
Used a spoon and fork	Dry during the day
Dry during the night	Achieved bowel movement
Built a tower of three bricks	Drew a circle
Began to understand sharing	Recognised parents

Pre-school children

A child between the ages of 3 and 5 is referred to as a PRE-SCHOOL CHILD. At this age a child is increasingly active and communicative.

Physical development

During this period in his or her life, a child continues to develop and perfect many of the physical skills which have been acquired since birth. Accomplishments include:

- running
- walking
- climbing
- riding a tricycle
- sitting cross-legged
- moving in time with music
- playing ball games.

Intellectual development

Between the ages of 3 and 5, a child will begin to speak grammatically, recount recent events accurately, enjoy jokes and be able to state their name, address, age and usually birthday.

The child will also be gaining control in writing and drawing. A recognisable person may be drawn, such as father or mother, also a house which has doors, windows and a roof. Pictures are coloured neatly and four or more primary colours can be named.

'Kate and Tom' by Kate, aged 3¾

Emotional and social development

By the age of 5, a child is able to use a fork, spoon and knife. He or she can dress and undress themselves, although they may have some difficulty with fastenings. They indulge in make-believe play and in general are more sensitive. They relate clock time to daily programmes of events. They will know when they have their dinner or tea and the time they usually go to bed.

Children of this age need the companionship of other children and begin to develop personal relationships. They gradually become more independent from their parents. They will play with other children and also by themselves. They will comfort playmates who are upset, choose their own friends, begin to understand the rules of games and understand what is fair play.

5 to 10 years of age

At this age, life revolves around the family, school and the community. Independence is increasing and variations in children's abilities to do different things become more obvious. At about 5 years of age, a child will usually start to attend school. What do we expect from a child of this age?

Physical development

The 5-year-old appears taller and slimmer than the toddler and his or her features have a more adult look. Movements are well co-ordinated and physical skill increases. The growth rate follows a steady, but slower, pattern until the age of puberty ends at about 18 years of age. Girls tend to develop more quickly than boys, physically and intellectually.

Intellectual development

The child begins to develop a greater capacity for DIRECTED THINKING (to concentrate on one thing) – he or she can concentrate on one task and finish it. When you work with children of this age group in school, you will see how they learn a range of activities. These activities are designed by teachers to help the children gain knowledge and skills.

Children who have never been separated from their parents before may experience problems of adjustment when they start school. They may be unable to settle, cry, become aggressive or angry. Carers working with children of this age should be sensitive to this situation. Think about your own first day at school and your feelings at that time. Discuss with your parents what your reactions were then.

Activity 2.3

Starting school for the first time may prove to be difficult experience for a 4- or 5-year-old child.

Produce an advice sheet to help parents prepare their child for starting school. Carry out some research by talking to teachers, care staff, parents and your friends first. Use a computer to produce the sheet, if you can.

Social development

A child first relates to his or her mother and then to the father, brothers, sisters and other relations. The range of contacts grows when school starts.

In school, the teacher may take on the role of parents in the child's eyes, but the teacher cannot to give undivided attention to every child. Sometimes, therefore, a child who is used to a lot of individual attention from his or her parents may find it difficult to adjust to school at first.

Between the ages of 5 and 10 girls tend to develop more rapidly than boys, both physically *and* intellectually. Boys tend not to play or develop relationships with girls – you may have noticed this during your work experience. Boys will tend to play football, 'rough and tumble' games and other activities in groups, while girls will have their own activities and games.

By the time a child is 9, special friendships will have been developed. However, 9-year-olds can be very critical of each other and may exclude individuals from their games. You will see this in any school playground.

Between the ages of 7 and 10 special friendships develop between children of the same sex. Some children are excluded

Emotional development

Boys and girls continue their emotional development. They experience the growth of feelings about themselves and others. They also begin to develop their self-image and identity.

By the age of 10, childhood is nearly finished and puberty is beginning. The skills of the 10-year-old bring together all that has been experienced and learned in childhood.

Adolescents

ADOLESCENCE is the name given to the period of life between the onset of PUBERTY at about 11 to the beginning of adult life at 18.

In our western society, adolescence coincides with a growth spurt. It is a time of social and biological change. In Victorian times children left school and were sent out to work at about the age of 6 or 7. They didn't have the opportunity that adolescents have today to gain experience and education. Today, the tendency is to prolong adolescence, and people stay on at school until 16 or 18.

Physical development

Puberty means 'age of manhood'. Physical changes occur because of increased production of sex hormones:

- OESTROGEN in girls
- TESTOSTERONE in boys.

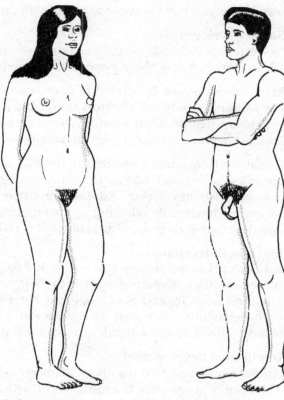

Puberty in girls   *Puberty in boys*

Puberty in girls

Changes in girls tend to start at 10 to 12 years of age, sometimes even earlier. These include:

- a growth spurt
- breast development
- appearance of pubic and armpit hair
- broadening of the hips
- a redistribution of fat
- menstruation.

Puberty in boys

In boys, the changes associated with puberty usually start at 12 to 14 years. These include:

- a growth spurt
- facial hair
- deepening of the voice
- enlargement of the penis, scrotum and testes
- appearance of pubic, chest and armpit hair

- the limbs lengthen and shoulders become broader
- the ability to ejaculate.

Physical changes can lead adolescent boys and girls to develop spots. While this is common and can develop into acne, it is a normal part of growing up and is treatable.

Adolescence is a period when a lot of social, intellectual and emotional changes occur. Adolescents have to grow physically into a new body as we have already seen. They also have to come to terms with new feelings and attitudes.

Social development

In western society adolescence is a time when a person is neither a child nor an adult. However, it is also a period when interest in the opposite sex begins.

Many of the issues associated to adolescence are PSYCHO-SOCIAL in nature. For example, spots are physical things but they may also cause psycho-social problems such as depression, shyness, embarrassment, and prevent a person socialising and developing personal relationships.

It is also a time when a person's individual identity (their own PERSONALITY) becomes established. Moral (right and wrong), social and personal responsibilities are also developed. Adolescents often do this by challenging accepted ways of behaving. By rebelling against their parents or teachers, they are testing and developing their own ideas of what is right and wrong.

Emotional development

Adolescents experience mood swings and feelings of ambivalence. For example, sometimes they may co-operate with their parents, but at other times they may 'dig their heels in' and not co-operate. Parents and friends may be confused by such behaviour. They may not understand what adolescents are thinking or feeling. This is a very difficult time for most parents and children.

Intellectual development

Adolescents begin to think about themselves and what others think about them. They begin to compare the ideal world with what they experience in reality, in terms of families, politics and religion.

What do adolescents say about this period in their life?

They will experiment with different identities. For example, they may try being a punk, a hippie or even a delinquent. Many of these may be the opposite of what their parents are or want for them. This role-playing may not be a bad thing. It allows adolescents to achieve their personal identity.

Adolescence is also a time when a person is starting to think about the future - a possible career or going on to university, for example.

Activity 2.4

Prepare a 'problem page' which might appear in a teenage magazine. Design the page using a computer, if you can.

a Start by finding out as much as you can about the problems associated with adolescence.

b Write a selection of letters asking for advice on a range of adolescent issues.

c From your reading and research, prepare clear answers for each letter.

Adults

Adult life begins at 18 years of age and ends at death. We will look at the years 18 to 64 here and the years 65+ on pages 50–3.

During adulthood most people reach the peak of their performance. Skeletal growth ends in the late teens or early twenties, and a person is at their peak at this time. From the age of 30 or so signs of ageing begin to show.

During childhood and adolescence the individual is dependent upon others. During adulthood, however, the individual is expected take responsibility for his or her own self, for children, for their own old age and perhaps for the care of older people.

The 18- to 25-year-olds

Who are this group? They are young people at the beginning of adult life who may still be involved in education or training. Perhaps they are at university or college and still receiving financial support in the form of grants, loans or assistance from parents.

In addition, they may have left the family home and be living in a different part of the country. They may be considering home ownership.

They may be employed or unemployed and receiving state benefits. This can be a time of freedom, providing financial stability has been achieved.

People may also be considering settling down as couples and starting families. The process of becoming a 'couple' will tend to follow a certain path:

• First, there is the single-sex group within which social activities occur.
• Then mixed groups start to form.
• Girls and boys begin to take an interest in forming relationships with each other. For girls, the approval of boys becomes more important than acceptance by their girlfriends.
• Mixed groups of couples appear, but later individual couples dominate the social scene.

- Couples may develop an interest in sexual relationships, hopefully within a framework of respect and caring.

Activity 2.5

a What do you think it means to be a 'couple'.

b What qualities do you think you will look for when choosing a partner?

c Complete the quiz below, writing your response on a sheet of paper.

Quiz

Qualities	Score									
	1	2	3	4	5	6	7	8	9	10
Good wage earner										
Good-looking										
Good sense of humour										
Handyman/woman										
Good with children										
Likes a good social life										
Rich										
Hardworking										
Manages money well										
Dresses well										

Give each quality a score out of ten, the higher score showing the importance you attach to each quality.

d Discuss the responses with your fellow students.

The 25- to 40-year olds
This group is made up of men and women who may be married or single, with or without children. They may live as couples or single people.

If employed, they will usually be concentrating on their career, hoping to consolidate their position and looking for promotion. Look at job adverts in magazines and newspapers – many employers are looking for people in this age group, because they have some experience and are still energetic and ambitious.

Often by the time people are in their late twenties they have formed a steady relationship. They may get engaged, get married or decide to live together as a couple in a stable relationship. However, many relationships end in separation or divorce.

During this stage, couples and single parents will be bringing up families, with the need for a reasonable income, housing and community facilities to help them to do so.

Activity 2.6

One in three marriages ends in divorce. Discuss in groups whether you think it is too easy for couples to obtain a divorce?

The 40- to 64-year-olds

People in this age group (often called 'middle age') may have experienced a career change, may have taken early retirement or may have been made redundant.

Children of people in this age group will probably be growing up and starting their own families and careers. The parents in this age group will be becoming elderly and possibly dependent on others.

Middle age can be a time of greater security in life. People will have brought up their own children, have greater financial security and will have achieved some, if not all, of their career goals. It should be a time to feel confident, relaxed and able to enjoy life.

However, people sometimes feel negative during this life stage. They may feel, perhaps, that they have lost the main role in their life – bringing up children. They may be faced with the prospect of caring for elderly relatives just when they would like to enjoy some independence. Dissatisfaction with achievements or lack of recognition at work can also cause concern.

People in this age group may experience some of the early symptoms of ageing, such as grey hair, long-sightedness and dental problems. Ill-health is also more common. People are more likely to die as a result of heart disease, cancer and respiratory disorders.

Women begin to experience the MENOPAUSE (the 'change of life') any time after 40. This involves a series of changes in hormones which eventually means the end of a woman's ability to have children.

Activity 2.7

Arrange to interview a person in this age group. Find out how they feel about their age and stage in life. You could ask your parents or grandparents or a neighbour.

Before you start, write down the questions you want to ask under these headings:
- Work/career
- Home life
- Relationships with parents/children
- Social life
- Physical state.

Elders

Old age is often viewed in a negative way – as a stage of life that just brings problems, such as the need for residential accommodation or health and social care. But people do not change simply because they have reached old age. They continue with their lives in the same way they have always done. Many remain independent for most, if not all, of their lives.

The poet Robert Browning expressed an optimistic view of old age:

'Grow old along with me
The best is yet to be
The last of life for which the first was made.'

Another poet, Dylan Thomas, felt that 'Old age should burn and rage at close of day'. Do you agree with this sentiment?

Old age can be divided into two stages:
- early old age (up to 75 years old)
- late old age (beyond 75 years).

Today, people are living longer than ever before. About 18 per cent of the population are now over retirement age. Women tend to outlive men by about five years on average (see the graph opposite). The length of time a person can expect to live in years is known as his or her LIFE EXPECTANCY. Things which can affect life expectancy include:

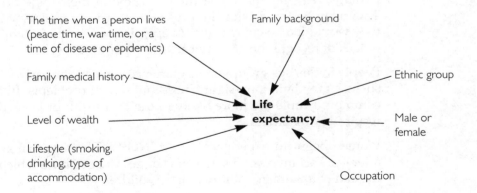

Physical changes in old age

Some of the physical changes that are happening throughout life and which become may become more obvious in old age include the following:
- **Skin** – dryness, wrinkling and loss of elasticity.
- **Hair** – growth slows, thinning occurs, men may go bald and all body hair goes grey.

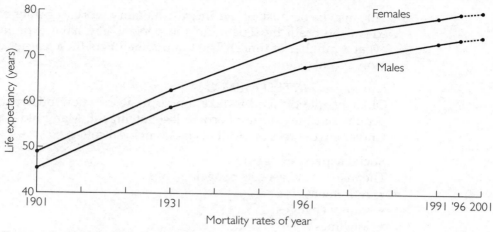

Expectation of life at birth, by sex

- **Eyesight** – long-sightedness may develop. People find it hard to distinguish colours. Changing from bright light to dark becomes a problem. Side vision becomes narrower. Cataracts and glaucoma can lead to blindness if left untreated.
- **Hearing** – the ability to hear deteriorates. Appreciation of high-pitch frequencies is lost first.
- **Smell and taste** – these senses deteriorate, sometimes causing loss of appetite.
- **Teeth** – may deteriorate quite early in life. Gum disease and decay are major problems. Carers need to be sensitive to this when providing food and attending to oral hygiene.
- **The lungs and respiratory system** – the lungs become less elastic and respiratory muscles weaken. Older people are more likely to be affected by physical disorders.
- **The heart and blood vessels** – the efficiency of the heart decreases. Blood vessels become less elastic and blood pressure may be raised.
- **The digestive system** – secretions of saliva and digestive juices decrease with age. Food takes much longer to pass through the body as muscles become weaker and less effective. Constipation can then become a problem.
- **The urinary system** – the kidneys become less efficient at filtering out waste products effectively.
- **The reproductive system** – in women the menopause will have marked the end of reproductive life.
- **The skeleton and muscles** – between the ages of 20 and 70 a person can lose two inches in height. Total bone mass is reduced and muscles become less flexible. Posture and mobility are likely to be altered considerably.

This all sounds negative. There is no denying that certain aspects of the ageing process can be very troublesome to some individuals, but not to everyone.

Psychological changes in old age

Personality

It is often said that old people do not like change. Like most of us, elderly people find familiar surroundings and situations a comfort. They are less likely to make mistakes in their own homes than when in hospital or residential care.

Memory

You may notice that some elderly people easily forget what has happened recently, but clearly remember things that have happened several decades ago.

This may be because of the way the memory works – earlier events are imprinted on the brain by repetition (the person may have experienced a particular event a number of times). The brain remembers these earlier events rather than more recent events.

Learning and INTELLIGENCE

Older people do tend to take longer to absorb new information than younger people, but they do not become less intelligent. Many older people take Open University degrees or enrol in classes in local colleges.

Social aspects of ageing

The main social aspects of ageing are:

- retirement
- family changes
- loneliness
- changing roles

Retirement

Retirement ages vary around the world – from 55 in Japan to 70 in the USA. When people leave work they feel that they lose their status in society. For example, a bank manager is no longer a bank manager or a teacher a teacher. People may lose their friendships, their income drops and their lifestyle changes.

Reduced income can give rise to problems. A retired person needs between 65 and 80 per cent of their previous income to maintain their standard of living at the same level. Most people's income drops by half and many drop by a lot more.

Family changes

When their children have grown up, many elderly people will become grand-parents and great-grandparents. Older people do have a considerable role to play in looking after their grandchildren, often in the form of child care and sometimes even financial help.

Drastic changes are brought about when one partner dies. A woman may have little experience of financial matters. She may not drive or feel confident to

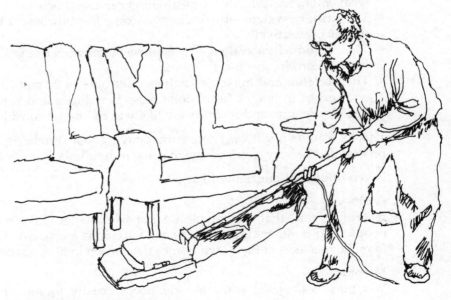

Adapting after losing a partner

attend functions by herself. A man may lack the ability to cook and care for himself and his home.

Loneliness

This may occur for a variety of reasons. People can be isolated in their own homes because of poor mobility or because they do not have many visitors or friends. It is also possible for people to feel extremely lonely when they live in residential homes. They may have difficulty in forming relationships with other residents and staff. Many people in residential care or hospital miss their own homes and familiar possessions.

Changing roles

Many elderly people worry that their declining health may cause them to be a burden to other people. An elderly person may become totally dependent on one of their children – the roles have been reversed.

Social factors affecting personal development

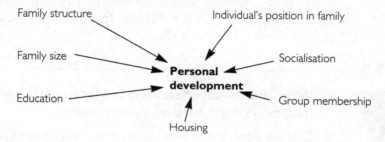

The family

Family structure

The image we see of families in magazines and on television is that they all live in beautifully decorated homes, that mothers are always glamorous, patient and perfectly groomed, and that fathers are well-built, smart and friendly. These parents are shown with their new car and their two 'designer' children. The reality may be something quite different.

Most people understand that the word 'family' refers to a group of people who may be related to each other by blood and by marriage. Everyone knows what a family is – a mum, a dad, sisters, brothers, grandparents.

Look around at your own family and compare it with those of your friends. It is clear that some families are large, some are small, some have two parents and others only one.

Activity 2.8

a Write down what you think a family is.

b Compare what you have written with other members of your group.

You may find that you have written down many similar points. Marriage or a partnership may have featured in some of your definitions, but of course they are many single-parent families.

Traditional marriage is declining and more people are living alone. In 1971 only

4 per cent of women were still unmarried by age 50. By 1987 this had risen to 17 per cent.

Today, more than one in four children are born to unmarried mothers. Most of these mothers are not lone parents, however. They live with partners, usually the father of the child.

However, the majority of people in the UK are married and living as a family unit, with or without children.

> A **family** is a group with relationships, created on the basis of blood relationship.
> A **family household** consists of family members who live together.

There are many ways in which the family can be organised and still carry out basic tasks. In some societies, the family structure is very different from that in the UK. For example, in the UK it is customary for one wife to have one husband. This is termed MONOGAMY. In Tibet, however, one woman may have several husbands – POLYANDRY. In other countries, one husband may have several wives – POLYGAMY.

Activity 2.9

a Write down what effect living in a family with more than two female parents (polygamy) might have on a young child.

b Discuss what you have written down with your class colleagues.

Family size
Families are now smaller than they used to be. In Victorian times the average family would have about six children. Today, the average is approximately two children.

Activity 2.10

a Write down what you think are the reasons for the fall in the average size of the family over the past hundred years.

b Compare a child living in a family of two children with a child living in a family of ten children. How do you think the size of the family affects a child's ability to develop personal relationships?

An individual's position in the family
A child's position in the family may affect how he or she behaves.
- A younger child may feel inferior. This may be because they have been looked after by older siblings (brother or sister). The younger child may feel that the older child is superior to them, or as being more like their parents.
- A younger child may have to work hard to get their views or wishes heard in a family with older children.
- An older child does not have to 'fight' to establish their place in the family.
- An older child, particularly the first-born, is more curious and interested in new situations and things. They tend to be less aggressive and show more responsibility than their younger siblings.

The family and emotional security

Some people stress the importance of the family in providing emotional satisfaction and security for its members. The family and home is a place where people can relax and be themselves, and test out relationships with confidence.

Other people argue that the family can restrict a person's ability to build relationships. They say that the family stifles personal development, causing strain, tension and discontent.

SOCIALISATION and education

A society needs its new members to be socialised into its patterns of behaviour, its values and its rules, such as:

- how to behave in public
- how to relate to older people
- what is 'right' and 'wrong'.

Socialisation means to become part of society, to make social. It begins with our families, especially our parents. Later, playgroup staff, nursery staff and teachers will also play a part in this process. Gradually, and unconsciously, children learn the 'rules' of the society they live in.

The process is never-ending – it continues throughout life as we meet new experiences. However, the part our families play is very important.

The intellectual needs of children are partly met by their time at school. There a child not only improves the skills learned at home, such as eating and drinking, but also learns how to relate to others and develop intellectual skills.

Schools offer linguistic (language) and intellectual stimulation. Children learn how to play and take part in creative activities. These activities will become more ordered as the child gets older, and the child will learn to read and use numbers (numeracy).

Those that stay at school until they are 16 will have the opportunity to obtain qualifications such as GCSEs and GNVQs. Staying at school or college until the age of 18 allows a student to gain vocational qualifications, BTEC or City & Guilds qualifications, or A-levels. These will allow a young person to enter higher education.

When a child is at school, he or she will be influenced by teachers. Think back to your days at primary school. Was there a teacher you liked? Did you work harder for this teacher? If you did, why do you think this was so?

Parents also play a part in the education their children. Early stimulation and the availability of opportunities for personal development provided by parents can make a great difference to a child's academic performance and ability to make personal relationships.

Children also learn how to behave and interact with other children and adults in a nursery, playgroup or school. (See also 'Peer groups' on page 58.)

Activity 2.11

In pairs or small groups, think about the skills that a child may not develop between birth and 5 years if he or she is denied all social contact. Make a list for your portfolio.

STEREOTYPING

Socialisation gives us our first lessons in stereotyping. As part of the socialisation process, we copy what our parents do. They decide the way we dress, the games and toys we play with and they tell which roles are appropriate in different social situations. Have you noticed that in many cases boys will tend to play with guns, and girls with dolls? Do they do this naturally or do they learn it from their parents and friends?

Activity 2.12

During your next placement at a nursery or school, observe how boys and girls behave while they are playing. What games do the girls play? Are they different in any way from the games played by the boys?

Housing

For many people, home is not only a place of accommodation, but also a source of their physical and mental well-being. Home should be a place where you can relax away from the tensions and pressures of the workplace. A person's house is regarded as their territory. People talk of 'home sickness' when they miss being at home.

People may be judged because of where they live, the type of house they live in, whether it is owned or rented. So housing is much more than bricks and mortar.

How can housing affect personal development?

During the Second World War, when many thousands of homes were damaged or destroyed, local authorities took the opportunity to clear away the slums and build new homes. In many instances, they replaced this poor housing with high-rise blocks of flats. The flats were generally of a higher standard than the housing they replaced. For the first time people had good sanitation, bathrooms and hot and cold water.

However, rehousing and slum clearances also meant destroying whole neighbourhoods and the feeling of community that existed in them. People who were moved often felt isolated, lonely and missed the support of the extended family – their brothers, sisters, grandparents or aunts or uncles.

The problems associated with high-rise flats caused, in many occupants, mental and emotional stress. Lack of social facilities caused frustration, which in a number of areas led to violence and vandalism. Many local authorities later realised that high-rise flats were a mistake. In recent years, therefore, authorities such as Sheffield, Leeds and Liverpool have demolished these flats and built conventional housing.

Activity 2.13

a What disadvantages can be associated with living in high-rise flats? You might like to consider some of the following:
- problems of noise
- lack of privacy
- access problems
- lack of play facilities
- lack of community spirit
- difficulties with stairs or lifts.

b How would living in these conditions help or hinder a person's ability to develop personal relationships?

Examine:
- teenagers
- adults
- elderly people.

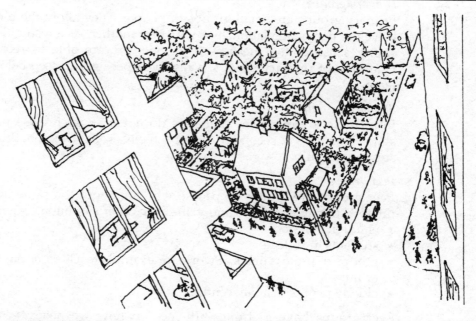

People who live in high-rise blocks often feel isolated and miss the support of friends, neighbours and extended families

Sheltered housing

Sheltered housing was developed during the 1920s and 1930s. It can be described as housing that has:
- a resident warden
- an alarm system fitted to each dwelling
- occupancy restricted to elderly people only
- accommodation all on one site.

Sheltered housing fulfils may housing needs:
- It meets the special needs of many elderly or disabled people.
- It reduces the possibility of emergencies occurring, as it has a resident warden.
- It offers more choice to people, as it is an alternative to residential care.
- It also helps to combat loneliness by offering the possibility of wide social contact, which also fosters independence.

Group membership

Most of us have been or are members of a group at some times in our lives. We form groups:
- for security
- to share common ideas and pleasures, for example to play football or basketball

- to help others, for example as a volunteer at a youth club
- to get things done, for example if you feel that the food is not up to standard at your college, you may form an action group to try to improve it
- to enjoy the companionship of others.

We feel safe and confident as one of a group sharing so much in common with other members.

Primary groups

Primary groups are small groups of people. They allow the members to establish close personal relationships with one another. As a result, the group forms a strong sense of togetherness. The members are able to rely on each other. Examples of primary groups: a family, a peer group (see below) or a football team.

Secondary groups

In secondary groups, the members do not have such close personal relationships. Examples of secondary groups: the National Union of Students, a football supporters' club.

Peer groups

Peer groups are groups of people who are about the same age, share similar interests or circumstances and value each other's opinions, such as:

- children at school
- students in college
- groups of professionals at work, for example teachers, social workers, doctors or nurses
- elderly people in a day centre.

Peer groups have a strong influence on how we behave. When you are at school, for example, peer groups are likely to influence your attitudes towards school work, the music you like, the way you dress and even the way you express yourself. They are an important part of the socialisation process (see pages 55 and 60).

A group of 3 to 4-year-olds at a playgroup – a peer group

Activity 2.14

a Make a list of the peer groups that you belong to.

b List how you think that the groups influence the way you behave.

Economic factors affecting personal development

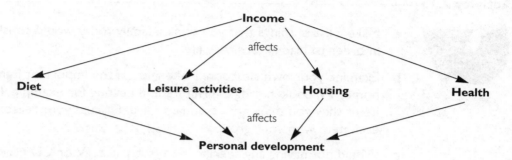

People receive income from a variety of sources, but mainly from:
- wages or a salary from an employer
- from the state in the form of Social Security or other benefits.

About one in five people live below the official poverty line. This is about £140 a week – about half the average weekly wage.

There are great differences between the lowest and highest paid jobs. The results of a recent survey of 8000 jobs advertised in a Job Shop showed that about 1000 jobs paid £3.50 per hour and 3000 paid £2.50 per hour. A person working 40 hours per week at £2.50 per hour would earn £100 a week, which is below the official poverty line.

On the other hand, the highest paid salaries can be very high indeed. A number of managers who manage large companies, such as electricity and water companies, can earn £200 000–£300 000 a year.

Many single and lone parents live in poor households. In the 1980s nearly one in three elderly women living alone and single parents living without partners were living below the poverty line. Only 28 per cent of all other households lived below the poverty line. In the early 1980s, the average income of single-parent households was less than 40 per cent of the income of two-parent families.

How can economic factors affect development?

Diet

People with little or no money may not be able to pay for food or heating. Children and older people, in particular, need good, nourishing food for their physical development, such as bone formation.

Leisure

People who have been unemployed for a long time, and who therefore have little money, are just able to buy the necessities for life: heating, food and shelter. They have little opportunity for leisure activities because of the cost. Being unable to take part in leisure activities, buy luxuries or visit friends can lead to depression and possibly ill-health.

Housing

Poorer people are more likely to live in cheap and poor housing and in crowded conditions. Cheaper accommodation is usually found in the middle of cities where the air may be polluted by car exhaust fumes and emissions from factories. Health can be affected by damp conditions and pollution. (See also social effects of housing, on page 56.)

Activity 2.15

a   Make a list of things that you think a family today would consider necessary in order to lead an ordinary life.

b   Examine your own situation. Make a list of the important items in your home, TV, cooker, fridge, furniture and heating for example. Highlight the items they you think are essential to live. Discuss your reasons for choosing each item with your group.

c   Would not having any specific item (such as a TV or CD player) hinder you ability to make personal relationships with other teenagers?

Personal relationships

Personal relationships give some of the greatest pleasures in life. Unfortunately they also cause problems for some people. Good personal relationships are based on mutual understanding and trust. Misunderstandings can cause misery and stress.

Childhood relationships

Children are not small adults. They are human beings that operate at a different intellectual, emotional and social level to that of adults. The development of relationships proceeds through a series of stages – a life-long process. The first two years of life are of vital importance in developing a person's PERSONALITY, IDENTITY and ability to form social and personal relationships.

Socialisation

In the UK men and women are expected to behave differently, perform various roles, which have a great effect on behaviour and personal relationships. A baby is not born with the knowledge of how to behave in social situations. It is acquired by the process of socialisation. As we have already seen, socialisation is the process by which we learn the patterns of behaviour which are expected of us. It is the process by which we learn language, the rules and regulations of society and what we believe in.

Activity 2.16

Write a definition of socialisation and give an example of how your experiences may have affected your ability to develop personal relationships.

Children learn by:
• repeating actions

- making associations between things
- observing and copying other people.

By watching others behave and observing the consequences of that behaviour for that person, the child identifies with the other person's behaviour.

Children learn by observing and copying other people

Learning is an active process and is done by the child. You cannot make a child learn, you can only provide the best situation possible for them to learn. For example if a child's behaviour results in a kiss or hug or other form of pleasant behaviour then the child has good reason to carry on doing whatever it was doing. On the other hand, if good behaviour does not result in a reward, the child may have no reason to improve its behaviour.

Children do not simply copy some actions. The relationship of the person to the child is also important. The child is more likely to copy someone who is important or nice to them, such as parents, teachers or playgroup staff.

As all families are not identical and behave in different ways towards children, some will be strict and others not so. So each child's personality and its ability to develop personal relationships will inevitably be quite different

LANGUAGE

Humans are the only species which have the ability to use language. Language is an organised system of symbols which humans use to communicate and establish relationships with one another.

Before children produce recognisable words, they produce sounds which become steadily more varied and deliberate. Before speaking recognisable words, many children pass through a stage of jargon. This is the stage that an adult may feel sure that a child has said words, but cannot make out what the words are. The mother's influence on a child's acquisition of language is important. Mothers hold power and influence in the family. They are often the first socialisers of their children.

Activity 2.17

Talk to a parent with a very young child. Ask what sounds the child produces and find out how the parent knows what the child is trying to communicate.

Certain groups of children lag behind others in their ability to develop speech and relationships. Middle-class children tend to talk more than children from working-class backgrounds. Why do you think this is so?

Children who have a good early experience of being loved, find it easier in later life to make loving relationships. To develop good relationships in later life, therefore, children need to experience affection, approval and tender physical closeness from their parents. If these are not experienced, it may be difficult to build up loving relationships later.

Loosening of ties between partners in a family, as a result of separation or divorce, can deeply influence relationships between children and their parents. However, in some cases it has been argued that single parents may be more child-centred than traditional families.

Adolescence

The importance of the peer group

Most teenagers become less and less reliant on their parents and involve themselves in a widening range of relationships. Many adolescents belong to peer groups which provide support while they establish new relationships. Teenagers breaking away from their parents feel safer if they belong to a group or are part of a crowd.

Belonging to a group gives teenagers a sense of identity, a feeling of being 'one of a gang'. Membership of a group also gives a feeling of SELF-ESTEEM. When you have self-esteem, you value yourself and feel confident, you know yourself and trust your judgement. Groups give a feeling of security and stability within which social skills can be developed. Social skills such as making friends both male and female can be practised.

Relationships with parents

Adolescence is a time of experimentation and rebellion. Although teenagers have disagreements with their parents, they still tend to agree with their parents on important issues such as need for honesty and integrity. Many value their parents' opinions. However, parents and teenagers do disagree about such things as clothes, music and hairstyle. Many teenagers find that parents are difficult to get on with, but relationships improve as they the teenager gets older.

Activity 2.18

Look back on your early teenage years. What can you remember of the relationship you had with your parents?

Write them down and discuss your examples with your class colleagues.

Adults

We have seen that childhood experiences will determine how easy or difficult it is for a person us to make relationships in later life. Making relationships in adult life is not something that comes as second nature. It is something that we have learned to do during our childhood. If children have had a loving stable relationship with their parents they will usually find it easier to develop good adult relationships.

Case study

Mary did not see much of her parents and when she did they kept her at a distance. Her parents were professional people with jobs that kept them away from the home for long periods during the day. When they did come home they brought work with them. They only had time to put Mary to bed.

Both parents had difficulty showing affection to Mary and she never learned how to give affection or trust in return. She never got close to her parents and had difficulty sharing her problems and concerns with them. She felt that she could not trust them with any intimate or important experiences.

When Mary grew up and began to form adult relationships, she had great difficulty in keeping friends or partners. She always wanted a lot of love and affection from them, but because of difficulty in giving love, the relationships never lasted very long.

Activity 2.19

a Read the case study regarding Mary.

b What kind of early relationships with her parents would have enabled her to establish positive personal relationships with people of her own age?

c Discuss your ideas with your class colleagues.

Relationships between clients and carers

In the past, health and social care workers controlled services and made decisions about the kind of help to offer to clients. The **power** was in the hands of the carers. This does not help to build a relationship with a client based on trust. The client needs to have some control, or power, too.

Establishing good relationships with clients

When working with clients we should help them to plan their own care by:
- not thinking that we know what they want or need better than they do
- involving them in all discussions about their future
- helping and supporting them to control their own situation
- helping them to recognise their abilities and life experience
- giving them accurate and honest information
- making sure that they have a choice.

To achieve this, we need to do the following:
- find out what the client's wants and needs are – this must only be done with the client's consent
- ensure that the client understands what is happening and agrees to any help offered
- involve all relevant carers and/or family in the process of finding out the client's needs or wants
- ensure that any care offered is based on agreement with all concerned – family, carer and client
- allow the client the greatest possible degree of choice in the services offered.

Health and social care services should be able to respond flexibly and sensitively to the needs of the client. This allows the client to feel independent and prevents their condition from getting worse.

Positive personal relationships can also be formed by focusing on the individual client and helping them within a charter of rights and a clear complaints procedure. That is, if the client sees that you are not judging them and that you are being objective about their situation, they are more likely to trust you and form a positive relationship with you. Helping is a contract between the carer and the client, one of trust and made within a positive relationship.

The needs of clients

We also build relationships with clients by showing them that we have up-to-date knowledge about the services that are available and how these services can help them.

Before you can give any advice, however, you need to find out what a client's needs are. How do we do this? We have to carry out an assessment of the client's situation – his or her abilities, expectations and aspirations. We do this by looking at their needs under the following headings:
- physical needs
- emotional needs
- intellectual needs
- social and cultural needs.

How are a client's needs assessed?

Maslow's Theory of Human Needs
This theory is a useful starting point. Maslow suggests that human needs are arranged in a series of five levels as shown in the diagram opposite.

The needs at Level 1, such as shelter, food and water, are the basic, essential requirements for any individual to live. The more complex needs shown from the middle of the pyramid upwards are only considered when the basic needs

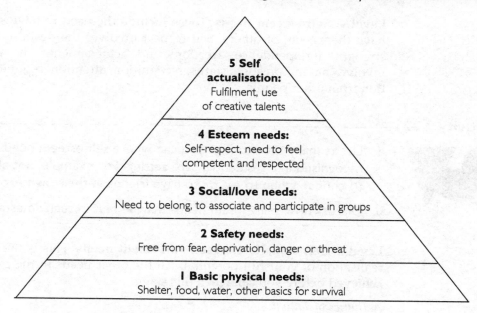

Maslow's hierarchy of needs

have been taken care of. For example, a homeless, hungry person needs shelter and food before they might worry about their social needs.

Level 1: Basic physical needs These include the need to satisfy hunger and thirst, the need for oxygen and the need to maintain temperature regulation. It also includes the need for sleep, sensory pleasures, maternal behaviour and sexual desire. If people are denied any of these needs, they may spend long periods of time looking for them. For example, if water or food is not readily available, most people's energies will be spent trying to obtain a supply.

Activity 2.20

Mrs Jones is elderly and confused. She has been missing for twenty-four hours. She is found in a local wood, very tired, hungry and thirsty.

What would you say are her most pressing needs?

Level 2: Safety needs Once basic physical needs have been met, a person's next concern is usually for safety and security, freedom from pain, threat of physical attack and protection from danger.

Level 3: Love and social needs These include affection, a sense of belonging, the need for social activities, friendships, and the giving and receiving of love.

Activity 2.21

Discuss with your class colleagues how children might have their love and social needs satisfied and in what situations might these needs occur.

Level 4: Self-esteem needs These include the need to have self-respect and to have the esteem of others. Self-respect involves the desire to have confidence, strength, independence, freedom and achievement. The esteem of others involves having prestige, status, recognition, attention, reputation and appreciation from other people.

Activity 2.22

a List as many situations as you can where self-esteem needs might not be recognised in a residential care setting. For example, not allowing residents to choose when to eat or to have friends in their own room.

b Discuss how self-esteem needs may be met in such an establishment.

Level 5: Self-actualisation/self-fulfilment needs This is the development and realisation of your full potential. All the other needs in the pyramid have to be achieved before you can reach this stage.

Activities of daily living
Another way to assess a client's needs is by using the 'activities of daily living' model. The assessor looks at the client's situation in relation to the everyday activities that people need to carry out. The activities include:

- **safe environment** – freedom from pain, comfort
- **body functions** – breathing comfortably, passing urine and faeces regularly, maintaining body temperature, etc.
- **nutrition** – a healthy diet, ability to eat, adequate and suitable fluids
- **personal cleaning and dressing** – mouth, teeth, eyes, ears, skin, suitable clothing, ability to dress and undress
- **mobility** – can the client get out of bed or exercise?
- **sleep** – sleep pattern, does the client wake during the night or sleep during the day?
- **sexuality** – is the client able to express their feelings? do they have the ability to enter into meaningful sexual relationships?
- **religion** – are the cultural needs of client being met? do they have the freedom to worship?
- **communication** – is the client able to communicate verbally, express emotions, use smell, touch?

Activity 2.23

a Decide what you think might be examples of the following needs:
  - religion needs
  - sexuality needs
  - nutritional needs
  - physical needs.

b With your class colleagues, discuss and decide at which levels of Maslow's pyramid these needs could be met, in a residential establishment.

How are people's needs met?

Physical needs
These may be met by:

- the provision of appropriate food and drink. For example, babies and people who are ill (such as someone suffering from diabetes) need different diets to a healthy adult.
- attending to personal hygiene. This is essential to prevent infection and spread of disease.

Intellectual and emotional needs
These may be more difficult to meet. It is important to:
- treat people as individuals
- respect people's individuality and opinions
- allow people to be as independent as possible.

For example, in a residential home for elderly people these needs may be met by allowing residents to:
- be independent
- choose their own meals
- make decisions about their own meal times, bed times, visiting times
- participate in social and educational activities in the establishment and outside of it.

Emotional needs are not separate from physical needs. People often feel better after a bath or a visit to the hairdresser. If they feel clean, they feel more secure when interacting with others. For example, someone who smells of urine will not feel emotionally secure when talking to relatives or friends. By meeting their physical need, their emotional need may also be met.

Social and cultural needs
These are an important aspect of a person's life. Social needs can be met by:
- encouraging people to socialise
- encouraging people to keep in touch with relatives and friends
- arranging for volunteers to visit them in their own homes if they are housebound.

Cultural needs are recognised when people are allowed to practise their cultural rituals and traditions. They can be met by recognising that people:
- need to practise their religion
- have cultural food preferences
- relate to individuals in their family according to their cultural practices

Activity 2.24

a Think about a client that you have been supporting in your work placement. Observe their behaviour over a period of time and using the information given in this section, list the needs that you think are being met and those that are not being met.

b Explain why you think so.

CONFIDENTIALITY

When, as a carer, you are involved in assessing a client, you will collect a lot of information. Because you have built up a relationship with your client, and because your client trusts you, he or she will feel able to tell you things that perhaps they have never told anyone else. They may say, for example, 'I've never told anyone else this, but . . .' or 'You won't tell my son, will you?' You can never be certain what your client might tell you.

Your client will trust you not to tell anyone about anything that has been said in confidence. All clients have a right to expect this, and all carers should respect their right to confidentiality.

However, you will need to record information for assessment and you should make sure that your client understands this. Reassure them that only people directly involved in the asssessment will have access to the records. They should be kept in a locked filing cabinet when not in use.

It might be tempting to chat about a client on the bus, in the staff lounge, with other clients, with your family or your client's family. However, you should make every effort not to do this. You will be abusing your client's trust in you.

Confidentiality establishes trust between carer and client

Why have confidentiality?
- It establishes a relationship of trust between carer and client.
- It enables the client to share information of a sensitive nature.
- The client will always know what happens to information given to a carer.
- It allows both the carer and client to respect each other.
- It prevents the client been exploited by others.

Confidentiality: client rights
Clients and patients have many rights in respect of confidential information. Some of these rights are set out in laws which outline the procedures for dealing with confidential information:
- the Mental Health Act
- the Medical Records Act
- the Access to Personal Files Act.

The Patient's Charter is not a legal document, but it does guarantee:
- confidentiality of health records
- access for patients to their health records

- that relatives and friends may only be given information about the patient if the patient agrees.

> **Things which help to form effective relationships**
> - seeing the client as an individual, not as a problem, such as a 'handicap' or an 'old person'
> - respecting people, their wishes and opinions
> - allowing and encouraging people to make choices for themselves
> - keeping confidential any information a client may give to you.
>
> **Things which hinder or act as barriers to forming effective relationships**
> - not respecting a client
> - being angry or aggressive towards a client
> - breaking confidentiality
> - not paying enough attention to a client, not having enough time to talk to them or help them.

Test yourself

1 When does the process of personal development begin?

2 What is the average weight of a new-born baby?

3 What is a pre-school child?

4 When does puberty usually begin?

5 When do women experience the menopause?

6 What does socialisation mean?

7 What problems can living in high-rise flats cause for people?

8 What is a peer group?

9 What are basic physical needs?

10 Why have confidentiality with clients?

Assignment A2.1
Personal development

This assignment is in the form of a report (word-processed, if possible) identifying when the main life stages occur and a description of their characteristics: physical, intellectual, emotional and social. You will be expected to comment upon how social and economic influences affect personal development and to identify the social, economic factors which have influenced your own personal development.

Your tasks

1 List the main life stages and when they occur.

2 Describe the characteristics of the main life stages.

3 Arrange to interview at least two of the following to obtain data about the main life stages:
   • a parent with an infant/child
   • an adolescent
   • an adult
   • an older adult.

   Use the information you gain to supplement the information asked for in Tasks 1 and 2.

4 Describe the social influences which can affect personal development. Use the following headings as a guide on which to base your report:
   • family (structure, size, position)
   • education (length, type, teacher influence)
   • environment (housing, open spaces, leisure facilities)
   • peer group membership.

5 Describe the effects of economic influences on personal development. Use the following headings as a guide on which to base your report:
   • income
   • financial commitments
   • how income is spent.

6 Give examples of the social and economic factors that may have influenced your own personal development.

Assignment A2.2
Personal relationships

This assignment will enable you to identify the personal relationships formed at each life stage and describe their main characteristics (sharing, supporting, physical attraction, power, dependency).

You will also be expected to describe the effects of forming positive relationships (self-esteem, sense of identity, social integration, social activity) and negative relationships (lack of self-esteem, loss of identity, isolation) at each life stage. You will also need to reflect on and identify how relationships you have formed have affected your own personal development. Word-process your work, if you can.

Your tasks

1 Describe the main characteristics of the following types of personal relationship:
   a friendships
   b sexual relationships

    c working relationships

    d parenting

      at each of the following life stages:

- infant
- child
- adolescent
- adult
- older adult.

2 Describe the effects of forming positive and negative relationships at each of the following life stages:

    a infant

    b child

    c adolescent

    d adult

    e older adult

    of each of the following types of relationships:

- sharing
- supporting
- physical attraction
- power
- dependency

    at each of the life stages.

3 Give examples of how a positive or negative relationship has affected your personal development.

Positive	Negative
self-esteem	lack of self-esteem
sense of identity	loss of identity
social integration	isolation
social activity	

Assignment A2.3
Relationships between clients and carers

In this assignment you will be expected to make a report (preferably word-processed) on the relationships of two different clients:

- one the subject of the case study
- the other from your work placement.

You will need tc identify what contributes to forming effective relationships, the needs of the two clients and how these needs are met by carers. You will also be expected to identify barriers to forming effective relationships.

Your tasks

I Read the following case study and write a report using the following headings:

- Things which help to form effective relationships
- Things which hinder or are barriers to forming good relationships
- The needs of the client and how these were met by the carers: physical, intellectual, emotional, social and cultural needs.

Case study

Mr Joe Doncaster is 90 years old. He is well-educated and has lived alone since his wife left him 40 years ago. Until his retirement at 70 years of age, he was a manager of a small steelworks. For the past 20 years he has worked as a volunteer financial adviser for a local voluntary organisation. He has led a very sociable life. He is a keen theatre-goer and is also a very good bowls player.

Joe has recently had a hip replacement which was not a great success. The after-effect of the operation has restricted his mobility and he finds it difficult to sit still for long periods or play bowls. As a result, his social life has been severely restricted.

Joe decided some months ago that he would like to enter residential care as he was feeling lonely. He was also finding it more and more difficult to look after himself after a recent fall, as a result of which he has lost his self-confidence. He was advised by a neighbour to ring his local Social Services Department and talk to the duty social worker.

The duty social worker promised him a visit to discuss his situation within two weeks. Five weeks later a social worker arrived without an appointment and in a great hurry. Joan, the social worker, indicated that she was running late with her appointments and as a consequence she could only give him 15 minutes of her time. Joe had not had time to compose himself for the interview. He became upset and angry with the social worker because of what he saw as an uncaring attitude.

However, as a result of his assessment by the social worker, it was agreed that Joe should be offered a place in Oakridge Elderly Person's Home, some miles from where he lived. The manager of Oakridge visited Joe to discuss with him the time and date of admission. She also asked him if he wanted to bring into the home any personal belongings or pets. They were able to agree on certain pieces of furniture and some books. Joe was very impressed by the manner in which the manager treated him. She discussed issues with him and allowed him to come to his own decisions.

Joe liked the home. It was democratic. He was able to get up in the morning when it suited him, and he had a choice of meals for lunch and dinner. He liked his room with his personal belongings. He felt safe and secure as he had a key to his room. However, he did not feel safe when having a bath so he had assistance from the care staff. He liked one member of staff in particular who listened to him. He told her about his life. He confided to her that after his wife had left him he had relationships with a number of women, none of which lasted very long.

One evening when this member of staff was off-duty, Joe asked another member of staff to assist him in having a bath, while she was doing so she said 'I must be careful with you, I hear you are a ladies' man.' This upset Joe very much. He felt that the other member of staff had betrayed him by passing on what he thought was confidential information. Joe became depressed after this episode and felt that he could not trust any of the staff.

2 Write a report on a young or adult client using the following headings:
   • Things which help to form effective relationships
   • Things which hinder or a barriers to forming good relationships
   • The needs of the client and how these were met by the carers: physical, intellectual, emotional, social and cultural needs.

Key words

After reading this chapter you should be able to understand the following words and phrases. If you do not, go back through the chapter and find out, or look them up in the Glossary.

Pre-school child	*Directed thinking*
Adolescence	*Puberty*
Oestrogen	*Testosterone*
Psycho-social	*Menopause*
Life expectancy	*Personality*
Intelligence	*Monogamy*
Polyandry	*Polygamy*
Socialisation	*Stereotyping*
Identity	*Language*
Self-esteem	*Confidentiality*

CHAPTER 3

Investigating Working in Health and Social Care

What is covered in this chapter

- Working in health and social care services in the UK
- Jobs in health and social care
- Planning for employment in health and social care

These are the resources you will need for your Investigating Working in Health and Social Care portfolio:

- job descriptions you have collected
- information about the roles of health and social care workers
- information from careers advisers
- your curriculum vitae
- your written answers to each of the activities in the chapter
- your written answers to the Test Yourself questions at the end of this chapter
- your completed assignments: A3.1, A3.2 and A3.3.

Introduction

After you have read this chapter and carried out the activities and assignments you will have an understanding of:

- employment opportunities in health and social care
- the range of jobs in health and social care and their purpose
- the skills and qualifications needed to obtain those jobs.

Working in health and social care services in the UK

The main providers of health and care

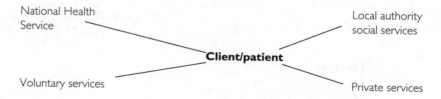

The National Health Service

Health care has not always been free in the UK, but today we do have a system of free health care – the National Health Service (NHS). What is the NHS and who are the people who work in it?

Until 1948 people had to pay for medical and social care. Many found this difficult to do because they were poor. One way to pay for these services was by taking out insurance, for example, through friendly societies or trade unions.

Then they knew the money would be there when they needed it.

In 1948 the government nationalised the health services and created the National Health Service. It brought various health and care services under the control of one person, the Minister of Health. The reason for this was to try to provide a fair and free service for everyone. However, there are still some people today who choose to pay for private health services.

The people who work in the NHS and who look after those who are sick do so in hospitals, health centres, nursing homes, general practitioners' centres or surgeries and also in the client's or patient's own home.

Hospitals

Hospitals are the places where people go for treatment when they are too ill to be cared for at home. They are normally referred to a hospital by their General Practitioner (see opposite). They may be seen first as an out-patient in a clinic and may later become an in-patient if they need special treatment or an operation.

Activity 3.1

Find out how many hospitals there are in your locality and the main services they provide.

Discuss your findings with your class colleagues.

Job roles in health care

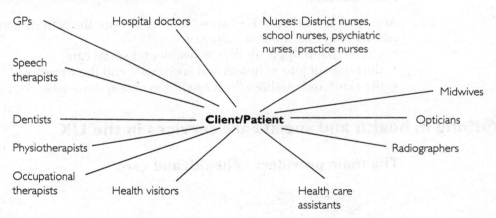

Doctors

Hospital doctors

In hospitals patients are looked after by teams of doctors, who specialise in particular areas, such as:
* paediatrics (children)
* obstetrics (childbirth)
* geriatrics (elderly people).

The senior doctors in the team may be referred to as specialists or consultants.

The role of the doctors is to:
* **diagnose** – find out what is wrong with the patient

- **prescribe** – decide on the treatment to help the patient
- **monitor** – review the condition of the patient and change the treatment if necessary.

The doctors are supported by other health and social care workers such as:
- nurses
- physiotherapists
- occupational therapists
- radiographers
- hospital social workers.

You will find out more about these workers later.

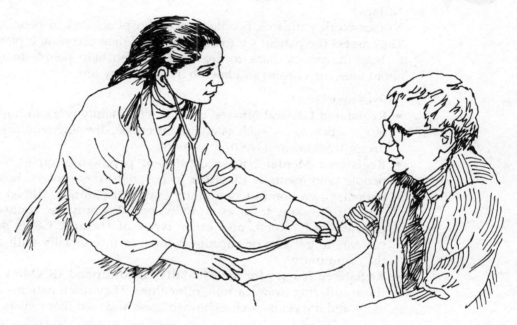

General Practitioners (GPs)

GPs (or family doctors) are the main route for most people to good health care. GPs are paid by the government through the local Family Health Service Authority (FHSA, see page 273). Their pay depends on the number and type of patients registered with them.

Most people select their own GP when they are over 16 years old from the list of GPs kept by the FHSA. GPs:
- diagnose and treat illness
- monitor patients with chronic (long-term) illness
- prevent disease through screening programmes
- refer patients to other services, such as hospitals and social services
- offer advice and support to patients, and also to their carers, relatives and family.

GPs work in the community. They are based in surgeries (or practices) covering particular areas. Sometimes a number of GPs work together in a group practice.

GPs employ receptionists and clerical staff to run their practices. They often also employ practice nurses. Social workers, health visitors and midwives are also often based at GP's practices. You will find out more about these workers later.

Training: Initially doctors undertake a five- or six-year degree course, before going on to specialise in a particular area of medicine or becoming a GP.

Entry requirements: A wide range of GCSEs, plus three or four A-levels in science subjects.

Activity 3.2

Find the address of your local FHSA. Ask your local FHSA for a list of GPs in your locality. How many of them work in group practices?

Nurses

Nurses work with sick people both in hospitals and in people's own homes. They assess the patient's nursing needs and then carry out a plan of health care to help the person back to health. They also help people to make decisions about their own health and how to live a healthy life.

Nurses may be:
- **Registered General Nurses** (RGNs) who mainly work in hospitals, carrying out practical tasks, such as giving injections, dressing wounds, administering drugs, washing and feeding patients.
- **Registered Mental Nurses** (RMN), or psychiatric nurses, who work with people who mentally ill, either in hospitals, day centres, hostels and in the patients' own homes (community psychiatric nurses, CPNs). The RMN carries out the same tasks as an RGN, but also provides counselling (for both patients and carers), and other types of therapy. CPNs sometimes help patients to get jobs or encourage them to mix socially with other people in the community.
- **Registered Nurses for the Mentally Handicapped** (RNMH) who work with those suffering from learning difficulties. They teach patients everyday social skills and life skills, such as how to dress and feed themselves.

Training: The RGN, RMN and RNMH qualifications have been replaced by a new training programme called PROJECT 2000. This is a three-year training programme for nurses. In the first half of the programme the student nurses study subjects which are common to all fields of nursing. When they have passed the first part, they can then decide to study a specialist area, either:
- adult nursing
- mental handicap nursing
- mental health nursing
- children's nursing.

Entry requirements:
- Age – over 17½
- At least five GCSE passes at grade C or above.
- Other equivalent qualifications – BTEC National Diplomas or appropriate GNVQs may also be considered.

In addition, you need to have:
- an interest in caring
- good communication skills
- the ability to work in a team
- the ability to remain calm under pressure.

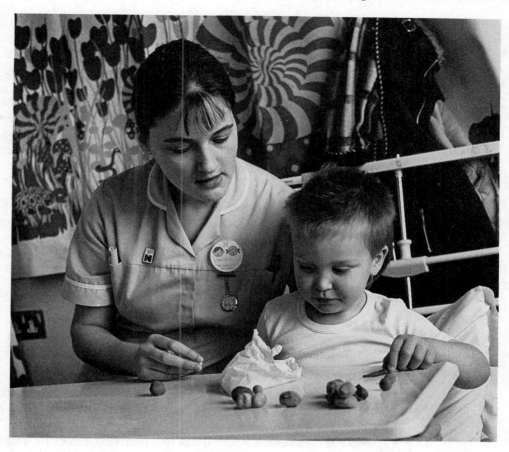

A nurse may decide to specialise in children's nursing

Practice nurses

Practice nurses are RGNs. They are usually employed directly by a local GP practice, where most of their work is carried out. They perform such tasks as:

- dressing patients' wounds
- blood and urine tests
- giving injections
- offering family planning advice.

There are approximately 4000 practice nurses employed.

District nurses

District nurses are RGNs. They are employed by local health authorities. They provide the link between hospitals and the primary health care team (GPs, nurses, social care staff and others) by MONITORING A PERSON'S ABILITY to cope in his or her own home.

They provide physical, social and emotional support and nursing care for acute (short-term) and chronic (long-term) patients and their families in their own homes. They carry out a range of tasks, including:

- assessing patients' needs
- giving injections
- changing dressings
- taking blood tests

- washing and feeding patients
- giving advice and teaching people about practical care.

There are approximately 20 000 district nurses employed.

Health visitors
Health visitors are RGNs who have had further training leading to the Health Visitor's Certificate. By law health visitors have to visit (or see) regularly all children under the age of 5 to ensure that their progress is physically, emotionally and socially normal. They also offer parents support and advice about feeding, safety and child development.

Other roles of health visitors include:
- health education – advising people how to keep healthy and prevent illness
- running antenatal classes for expectant mothers
- running child health clinics
- supporting patients, particularly elderly people, in their own homes and helping ill people to live with their disabilities.

There are about 13 000 health visitors working in England, Wales and Scotland.

Midwives
Midwives are independent, professional nurses in their own right. They are usually RGNs who have completed an 18-month midwife course.

They are responsible for:
- supervising the antenatal care of pregnant women – monitoring the health of the mother and the unborn baby, and offering advice on diet, exercise, parenthood and care of the baby
- postnatal care once a woman has had her baby, either in hospital or at home – they look after the mother and baby for ten days after birth, when the health visitor takes over
- delivering babies themselves, or in difficult situations assisting a doctor to deliver a baby.

School nurses
The school nurse is an RGN. She gives advice on health matters in schools, and looks after the children, making regular screening checks, and giving advice about such matters as immunisation.

While the main, face-to-face delivery of care is from nurses and doctors, there is a large range of professions allied to medicine. They support the doctor in looking after and treating the patient.

Radiographers
Radiographers use:
- X-rays and ultrasound to look at internal organs, for example the ultrasound, or 'scan', in pregnancy to look at the unborn baby
- X-rays and gamma rays to destroy tissues in illnesses such as cancer.

The radiographer is a technician, instructed by a **radiologist** – a specialist doctor who, for example, interprets X-ray pictures and produces reports for the doctor requesting the X-ray.

Training: Radiographers have to undertake a three-year course leading to a diploma or degree in radiography.

Entry requirements: Three GCSEs at grades A-C, and two A-levels.

Physiotherapists

Physiotherapists help people to overcome problems caused by a wide range of illness and physical conditions. They treat people of all ages, either in hospital or in their own homes. They play an important role in the mobility of patients using supportive and manipulative exercises to develop muscles for movement. For example, a person who has had a broken arm and has just had the plaster removed may need help to build up the muscles or loosen stiff joints. Physiotherapists also provide treatment to relieve pain.

Patients are usually referred to physiotherapists by doctors. The physiotherapists then work in co-operation with doctors in planning the patients' physiotherapy programmes, and also discusses treatment with the patient.

A physiotherapist at work

Training: Physiotherapists have to undertake a three-year degree course in physiotherapy.

Entry requirements: Five GCSEs at grades A-C, including English and two science subjects, plus two A-levels. Three A-levels are required for entry to many courses.

Academic requirements are important, but a physiotherapist should also have:
- an interest in people
- compassion
- patience
- fitness
- confidence
- the ability to work in a team.

There are now approximately 9500 physiotherapists working in the NHS. Some have private practices.

Occupational therapists

Occupational therapists (OTs) treat physical and mental illness with activity. They help people to overcome the effects of illness, disability or severe injury by first assessing their capabilities and then helping them to overcome difficulties and learn to carry out tasks by themselves. They advise on aids and adaptations that might help a client to manage better in their home.

A large part of their work is with people suffering from physical or learning difficulties. They work on a one-to-one basis and with groups. Their work requires a great deal of tact, sympathy and understanding.

Many OTs work in the community and in social services departments. In the community their job is to visit clients in their own homes and assess with their carers how they manage daily tasks, such as washing, dressing and getting in and out of bed.

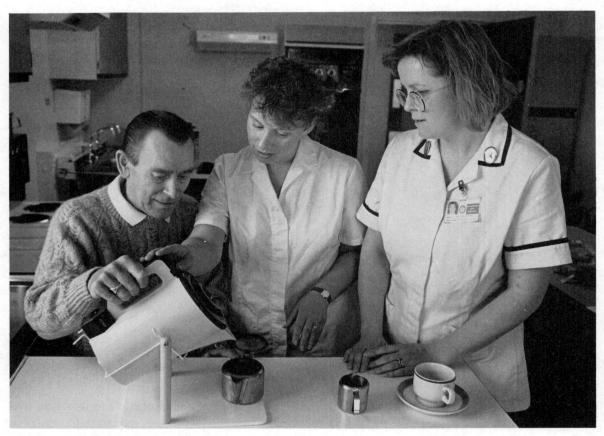

Occupational therapists assessing a client performing daily tasks

Training: Occupational therapists have to undertake a three-year training course.

Entry requirements: Minimum of two A-levels and three GCSEs at grade C or higher, which must include English Language and a science subject. A BTEC or appropriate GNVQ qualification may also be accepted.

Currently, nearly 5000 occupational therapists (OTs) work in the NHS.

Activity 3.3

Contact your local social services department and find out if they employ occupational therapists. Make arrangements to visit the OT and talk to him or her about their job and the people they support.

Speech therapists

Speech is an important part of everyday life. Speech therapists help people with speech disorders, ranging from children with delayed speech development to older people recovering from a stroke. Most of their work is with children. Many work in hospitals, but others work in schools and clinics.

The skills of the speech therapist are directed towards helping people gain some independence and intelligible communication. They use their practical skills to rehabilitate, educate and counsel patients and their families.

Training: A three- or four-year degree course, or a two-year postgraduate diploma.

Entry requirements: Five GCSEs at grade A–C, including English Language, a biological science and sometimes a modern language, plus two A-levels or a BTEC National Diploma.

The personal qualities needed are:
- the ability to build a one-to-one relationship with people
- flexibility
- patience
- the ability to listen, explain and reassure people.

Health care support workers

The HEALTH CARE SUPPORT WORKER (or health care assistant – HCA) is someone who assists health care professionals in hospitals, clinics and community nursing. They:
- help maintain stock on the ward, and equipment and materials in their workplace
- help patients in and out of bed
- help patients to dress
- make beds
- prepare drinks for patients.

They may also take patients' temperatures, perform simple urine tests and change simple dressings.

Training: Training is on-the-job and many support workers complete Levels 2 and 3 National Vocational Qualifications in Health and Social Care.

Entry requirements: There are no minimum entry requirements for this type of work. However, most hospitals set their own entrance tests.

Dentists

Dentists in general practice carry out all types of dentistry:
- fillings
- fitting dentures
- putting crowns on teeth
- cleaning teeth
- advising people on dental hygiene and how to look after their teeth.

Training: A five-year degree course provides the basic training for the work.

Entry requirements: Usually three A-levels and a number of GCSEs are necessary for entry to university.

To be an effective dentist you must:
- have a liking for people
- have an interest in their welfare
- be able to put tense and nervous people at ease.

Over 23 000 dentists work in the UK. Most do some work for the NHS.

Opticians

Opticians measure people's eyesight, and advise whether glasses should be worn. They fit glasses and contact lenses. This is done in optician shops or sometimes in hospitals or clinics. Most people have to pay the full cost for testing, glasses or contact lenses. Full-time students and children obtain the service free or pay some contribution towards the cost.

Training: A three-year degree course followed by further training for professional examinations and registration.

Entry requirements: Five GCSEs and two A-levels.

Community and social services

Social service departments (SSDs) were set up by local authorities to provide community-based services for people in their own homes. The service is available to everyone, but is particularly concerned with families.

The Social Services Committee of every local authority (council) oversees the four main responsibilities of its social services department:
- to provide childcare as specified in the various Children's Acts and adoption Acts, including the 1989 Children Act
- to provide and regulate residential accommodation for older people and

people with disabilities as specified in the 1948 National Assistance Act and the 1984 Registered Homes Act

- to provide welfare services for older people, people with disabilities and people who are chronically (long-term) ill and to act as set out in the various mental health acts
- to refer clients to other organisations, such as voluntary organisations, for services.

Activity 3.4

Ask your local social services department for a copy of their Community Care Plan. This plan has to be published every year and is available to the public. Your public library will also have a copy. Make notes on the services provided by the social service department.

Job roles in community services

Social worker

The first worker we think of in the social care field is the social worker. Social workers provide support for individuals and families in terms of social rehabilitation and community services. They work in the community or in hospitals (hospital social workers). They specialise in:

- childcare work
- helping elderly people
- working with people suffering from mental illness.

Training: Qualified social workers have obtained a qualification covering all areas of social work. They may specialise in one area later.

The qualification that most social workers have is the Certificate of Qualification in Social Work (CQSW). Residential and day-care staff may have obtained the Certificate in Social Service (CSS). However, recent changes to training have involved the development of a new qualification to replace these – the DIPLOMA IN SOCIAL WORK (Dip.SW).

The Diploma in Social Work is now the professional qualification for all social workers (field and residential). It involves two years of study and practice supervised by a qualified social worker.

Entry requirements: Two A-levels at grade A–E and three GCSE passes at grade A–C. A GNVQ at Advanced level or a BTEC National Diploma are also accepted.

Home care staff

A number of staff provide the everyday emotional, social and practical support to clients living in their own homes. By law, local authorities must provide home care assistants (formerly called home-helps). They carry out such tasks as:

- simple cleaning
- lighting fires
- shopping
- cooking
- basic personal tasks.

Most of their work is concerned with supporting elderly people, but they do also work with people with physical disabilities and families with young children.

Training: Short training courses are offered by employers.

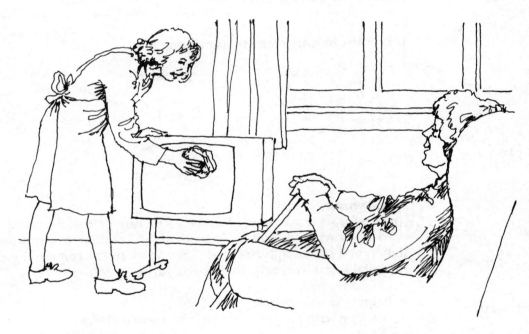

A home carer

Meals-on-wheels
This service is becoming increasingly important as more and more elderly dependent people chose to live in their own homes. About 33 million meals are provided every year to people in their own homes in England. This service is provided by the local authority in many areas but it is still also offered by voluntary agencies such as the Women's Royal Voluntary Service (WRVS) or Women's Institute (WI) in rural areas.

Nursery nurses
The Children Act 1989 made it law that local authorities should provide day care for children in need aged under 5 years. Day nurseries for children between 6 weeks and 5 years old are staffed by workers with qualifications in child care. There are also privately-run day nurseries.

Meals-on-wheels

The tasks of a nursery nurse involve all aspects of routine care, such as:
• feeding
• washing
• toilet training
• play activities.

A nursery nurse is both supervisor and friend to the children in his or her care.

Training: The special skills required for this type of care are recognised and nursery nurses have either National Nursery Examinations Board (NNEB) Diploma, a BTEC National Diploma or a Certificate in Caring Services (Nursery Nursing). Courses leading to these qualification are still available in colleges in the UK. However, since 1994 many courses have been organised so that a student can obtain all or part of an NVQ (see page 88) in Child Care and Education.

NVQs in Child Care and Education are available at level 2 in such areas as:
• Work with Babies
• Work in a Community-Run Pre-School Group
• Work in a Pre-School Group
• Work in Support of Others

and at level 3 in such areas as:
• Family Day Care
• Group and Education
• Pre-School provision.

Most of these qualifications can only be obtained by on-the-job training which is more relevant than learning from books or in college without work experience placements.

Entry requirements: No formal requirements, but a good level of education, such as three GCSEs or a GNVQ Intermediate in Health and Social Care.

Activity 3.5

Talk to the manager of your college nursery (if there is one) or a local nursery or playgroup. Arrange to visit the manager and discuss with him or her the type of work that is available locally in the childcare field. Make notes and compare them with those of your classmates.

National Vocational Qualifications (NVQs) in Health and Social Care

In the past many areas of social care were staffed with untrained, unqualified staff, but now there are qualifications which recognise the skills of the these people. In recent years the government in the UK has encouraged a new form of training, NATIONAL VOCATIONAL QUALIFICATIONS (NVQs). At the moment these new qualifications are for people employed in hospitals, residential, day or home care situations.

To obtain an NVQ in Health and Social Care, students have to show that they are competent (able) to do the job for which they are being assessed. NVQs measure what you can do, as well as how much you know and understand about the job.

If you want to know more about NVQs, talk to your tutor or careers adviser, or write to the National Council for Vocational Qualifications, 222 Euston Road, London NW1 2BZ.

Other jobs in health and social care

There are many other people who have an important role to play in supporting the people who work face-to-face with clients. Some like receptionists have direct contact with clients or patients, while others work in the background, for example maintenance staff and catering staff. These jobs can be described as **indirect care.**

Receptionists and clerical jobs
Receptionists are often the first health and social care workers that people come into contact with. Receptionists work in hospitals, clinics, day centres, GP's practices and health centres. They keep records, look after waiting lists and make appointments. As they are dealing with people under stress, they need tact and understanding to do the job properly. Clerical staff also keep and up-date patient and client records.

Administrators and managers
Managers are responsible for planning, developing and monitoring services. The manager of a hospital usually has degree in management. However, there are some doctors and nurses who have become hospital directors, and no longer practise medicine.

Domestic and maintenance staff
Domestic staff work in hospital wards, residential care and day centres. They support the care staff by cleaning, washing up and also talking to clients and patients. Maintenance staff look after equipment, keeping such things as lifts and lights in working order. In care settings they also keep clients' aids and equipment in order.

Voluntary services

Some services are provided by voluntary organisations. This means that some, or all, of their workers are volunteers – they are not paid. Many of them are charities and have to raise money to enable them to provide their services.

The WRVS is a voluntary organisation which provides a wide range of services to people of all ages, for example playgroups, clubs for elderly people, meals-on-wheels, shops in prisons and hospitals.

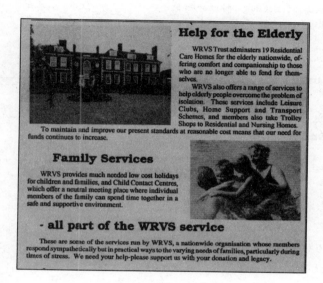

Help for the Elderly

WRVS Trust adminsters 19 Residential Care Homes for the elderly nationwide, offering comfort and companionship to those who are no longer able to fend for themselves.

WRVS also offers a range of services to help elderly people overcome the problem of isolation. These services include Leisure Clubs, Home Support and Transport Schemes, and members also take Trolley Shops to Residential and Nursing Homes.

To maintain and improve our present standards at reasonable cost means that our need for funds continues to increase.

Family Services

WRVS provides much needed low cost holidays for children and families, and Child Contact Centres, which offer a neutral meeting place where individual members of the family can spend time together in a safe and supportive environment.

- all part of the WRVS service

These are some of the services run by WRVS, a nationwide organisation whose members respond sympathetically but in practical ways to the varying needs of families, particularly during times of stress. We need your help-please support us with your donation and legacy.

Private services

Some patients and clients prefer to pay for their health and social care. They may take out insurance to help pay for these services. Many services provided by the NHS and local authorities may also be provided by private organisations, such as:
- private day nurseries
- private specialist clinics
- private hospitals
- private nursing homes.

Jobs in health and social care

Assignment A3.2 at the end of this chapter will give you the opportunity to identify some jobs in the health and social care field that might suit your skills, experience and ambitions. You will be asked to look at two jobs, one which you might like to go into when you finish this course or the GNVQ Intermediate course, and a second job that you might progress to after you have gained more experience and qualifications.

To give you some help with this task we will look at two jobs in more detail:
- the care assistant
- the nursery nurse.

We will consider the tasks and responsibilities of each job, and the skills and

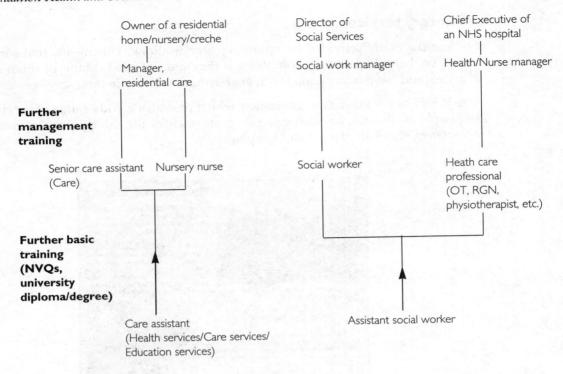

Career paths in health and social care

qualifications needed. In the final section of this chapter we will look at how you might apply for such jobs.

The care assistant

The job of a basic grade care assistant looking after children, adults or elderly people is the first rung on the ladder of a career in health and social care.

Mary Jackson works as a care assistant in a home for elderly people. She spent two years at college. In her first year she completed a one-year preparation for vocational work (CPVE) course, and in her second a BTEC First Diploma in Social Care.

The CPVE course was something like the course you are now completing and the BTEC First Diploma is the equivalent to the GNVQ Intermediate qualification. When she had left school she was determined not to do her A-levels. She wanted to go to a large college where she could have a wide choice of courses. She chose the CPVE course because, like the GNVQ Foundation course, it allowed her to gain experience of care and also gave her the opportunity to find out about other subjects, such as leisure and tourism, the performing arts or art and design.

Mary had at first wanted to work with children. However, after work experience in an home for elderly people, she changed her mind. Many students come to college or schools thinking they know exactly what they want to do. However, one of the main characteristics of a good care worker is flexibility and a willingness to learn from experience. This Mary had obviously done.

> 'The CPVE course allowed me to test out a number of care situations. I knew from the start that I didn't want to gain experience in art or acting. At first, I had wanted to work with children. I obtained work experience in a children's playgroup, a nursery, an old people's home and a casualty department. It was during this work experience that I found that I wanted a job helping old people, and not children as I had originally thought.
>
> I enjoyed working with children but I got great satisfaction from working in the old people's home. I felt at home with old people and I think they liked me. During my work experience I found that many of the care assistants had BTEC or City and Guilds qualifications. I was lucky to be able to progress to the BTEC First course in Care at the college where I did the CPVE course. The tutors were very nice. Because I had a number of work experiences on the CPVE course, they allowed me to spend most of my BTEC work experience working with elderly people at day centres and residential homes.'

She had also kept her ears and eyes open during her work experience. When she found out that many of the care staff had either BTEC or City and Guilds qualifications, she was determined to get on to such a course if she could. She applied for the BTEC course and was lucky to obtain a place.

Once Mary had completed the BTEC First Diploma course, she applied for a job as a care assistant at an establishment near her home. She was told later that she was successful in getting the job because she had submitted an excellent application form and had impressed the selection panel by her confidence and her obvious love of working with elderly people. A good reference from her tutor was also helpful, but more important was the references she had got from the people in charge of the establishments where she had her work experience.

> 'The job suits me. My manager has told me the she will put me forward for more training when I get some experience. I think it is important to get as much training as you can. It helps you to do the job properly and you owe it to the clients to be as skilled as possible.
>
> At the moment I work under a senior care assistant who helps me when I have problems or when want to know something. I mostly help the residents with dressing and undressing, bathing, and I help those with mobility problems to get around. I also change beds and empty commodes.
>
> What I like best is talking to the elderly people and their visitors and going on outings with the residents. They are such interesting people and have lived such varied lives.'

Activity 3.6

Visit the careers library in your college or school. Make a list of courses and training programmes which would be suitable for Mary to further her career.

Mary has a varied work routine and no two days are quite the same, but there *is* a routine. She is always aware of the fact that the residents come first and that she must never impose her ideas or views on them. If she is worried

91

What May likes best is talking to the elderly people

because someone doesn't take their pills or eat their meals, she always tells a senior member of staff. She is aware that the establishment is the residents' home, and she treats them as she would if she was in their own home.

'I get to work about 7 o'clock in the morning. The staff who have been working during the night tell us of any problems that may have happened during the night. My first job is to lay the tables for breakfast. Residents can come for breakfast at any time during the morning up to about 11.30 when we have to get ready for lunch.

We work in teams. Each team is responsible for looking after about ten residents. That way you get to know them really well. It doesn't mean that we don't talk to or help the others. It just means that we concentrate on our residents. I help get anyone up out of bed if they ask. We always knock on the door of their room before entering. One or two residents, if they are not too well, may have their meals in bed.

When breakfast is finished, I help clear away the tables and help those who ask for support to go to their own rooms, to the TV or to the activities room. I have plenty of time to talk to and listen to residents. I like doing this. I also like going out to the library, pub or shops with the residents.

I make drinks for residents and visitors. At lunch time I help to feed any residents who may have difficulty feeding themselves. After lunch I help clear up and find out what the residents want to do after lunch. I finish work at 1 o'clock.

Some days we have meetings at which we talk about the residents. We discuss how they are getting on and the best way to help them. Sometimes a resident's GP is present as is also the district nurse.

I am expected to write any unusual happenings in a reporting book, such as a resident not taking their tablets, not eating or perhaps if they had an accident. I also see one of the senior managers once a week for supervision sessions. We talk about how I am getting on and how I do things. I also discuss how I could do things better. I look forward to these sessions and am disappointed if they have to be cancelled because of an emergency in the home. We also report if the resident has had a visit from relatives or friends. This is not to check on the residents. If we know that a person doesn't get visits, we can make sure that they don't feel lonely.'

We can see from what Mary has said that she has the qualities necessary to do this job. She is pleasant, caring, willing to talk to people and, most importantly, she listens to them. She respects other people's views, does not impose her views on others and tries to find out what people really want. She is willing to work as part of a team and to be flexible. Importantly she realises that you do not stop learning when you get a job. She likes supervision sessions when she can discuss her job and how to do it better. She is also aware that she needs further training to become better at her job.

'I feel positive about the idea of further training. However I would like to wait a few years. I am not sure that I want to become a manager of a residential establishment. I might like to work with elderly people in their own homes.

If I stay in residential care work I shall do my NVQ qualification in care. I don't have to leave work to do this and there are no exams. I am assessed by my supervisor as to how competently I am in doing my job. After looking at me doing certain tasks a number of times, and me telling her why I did certain tasks in a certain way, I become competent and can be awarded the NVQ in Care at level 2. I can go on to take levels 3 or 4 later.'

Activity 3.7

List the personal qualities you think are necessary for an individual to be able to carry out the role of care assistant in a nursery school.

So Mary has a number of options open to her. She can stay working in residential care and gain NVQ qualifications. She may wish to leave residential care and work in the community as a social worker. If she does this she will need further training and obtain the Diploma in Social Work at a local college or university. What would you do?

The nursery nurse

Nursery nurses play an important role in the early years of many children's lives. The nursery nurse training, like that for social work or for teachers, offers training which allows them to take responsibility for the overall care of children in many situations. Nursery nurses work in a variety of situations:
- schools
- day nurseries

- creches
- residential nurseries
- hospitals
- private homes.

‘I always wanted to be a nursery nurse, ever since I left school at 16 with six GCSEs. I attended my local college to do my two-year full-time NNEB training. I felt strange at first being only one of two lads in a class of 22 girls. However the teaching staff made me feel very welcome and supported me through the two years.’

It is rare for males to do nursery nurse training but it is by no means uncommon, as it is now recognised that they have the qualities to do the job. John had more than the usual entry qualifications for the NNEB course. The usual entry requirement were three GCSEs at A–C, but in parts of the country where competition for places is high you may need A-levels also.

‘The two days a week that I spent gaining practical work experience in different childcare situations helped me to make up my mind that I wanted to work in a day nursery. I liked working with children from all kinds of background. Some parents paid the full cost of the child's place, while other parents got the place free – paid for by social services. Some children had behaviour problems and we had to plan how to help them when they were at the nursery.’

The NNEB course gave John the chance to experience different childcare work experiences. It allowed him to make his mind up about what area he would like to work in. He chose a day nursery, thus giving himself much choice. Day nurseries can be either private or run by local authorities.

‘The nursery I work in at the moment is run by a local college and is open to children of students and staff. Some places are also available to children from the local community. We open at 8 o'clock in the morning and close at 5 o'clock in the evening. We are open all the year around, taking more children from the local community during the school holidays.

I am involved in the routine care of children at the nursery. This involves feeding, washing, dressing and toileting them. First thing in the morning I help set the play equipment and play activities. I am able to play with the children and I become a friend to many of them. I sometimes give first aid to those children who have minor cuts and bruises.

One of the aspects of the job I like best is monitoring the development of a child during his or her stay at the nursery. I have to be very observant and try to identify any problems either before they arise or as they occur. This requires a responsible and caring attitude as well as sound judgement. I also like the teaching part of the job. I teach children to tie shoelaces, life and social skills, table manners. I also do some pre-reading and number work.

John likes the teaching part of his job – he does some pre-reading and number work with the older children

I like the job very much as every day is different. Some days I spend most of the time outside overseeing the children's play. Other days I assist with meals. I see myself staying at this job for some time to come. I hope one day to own and run my own day nursery. **'**

Activity 3.8

Visit a nursery. Observe and make notes about the daily routine of the unit.

In day nurseries nursery nurses work as a team, using a wide range of communication skills to enable them to express their ideas to adults and children. Nursery nurses need patience and to be fit, as children can be noisy, disruptive and lively.

Planning for employment in health and social care

The main stages of RECRUITMENT (finding someone to fill a vacancy) are the same for any job:
• the employer advertises the job
• the applicants apply for the job

- the employer selects the most suitable applicants to interview
- the applicants attend for interviews
- the employer decides which applicant to employ and offers them the job.

The job ADVERTISEMENT

Organisations use the following methods to advertise and recruit people for health and care jobs:

- the press:
  – national newspapers
  – local newspapers, especially for basic grade health and social care jobs
- specialist journals and magazines, such as:
  – *The Nursing Mirror* for nursing jobs
  – *Community Care* and *Care Weekly* for social care jobs
  – *The British Medical Journal* for doctors
- publications for minority groups, such as *The Afro-Caribbean Times*, and specialist newspapers aimed at people with disabilities
- job centres
- youth training or adult training schemes
- careers offices
- employment agencies (both for permanent and temporary posts) – see the back pages of *Community Care* for examples of employment agencies for social care staff
- specialist recruitment agencies
- visits to schools, colleges and universities
- job clubs
- careers conventions
- the Placing, Assessment and Counselling Team based at the local job centre or employment service who deal with workers with disabilities.

Job advertisements should at least show the following information:

- the organisation's name and address
- an outline of the major duties

Qualified Social Worker

£13,434 - £19,398 - Newcastle

Required to join a busy children's duty team, providing a service of assessment, support and child protection investigation to local families. You will divide your time between the Duty Service and carry your own small case load of mixed short- and long-term work. This area office serves a small inner-city area with a high level of social need indicators. A high proportion of the population belong to ethnic minority communities.

We would particularly welcome applications from social workers with Asian or Afro-Caribbean origins as these groups are under-represented in our teams serving the inner-city multi-cultural community.

For further information contact: J. Anderson, Team Manager, on 998 567893.

Applications forms are available from Personnel Section, Central Area Office, on 998 567894 quoting reference NWR176.

Closing date 15 February 199-. Interview date 28 and 29 March 199-.

Primrose Residential Home For the Elderly

Care Assistant
Salary £6000-£9500

A vacancy has arisen for a care assistant with the promotion of the present postholder. We are looking for a hard-working person, willing to work unsociable hours. Must have a caring nature and be willing to work as part of a team. A willingness to undergo training would be an advantage.

Further particulars from: Mrs Willis, Manager, Primrose Residential Home, West Street.

Please write for application form to be returned within two weeks of the date of this advertisement.

Examples of job advertisements

- qualifications and experience required
- salary
- benefits, such as pension, car allowance, etc.

Activity 3.9

a Visit your college, school or local library. Ask the librarian for a number of journals which advertise job vacancies. Make a list of the kind of vacancies that are advertised in each journal.

b Read the situations vacant section of a social care or health journal. Make a note of all the details of four or five advertisements. Do they provide sufficient information to give you all the information you need? Do you think more details are needed?

Discuss your views with your class colleagues.

Finding out more about a job

Before you decide to make an application for a post that you may be interested in, it is important to gather as much information about the job as possible. How can you do this?

Most employers will supply written information about the job and conditions of employment. Your first task is to write for that information and also ask for an application form. The information will describe the skills required for the job, the knowledge, education and qualifications needed. The employer will also explain any other special requirements necessary, such as age, health, physical characteristics, locality and availability to start work.

The **job description** describes as closely as possible the actual work to be done.

Job description

Post: Care Assistant, Primrose House

Responsible to: Manager of home (through assistant managers)

Main responsibilities:
* Assist residents with dressing, undressing, bathing and
  toilet as required
* Care for residents who are sick and needing minor
  dressings or bed nursing
* Support residents who have problems with mobility
* Help residents with the use of and care of aids and
  personal equipment
* Make and change beds, empty commodes and tidy room
* At meal times, set tables and trays, serve meals, feed
  those who need help, clear and tidy dining room
* Greet visitors, answer door bell, telephone and emergency bell
* Read and write reports, take part in training activi-
  ties as required
* Take part in residents' meetings and managers' meetings
  as required
* Support residents by talking to them, taking part in
  their activities, taking them out, participating in
  their hobbies, etc.
* Such other duties that may be required by the manager
  as are reasonable.

An example of a job description

Activity 3.10

a From a local newspaper, specialist journal or local newspaper, select an appropriate job advertisement and obtain information about the post from the employer.

b Discuss the information you have obtained with your colleagues. Was there enough information to let you know what the job is and what qualification and experience the employer is looking for?

Applying for a job

When you have found out as much as you can about the job it is time to make an application. This requires very careful thought and preparation. You will not get a second chance if the application does not result in you being invited for interview.

The job advertisement will often say how you should apply, usually in one of the following ways:
- by sending a CURRICULUM VITAE (CV) – a summary of the relevant information that the employer needs to know. You write the CV yourself and send it with a COVERING LETTER.
- by completing an APPLICATION FORM which is supplied by the employer.

Why send a CV?

The purpose of a CV is to let the employer know your personal details and experience. It is your chance to sell yourself to a prospective employer. One of the good points about a CV is that you can design it yourself and tailor it to suit each job you apply for. A standard CV is not the most effective means of selling yourself for a specific job.

If you are writing to someone to see if they have any vacant jobs, a CV with a covering letter is essential.

To create a good impression your CV should:
- be easy to read, concise and well designed (a clear layout)
- give details of your experience that are relevant to the specific job that you are applying for
- include actual facts and figures, such as grades achieved in examinations and relevant voluntary work or work experience that you have done.
- be typed.

You must encourage the person making the selection to read your CV rather than putting it in the wastepaper bin.

What should you put in your CV?

What you put in you CV will depend on the job that you are applying for. For example, a CV for the post of kitchen cleaner will have a different emphasis from that for a care assistant or a nursery nurse, where you would need to put greater emphasis on your caring experience.

Writing your CV

The first stage of producing a CV is to write a draft. You may have to do a number of drafts before you are happy with what you have done.

The length of your CV should be no more than two sides of A4. There will many CVs sent in for any one job and the employer needs to be able to read then quickly and gain an impression of your suitability for the post.

Your style of writing should be concise and to the point. Use words that suggest you are keen and willing to do things. Verbs such as 'produced', 'arranged', 'wrote', 'contributed' and 'accomplished' should be used. They suggest that you are a person who has done things. Just include facts.

The tone of your writing should be positive and optimistic. The different sections should be well-spaced and you should also leave wide margins.

Remember
A CV is not your complete life story. It is a summary of the relevant things you wish the prospective employer to know.

CURRICULUM VITAE

Personal details

Name	Ann Mary Jones
Date of birth	16 May 1978
Home address	26 West Hill, Derby DB66 7JJ
Telephone no.	0189 123456
Nationality	British
Marital status	Single

Education and qualifications

1989-1994	Queensway School, Derby GCSEs: English (E), Mathematics (E), Child Care (C), History (D)
1994-to date	Ashton College GNVQ Foundation Health and Social Care GCSE: Sociology – Welfare in Society

Work experience

1992	Two weeks working in Westcott Old People's Home
1993	One week on Geriatric Ward of St Thomas' Hospital
1994/5	I have had a number of placements: Apple Day Centre Bush House Residential Home Beacon School

Other skills
I have done baby-sitting for my sister and neighbours for the past three years. I also help out at a club for mentally handicapped children on Saturdays. I like horse-riding and going to dances. On Sunday I work for a few hours at a local store.

An example of a CV

When you have produced a draft of your CV, ask another person, perhaps your teacher or classmate, to read it through. Ask them to tell you if it is appropriate and whether it creates a good impression.

When you are satisfied that you have produced a good CV either type it yourself or ask someone else to do it for you. Never send a hand-written CV to a prospective employer. (Sometimes, however, employers will request that the application form or the covering letter is completed in your own handwriting.)

Post the CV to the employer with a covering letter. The letter will introduce you to the employer and it will encourage him or her to read your CV.

What should you put in the covering letter?
- The job for which you are applying
- The reference number (this will be found in the advertisement)
- The reason why you are applying for the job
- Where you saw the job advertised
- Relevant details related to your work experience, skills or qualifications – important facts that will catch the eye and make the person want to read your CV.

Remember
- Draft out what you want to say in rough first.
- Write clearly, using plain paper, pen and ink or a ball point pen – do not use pencil.
- Type the letter if you can, especially if your handwriting is not tidy.
- Keep the letter short and to the point.
- Check your spelling, punctuation and grammar.
- Say which job you are interested in and where you saw it advertised.
- Make the information you give relevant to the position. So read the advertisement again carefully.
- State why you are interested in the job and what skills and experience you have.
- Print you name clearly under your signature.

---

26 West Hill
Derby
DB66 7JJ

26 January 199–

Ms J. W. Harris
Manager
St Vincent's Residential Home for the Elderly
88 Leafy Glade
Derby
DB66 2HH

Dear Ms Harris

Care Assistant Post – Reference No. 12345

I read with interest the information about the above vacancy in The Star newspaper last Monday. I would like to be considered for the post and I enclose my curriculum vitae.

As you will see from my CV, I am just about to finish my Foundation GNVQ course in Health and Social Care. This is an introductory course to social care. The work experience that I have had over the past year has only served to increase my interest in wanting to work in the care field.

The job you have advertised appeals to me because I have always wanted to work with the elderly and it is also within easy travelling distance from my home.

I look forward to hearing from you soon.

Yours sincerely

Ann Jones

Ann Jones (Miss)

An example of a covering letter

Activity 3.11

a Read and give very careful consideration to the advertisement for a nursing assistant below. Write a CV giving relevant information, which you think would get you an interview for the post.

North Area Hospital
Johnson Ward

Nursing Assistant
Salary £6000 - £7500 p.a. inc.
38 hrs per week on a shift basis

Johnson Ward is based in a new Community Unit. At present it has 16 male and 8 female clients with long-term mental health needs. The duties of the nursing assistant will include the daily support and the personal care of the clients. Previous experience of caring for people would be desirable but it is not essential. However, you will need to have an interest in working with people with long-term mental health needs. You will need to be flexible and willing to work as part of a team. It is essential that you possess good communication skills and a positive caring attitude.

Telephone Mrs H. Maloney for an informal chat about the job on 888 98000 ext. 1234

Application is by CV to:
Personnel Officer, 24 Jackson Road, Doncaster DN56 8MF
Please quote ref. BN 678

Closing date 26 January 199-

---

b Discuss and compare your completed CV with your class colleagues.

Filling in an application form
Employers use application forms to make decisions about who to call for interview. They can find out more about an applicant from an application form than from a CV. This is because they can ask for the precise information they need to know.

Many employers still ask questions about marital status, number of children and ethnic origin. Do you think this is necessary? Does it matter if a person has three children, is married or what their ethnic group is? Would any of these things stop someone from carrying out the job? Personal information like this can lead to employers making subjective and inaccurate impressions of candidates. This can lead to **prejudice** and **discrimination**. A person should be selected for interview or the job on their ability to do the job.

The interview
Before an employer advertises a job, he or she will have drawn up a **job specification**. This will include not only details of the actual work to be done (the job description, see page 98), but also the sorts of things they would like to see

Oldcastle Social Services Department
Civic Offices
Downtown SC56 2TR

APPLICATION FOR EMPLOYMENT

Please print clearly

Position: Care assistant
Post no.: 123

Personal details
Surname .... Forenames ....
Address .... Date of birth ....
.... Telephone no. ....
.... Post code .... Do you have a full driving licence YES/NO

Present employment
Name and address of employer   From   Salary
....
....
Job title ....

Previous employment
List below your past employment, beginning with the most recent.
Name and address of employer   From   To   Salary
....
....
Job title .... Reason for leaving ....

Name and address of employer   From   To   Salary
....
....
Job title .... Reason for leaving ....

Name and address of employer   From   To   Salary
....
....
Job title .... Reason for leaving ....

Education
Secondary School   From   To   Examinations/Results
....
Further/Higher Education   From   To   Courses/Results
....
Other courses and training From   To   Results
....

Membership of professional organisations

Interests/Experience and skills
Outline your experience, either paid or voluntary, which is relevant to this application.

References
Name ....   Name ....
Occupation ....   Occupation ....
Address ....   Address ....
Telephone ....   Telephone ....
May we contact your referees before an offer of interview?   YES/NO

Signed ....   Date ....

An example of an application form

103

in the applicant – the ideal type of person for the job. The specification will detail the knowledge, skills, experience and qualifications required, and also any other requirements such as age, sex, ethnic group and physical characteristics.

Employers can request special permission to advertise for a man or a woman or someone of a particular ethnic origin. For example, if a playgroup only admits black children, the employer could make a case for looking for a black worker.

The employer will compare the information in your CV or application form with the specification. If your application meets the specification, you may be invited for interview. You will be notified of:
• the date and time of the interview
• how long the interview will last
• the place where the interview will be held
• the name of the person to report to
• whether you will be told of the outcome of the interview on the day.

The interview has a number of aims:
• to help the employer decide if you are a suitable person for the job
• to give you the chance to see if you could do the job
• to give you an opportunity to decide if you want the job or not.

Preparing for the interview
The more you can find out about the job and the employer's business before the interview, the more prepared you will be. You will need to think about:
• why you have applied for the post
• your ambitions
• the skills you can offer the employer
• why you would find the job interesting
• your previous achievements.

Make sure you know exactly when the interview will be held, how you are going to get there, who you are going to see and the time of the interview.

What should you wear?
You should give careful thought to the clothes you will wear for the interview. Things you should think about:
• do your clothes need dry cleaning?
• what would be appropriate for the interview
• your footwear
• your hairstyle.

Appearance and grooming are important because they help to create that vital first impression that the interviewer will get of you. Use your common sense about appearance.

What questions might you be asked?
Be prepared. It is useful to have some idea of the kinds of question that you may be asked in the interview. Show a genuine interest in the work of the organisation to which you have applied – find out what you can about it beforehand. This will help you prepare so that you will not be taken by surprise. It will also boost your confidence.

If you were the interviewer what questions would you ask? Imagine that you are interviewing an applicant for a job as an assistant in a nursery. What questions would you ask?

Appearance and grooming create that vital first impression

- Tell me about yourself.
- Why are you applying for this post?
- Why do you want to work at this nursery?
- What experience have you had of working with children?
- How would you make sure that you treated boys and girls equally?
- What skills do you have that make you think you can do the job?
- What do you do in your spare time?
- What is your ultimate ambition?

What questions would you think that the person applying for the post might like to ask?

- What are the normal hours of work?
- Are there any unsociable working hours?
- What is the pay? Will I be paid weekly or monthly?
- What are the holiday arrangements?
- What are the promotion prospects?
- Will I be offered training opportunities?

How can you make a good impression during the interview?

- Be pleasant and polite.
- Don't sit down until offered a chair.
- Don't smoke.
- Relax and sit upright in the chair. Don't fidget.
- Try and be positive and optimistic when replying to questions.
- Always look at the interviewer and members of the panel.
- If you do not understand a question, ask for it to be repeated.
- Don't be flippant. Don't make any silly remarks to hide your nerves.
- Try to hide your nerves by controlling your voice. Use pauses in speech to stress important points.
- Be honest. Don't invent answers. If you cannot answer a question, say so.
- Make sure you know the names of the interviewers.
- At the end of the interview, thank the interviewers.

At the end of the interview you should always ask two or three questions. When the interview ends, always shake the hand of the interviewer.

National Record of Achievement

We have already discussed how to present information in the form of a curriculum vitae or application form. You can also take your National Record of Achievement to the interview and ask if you can show it to the interviewer. Make sure that is it neat and tidy and has all the relevant information in it, such as:

- certificates
- sports achievement
- letter of recommendation from work experience
- school reports.

Test yourself

1 What groups of staff support doctors in hospitals to look after patients?

2 What training programme has replaced the RGN course?

3 What are the four main responsibilities of the local authority Social Services Committee?

4 What is the new social work qualification called?

5 What training opportunities are available for those wishing to train as nursery nurses?

6 List six places where you could find out about jobs in health and social care.

7 What five main pieces of information should a job advertisement give?

8 What is a curriculum vitae?

9 When you are invited for interview, what five main things should you be notified of?

10 What is an application form?

Assignment A3.1
Working in health and social care

This assignment will give you the opportunity to investigate some health and social care services. You will be asked to outline the main providers of health and social care and give examples of the services they provide and describe the job roles. Use information technology wherever possible in your work.

Your tasks

1 **a** Draw a map of your locality or use a street map.

   b Find out where the following types of service are and mark them on the map:
  - hospitals
  - social service department offices
  - day centres
  - residential care establishments
  - offices of voluntary services such as the NSPCC
  - any private care services.

2 Choose four examples of each of the four main providers of services:

   a NHS

   b social services

   c voluntary organisations

   d private organisations.

Describe the services each one offers to clients.
This information is available from pamphlets and books, but one good way to find out what services are provided is to make arrangements to visit the relevant establishments, and ask the staff and, if possible, the clients too.

3 **a** Make arrangements to interview four people who work in health care services, such as a GP, a health visitor, a physiotherapist and a district nurse.

   b Ask them about their jobs. Ask them what they do and make notes of what they tell you.

4 **a** Make arrangements to interview four people who work in the community and social care services, such as a social worker, a care assistant, a home care assistant, a child minder, a nanny or a nursery nurse.

   b Ask them about their jobs. Ask them what they do and make notes of what they tell you.

5 **a** Make arrangements to interview four people who work in indirect care services, such as porters, receptionists or domestic staff.

   b Ask them about their jobs. Ask them what they do and make notes of what they tell you.

Assignment A3.2
Jobs in health and social care

The aim of this assignment is to investigate two jobs in health and social care which might be likely to suit you.

Your tasks

1 Choose two jobs that might be suitable for you:

   a a job that you might like to do when you have finished this course

   b a job that you might like to do in some years' time after further training and experience.

2 Write a description each job's main purpose.
One way to do this is to get information from books, job descriptions and discussions with people already in a similar jobs. Use a word-processor for your work, wherever possible.

3 For both jobs, list the main skills that you would need to carry out the jobs. Use the following headings:

   a Practical skills

   b Emotional skills

   c Communication skills.

4 List the qualifications and training needed for both jobs.

5 Describe how you would gain the skills, training and qualifications appropriate to each of the jobs you have chosen.

6 Explain why your think the two jobs you have chosen are suitable for you.

Assignment A3.3
Finding work in health and social care

In this assignment you will describe the procedure for finding a job, and then produce your own CV.

Your tasks

1 List the main ways in which employers advertise job vacancies.

2 Describe the main stages in the recruitment process.

3 Describe the ways of presenting information about yourself to a prospective employer.

4 Draw up a curriculum vitae (CV) outlining your personal information. Use a word-processor to do this, if you can.

Key words

After reading this chapter, you should be able to understand the following words and phrases. If you do not, go back through the chapter and find out, or look them up in the Glossary.

Registered General Nurse (RGN)

Project 2000

Monitoring the person's ability

Health care support worker

Diploma in Social Work

National Vocational Qualifications (NVQs)

Advertisements

Curriculum vitae

Covering letter

Application form

Recruitment

CHAPTER 4

Contributing to a Team Activity

What is covered in this chapter

- Planning an activity with a team
- Undertaking a role in a team activity
- Reviewing the team activity

These are the resources you will need for your Contributing to a Team Activity portfolio:
- the team plan
- your individual action plan
- a record of your performance in the team
- a record of completing your activities in your individual action plan
- your review of the team plan
- your suggestions for any improvements as a result of the review
- your written answers to the Test Yourself questions at the end of this chapter.

Introduction

This chapter focuses on developing your skills in working with others in a team and carrying out a specific activity. The activity that your and your colleagues decide to carry out must be related to **caring for people**, such as:
- organising a day out for children or older people
- organising a birthday party of an elderly resident in a home.

When carrying out the activity you should use the knowledge you have gained from the other Foundation units you have completed. This chapter will also give you the opportunity to complete a number of core skills.

Your tutor or teacher will help you with the team activity by meeting with you as a team on a regular basis and reviewing with you individually how you have undertaken the activities. This will enable the tutor to assess what you have learned from the activity and why you contributed what you did in team discussions. Either you or the tutor will keep a written record of these discussions.

Planning an activity with a team

Working as a team or group

We all have a need to belong to one sort of group or another. We form groups:
- **for security** – people are naturally sociable and want to be with others, sharing common ideas, values and pleasures
- **to help others** – this could be a voluntary group or charity
- **to get things done** – we can often achieve things we want to do as part of a group that would not otherwise be possible on our own.

A group at work

Membership of a group or team can have the following benefits:
- pleasure and satisfaction from sharing a common interest
- security, which can give you confidence
- learning opportunities – you can learn skills in the group which can be practised in your personal life
- opportunities to develop leadership skills
- experience the democratic processes.

When you have completed this team activity you should:
- be able to understand and accept other members of the team
- have improved your communication skills as a result of working together, sharing ideas and discussing how to do things
- be more able to take responsibility for your own learning and behaviour
- co-operate with one another in planning, carrying out and reviewing tasks and activities
- understand the need to have a process for making decisions
- feel free within the team to discuss problems and resolving and conflicts constructively.

These things will not just happen, your tutor or teacher will help you to **set targets**, **plan activities** and **review them**.

Getting to know other members of the team

Before you decide what team activity to do, the members of the team need to be able to trust one another. To do this, you have to get to know each other well. You have to reveal things about yourself to the other members of the team. When you have done this, they will be more willing to reveal something of themselves.

This MUTUAL EXCHANGE of personal information leads to better understanding and acceptance of each other. When you have reached this stage you will feel more comfortable with each other. As a result, you will not be afraid to make suggestions and contributions to the team action plan.

Activity 4.1

a Complete as many of these incomplete statements as you wish. You do not have to complete them all.

My name is . . .
My age is . . .
I live . . .
I was born in . . .
My marital status is . . .
My friends . . .
My hobbies . . .
I want to get a job as . . .
At this very minute, I feel . . .
My ambition . . .
Things I find difficult . . .
My religious beliefs . . .
To me being black/white . . .

b Read the completed statements out to the rest of the team. Anyone in the team can comment on any of the statements. (You will get the chance to do the same when the rest of the team read out their statements.)

You can stop discussing your statements whenever you like. There must be no compulsion for anyone to discuss something they do not wish to.

c When you have finished this activity, ask yourself:
- How do you feel?
- How honest were you in revealing your feelings?
- Were you more open about some things than others?

Telling the team about yourself will involve you in exchanging facts, feelings and opinions with other members. This sharing of details allows you to discover things that you have in common with each other. It will help you to develop trust and make members of the team more open and communicative with each other.

Deciding on what activity to carry out as a team

When you have got to know and trust the rest of your team, you are ready to decide what activity you would like to do. There are many activities that you can choose from:
- organising a party for a group of children or elderly people
- producing a booklet containing a list of voluntary care organisations in your locality
- planning and organising a playgroup for children during half term in your college
- preparing and printing a newspaper for your school or college
- producing a booklet giving healthy-living advice for a specific group of people.

These are just a few ideas. Use them to prompt other ideas in your team.

You might decide to organise a playgroup outing as in this photograph

How can you decide what activity to carry out?

To help the team decide what activity to carry out, you can have a BRAIN-STORMING session. This simply means that all the members of your team individually write down as many ideas as they can think of. Then they discuss the ideas in the group and select one activity that you are all happy with.

Brainstorming helps to overcome the problems of making decisions too quickly or doing things in a certain way just because that is the way we always do it. Brainstorming helps you to look at things in a new and imaginative way – try it out in Activity 4.2.

Activity 4.2

a Write down the answer to the following question:

What possible uses can metal paper clips be put to?

Do not worry how silly or unusual some of the uses are.

b Discuss what you have written down with the rest of the team. As a team you may have written down a few uses, such as, clipping two pieces of paper together, or use as a pipe cleaner.

As a group, choose the most original idea.

Did your list include any of the following possible uses:
- made into chains?
- hooks?
- unlocking car doors?
- their sharp ends can punch holes in paper?
- cocktail stick?
- toothpick?

A brainstorming session

Brainstorming can be used effectively in small teams. Each member can shout out possible solutions to the problem. One member of the team should write each suggestion on a flip chart. Only when all the team members' ideas are exhausted, should a full discussion of the suggestions take place. The team can then make a final decision on the best solution or idea to follow up.

> **Remember**
> Never put down, ridicule, criticise, tease or embarrass other members of the team or their ideas.

The team should now be in a position to select an activity which will allow each member to play an individual as well as a team role.

TIME MANAGEMENT: how to organise the team's activity

Planning is an important part of carrying out any task or activity. When the team has selected an activity, you will need to consider how long you have been given to carry it out and whether you can fit in all the tasks to complete the activity. This is called **time management**. As yourselves the following questions:

- How long have we got to carry out the activity?
- How available are the resources, the things we might need to complete the activity? (people, money, accommodation, transport, etc.)
- How easy is it to get the information we might want? (cost, etc.)
- Can we do all we want to do in the time given?
- Do the team members have the individual skills to complete the activity? (people who can organise, manage money, write letters, etc.)

As a example, let us suppose you are going to organise a party for a group of children who attend a school for children with learning difficulties. Your time plan might look like this:

Task	Estimated time needed to carry out task (weeks)
Discussion within team and agreement of activity	1
Agreeing the team action plan	1
Agreeing your individual action plans	1
Discussion and agreement with school	2
Organisation of party	4
Review of activity, team and individual	2
Preparation of evidence for portfolio	2
Total	**13 weeks**

An example of team management

You can see from the list of tasks in the above example that for an activity such as organising a party you may need to think in terms of at least 13 weeks. Planning your time is a very important aspect of carrying out an activity.

Activity 4.3

As a team you have been given the task of producing an information leaflet about the Foundation GNVQ in Health and Social Care for new students. You have to design the leaflet and decide what it should include.

List the tasks that you might have to do complete the activity and the time that you might take to them. Use a table like the one below.

Task	Estimated time needed to carry out task (weeks)
Total	. . . . . weeks

Did you include any of the following tasks:
Gather information on course?
Decide on the layout?
Decide on the lettering
Time to print the leaflet?
Time to review the activity?

Contacting people

To complete an activity you will need to contact other people with expertise or access to resources. These people may be individuals or they may represent organisations, for example a social worker may represent the local Social Services Department.

There are a number of different way that you can contact people:

By phone   By letter or fax

By visiting and talking to them in person

The method you chose will depend on a number of things:
- the distance from you that the person lives
- how busy they are
- whether they are on the telephone or have a fax machine.

Whatever method you choose you must keep in mind the following:
- **Who do you need to contact?**
  If you wish to invite a group of children from a school to a party who should you contact? The head of the school, perhaps.
- **Arrangements to contact people**
  You can telephone people on the off-chance that they may have time to talk to you. But it is better to telephone to agree a specific time to telephone again. By doing this, you will be sure of speaking to the person you wish to. Never visit without making an appointment. Make an appointment by letter or telephone, telling the person:
  – who you are
  – the organisation you represent
  – why you wish to see them.
  If you are writing to people, do not forget to enclose a stamped, addressed envelope. If you do this, they are more likely to reply to your letter.
- **What is it you want them to do?**
  You must be clear in your own mind what you want them to do. Remember that they are busy people. They will be more likely to help you if you know exactly what it is you want them to do. Make a list of the things you want to say or know before you see or ring them.

The example on page 118 makes it clear who the letter is written to and what it is you want the person to do.

Remember
Each member of the team will need to write their own copy of a letter, not to send to the individual or organisation, but to keep as evidence that you are capable of writing such a letter. You must keep a copy this letter in your portfolio as evidence. A copy of the actual letter sent will not do, unless of course you actually wrote it.

```
                                                      Best College
                                                      Circle Road

                                                 12 December 199-

  Mrs Jackson
  Head of St Ann's Centre
  Straight Street
  Any Town S1 0TY

  Dear Mrs Jackson

  Party for Elderly People February 199-

  I am a student on a GNVQ Foundation Course at Best College. My
  class has decided that we would like to organise a party for the
  elderly people who attend your day centre.  Could I please make
  an appointment to visit you so that I can discuss this with you?

  I am free every Wednesday afternoon and Friday mornings. Would
  either of these days suit you? Please let me know which date and
  time you could see me.

  I enclose a stamped addressed envelope for your reply.

  Yours sincerely

  Mary Thorn

  Mary Thorn
```

An example of a letter to a head of a day centre

Activity 4.4

The team has asked you to write a letter to the head of the local youth club requesting the following:
- permission to use a room in the club for a meeting
- the cost of hiring the room
- dates when a room would be available.

Write the letter, taking into account the points above. Remember to use capital letters and full stops in the appropriate places.

NOTE-TAKING to give feedback to the team

Remember to take notes of any conversations you may have or agreements that you may make with any individual or organisation. You can use notes you have taken when reporting back on your actions to the team.

Note-taking is a very important aspect of your work. If you are going to work in health or social care, it is a skill that you must practise and develop. Note-taking provides a written record of what you have been studying or the information that you have been collecting. To be useful the notes must be accurately taken and, later, accurately presented.

You should take notes in a consistent format:

- In class a loose-leaf binder is better than an exercise book because you can rearrange your notes for discussions, tutorials or revision.
- If you are observing a situation and taking notes, or interviewing someone, than a less-obvious method is best – perhaps a small notebook or tape recorder. **Remember to ask permission before you tape record anyone or any situation.**

Preparation of interview notes

Make a note of key points

When recording any conversation, or when note-taking in class, you should take clear, brief notes that will allow you to recall the important points later. You need to capture the important points of agreement, or the important line of argument. When interviewing anyone, concentrate on following the flow of argument and just jot down any key points with a structure that you can understand later.

Be sure you know what you want to talk to the other person about

Before you interview anyone you should be very clear in your mind what it is you wish to get out of the interview, what is it you want to find out or get agreement for. Plan the interview and the questions you will ask. Work out what notes you will want to make.

Plan the questions you will ask

Make notes in your own words

The process of converting ideas or conversation of the person you are interviewing into you own language will also ensure that you understand the content – what you write down. Add you own comments where appropriate.

Activity 4.5

a Read the first four pages of Chapter 5.
   Make notes of the main points that are made in the text.

b Compare and check what you have written with the other team members. Discuss the different way each of you took notes and what you have written.

Preparing your team action plan

When you have permission from the organisation or individual to carry out the activity, the team is in a position to draw up a TEAM ACTION PLAN. Ask yourselves:

- Can we carry out our plans?
- How long do we have to complete the activity?
- Has each member of the team the ability to carry out their individual action plan as agreed originally?
- Is the team in a position to prepare a team action plan?

What is action planning?

Planning is an essential part of the process of learning, doing or accomplishing something. With small tasks or problems, it is often an automatic process. For example, after travelling to a distant town by bus or train, you may use this experience automatically next time you want to plan a journey. You do not have to find out again where to buy a ticket or catch the bus. With new or big activities, this system may not work. What we need is a plan to help us organise what to do – an **action plan**.

Action plans can be developed by individuals or teams. When we work as part of a team action planning is a must. It helps to co-ordinate what each individual member and the team itself will do. When developing an action plan you must **record and agree each member's task**, for example 'Mary will contact the head of the school by a certain date and Jack will write the invitations to the children.' This is a form of agreement, or contract, between the people involved in carrying out the activity.

The essential parts of an action plan are:

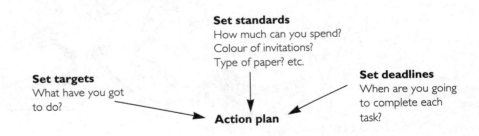

Set standards
How much can you spend?
Colour of invitations?
Type of paper? etc.

Set targets
What have you got
to do?

Action plan

Set deadlines
When are you going
to complete each
task?

For example, opposite is a list of some of the tasks you might have to do both as a team and as individuals to organise and plan a party for a group of elderly people. Each of the tasks has to be agreed by the team members and some of the tasks allocated to individual members of the team.

To help you plan either an individual or team action plan, you must list all the things to be done. Then you need to decide **who is to do them** and **how long they will take** to finish the task.

The team will need to draw up a team action plan like the one on page 122. Each individual member of the team will also have to make an **individual action plan** (see page 127).

Time and day of party
When are you going to have the party?
What day is best for the party?
At what time of day will you have the party?

Premises
Where will the party be held?
What facilities will be needed?
How many plates, cups, etc. will be needed?
What facilities are needed for storage of food, etc.?
Will the team have to pay for premises? If so, how much can the team afford to pay?
Types of premises to think about: community centres, youth clubs, college refectories, scout halls or church halls.

Collection of elderly people from their own homes
Who will decide who is to be invited?
How will those attending the party be transported?
Types of transport: private cars, college mini-bus, hired bus.

Timing of the party
When should the party take place?
What day is most suitable?
What time during the day best suits the participants?
Things to consider: age of people attending, time of year.

Publicity
What kinds of invitation will you use?
How will they be delivered?
How will those invited let you know that they accept the invitation?
Consider: letter, cards, postal delivery, hand delivery.

Money
How will you pay for food, transport, the venue, invitations?
What kind of accounting system will you need to let people see how you are spending the money?
Where will you keep the money?

Food
Who is going to prepare the food?
Who is going to pay for the food?
Who will serve the food?
Who is going to wash up?

Finishing up
Who is going to clear away?
Who is going to write thank-you letters?
Who is going to find out if the elderly people enjoyed the party?

The tasks necessary to organise a party for a group of elderly people

```
┌──────────────────────────────────────────────────────────────────────┐
│                                                                        │
│  TEAM ACTION PLAN SCHEDULE                                             │
│                                                                        │
│  Tasks to be carried out        Date to be        Person to           │
│  (Goals)                        completed           carry             │
│                                                    out task           │
│                                                                        │
│                                                                        │
│  Collection of elderly people                                         │
│  from their own homes                                                 │
│  Who will decide who is to be                                         │
│  invited?                       10.12.95              Mary            │
│  How will those attending the                                         │
│  party be transported?          10.2.96               Team            │
│                                                                        │
│  Publicity                                                            │
│  What kinds of invitation will                                        │
│  you use?                       14.12.95              Team            │
│  Who will design them?                               Susan            │
│  Who will get them printed?     4.1.96               Susan            │
│  How will they be delivered?    6.1.96                Team            │
│  Who will deliver them?                        John/Mary/Helen        │
│  How will those invited let                                           │
│  you know they accept the                                             │
│  invitation?                                          Team            │
│                                                                        │
│  Money                                                                │
│  How will you pay for food,                                           │
│  transport, the venue,                                                │
│  invitations?                   10.12.95              Team            │
│  Who will look after the money?                       Jack            │
│  What kind of accounting system                                       │
│  will you need to let people                                          │
│  see how you are spending the                                         │
│  money?                                               Team            │
│  Where will you keep the money?                       Team            │
│                                                                        │
│  Food                                                                 │
│  Who is going to prepare the                                          │
│  food?                          25.1.96               Team            │
│  Who is going to pay for the                                          │
│  food?                                                Team            │
│  Who will serve the food?                             All             │
│  Who is going to wash up?                             Team            │
│                                                                        │
│  Finishing up                                                         │
│  Who is going to clear away?                          Team            │
│  Who is going to write thank-                                         │
│  you letters?                                       Michelle          │
│  Who is going to find out if                                          │
│  the elderly people enjoyed                                           │
│  the party?                     1.3.96               Joanne           │
│                                                                        │
│                                                                        │
└──────────────────────────────────────────────────────────────────────┘
```

An example of a team action plan

Activity 4.6

The team has decided to paint the room in the college used by a voluntary playgroup. They will need to consider:

- how long they have to carry out the task
- how much it will cost
- how much money they have
- what colours to use
- who will do the painting
- who will clear up afterwards
- who will liaise with the playgroup organiser.

Use the schedule below to draw up a team action plan.

TEAM ACTION PLAN SCHEDULE		
Tasks to be carried out (Goals)	**Date to be completed**	**Person to carry out task**

RECORDING what you do as a team

Remember that you must provide evidence in your portfolio of your ability:
- to work as a member of a team
- to work on an individual basis, on your own.

It is, therefore, very important that you devise a method of recording individual contributions in the team. You will need to provide evidence that the team can:
- identify the resources that are available
- identify which member of the team is going to carry out which task.

This will be shown in the team action plan that we discussed above.

Recording what individuals do within a team

However, you must also provide evidence that you contributed to team discussions and in making decisions within the team. Your tutor can watch what you do in the team, but you yourselves can also record who made contributions, decisions and identified resources.

Activity 4.7 describes one method that you can use to show who did what in the team.

Activity 4.7

The aim of this activity is for half the team to observe the other half performing a team task.

a   As a team, decide on a task, which may be as simple as a topic for discussion.

The members who are to carry out the task sit in a circle or around a table. The observers place themselves where they can see what the others in the team are doing. See the example below.

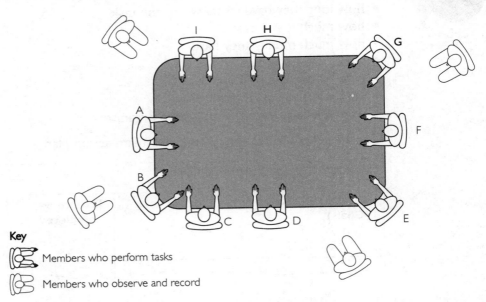

Key

Members who perform tasks

Members who observe and record

b Begin the task. The observers should observe and record what they see. They should look for:
- Who speaks to whom?
- Who identifies resources that are available?
- Who agrees to carry out different activities?
- Who contributes to the development of the team action plan?

To record what goes on within the team (the interactions between the members), use a table like the one below.

Who identifies resources that are available?	A	C	H	I	B
Who agrees to carry out different activities?	B	D	C	H	A
Who contributes to the development of the team action plan?	B	I	H	K	C

c At the end of the task, the observers and participants in the task can swop roles, so that everyone has a chance to provide evidence for their portfolio.

You may have noticed that certain members of the group say very little, while others say a lot. Some may be intimidated by those who are aggressive or say a lot. Why does this happen? Communication between people is called INTER-PERSONAL COMMUNICATION.

What stops people from communicating?
Although everyone communicates, it is true to say that good communicators are made. Most of us will have **learnt** communication skills from the people that we lived with (starting with our families) and went to school with.

Communication is not always easy. There are a number of factors that can create barriers between ourselves and other members of the team. We may not want to, or may be unable to, communicate with colleagues for many reasons. Colleagues may be confused, tired, shy or embarrassed, disabled, in pain or emotionally distressed. We may:

- be from a different ethnic background
- be from a different social class
- have different cultural or religious beliefs
- have different social values
- even be of the opposite sex.

Health and safety considerations

When working in the health and social care services, we must make sure that what we do does not make it hazardous for either the client or ourselves. You must, therefore, take into consideration any health and safety factors of the activity you are organising. Read Chapter 5 before you start the activity. It will give you a basic understanding of health and safety procedures.

When planning the activity, remember to examine and identify any common hazards which might be likely to occur, such as:

- danger of fire
- unsafe equipment
- problems caused by possibility of infections.

Is the environment safe? Make sure that any equipment or accommodation you use is safe. In particular, consider:

- first aid equipment
- safety precautions (fire or evacuation procedures, etc.)
- safe working practices (fire guards, etc.)
- alarms and emergency systems, such as fire alarms.

The benefits of this will be:

- the prevention of accidents
- improved and safe working conditions
- improved and safe services for clients.

Review of the team action plan

Before the team moves on to allocating and agreeing individual action plans, it is useful to sit down and look at everything you have done so far. There are two parts to this review:

1 **What have you done so far?**
   - Have you a written record of the team's activities?
   - Have you all agreed on the activity to be undertaken?
   - Is the plan going as you would have hoped?
   - Has everyone in the team made a contribution?
   - Have your tutors helped you? Is there any way they could help you in the future?

2 **What needs to be done to put the team plan into action?**
   - How can you overcome any problems that you have identified in 1 above?
   - Do you want to make any changes to the plan?
   - What resources will you need to continue?

```
TEAM ACTION PLAN REVIEW SCHEDULE
```

Tasks to be carried out (Goals)	Task completed Yes	No	What needs to be done?
Have you agreed:			
on a party?	✓		-
on transport?	✓		-
who is attending?	✓		-
the kinds of invitation will you use?		✓	Agree design
printers for the invitations?	✓		-
how to deliver the invitations?		✓	Post or by hand
how activity will be paid for?			-
the accounting system to be used?		✓	Advice from tutor
where the money will be kept?		✓	-
who will prepare the food?	✓		-
who is going to buy the food?		✓	Advice from catering students
who will serve the food?	✓		-
who is going to clear away?	✓		-
who is going to write thank-you letters?	✓		-
who is going to find out if the elderly people enjoyed the party?		✓	Further discussion
Did all members take part in decision-making?	✓		-
Have you considered Health and Safety factors?		✓	Read Ch. 5 and talk to tutor

An example of a review of a team action plan

Use a review sheet like the one above to help you review the team action plan. As you can see, there are still one or two activities to be decided upon. The team should either decide upon these issues themselves or ask their tutor for advice.

Undertaking a role in a team activity

Before you begin to undertake any role as an individual member of the team, you must draw up an **individual action plan**. This looks very similar to the team action plan except that it only relates to the job or jobs that you have agreed to do. It should indicate:

- the job you will do
- when you hope to finish it
- the resources you will need to complete successfully.

See the example below.

| Name | John Kendall | | Class or group | 1a |
| Tutor | Helen Sullivan | | | |

Activity   Organising an outing for children in the college nursery

Individual tasks	Date to be done by	Resources needed
Telephone head of nursery	3.6.9–	Telephone
Get list of children	6.6.9–	From teacher
Find out if any children have medication	10.6.9–	List from teacher
Arrange transport	16.6.9–	Minibus
Report back to team	20.6.9–	Written report

An example of an individual action plan

Making the best use of available resources

How do you make the best use of available resources? Let us look at an example from the individual action plan above – deciding which form of transport to use to take children from the college nursery on a outing. What kind of questions should you ask yourself?

- How many children are going on the outing?
- What health and safety considerations do I need to take account of?
- How many staff will be needed to escort the children?
- Do any of them use a wheelchair?
- What kind of transport will be able to accommodate a wheelchair?
- How many seats are in a mini-bus?
- How many children will a mini-bus carry?
- What is the cost of a mini-bus?
- What is the cost of a 50+ seater bus? Can it accommodate a wheelchair?
- Who much money do I have to spend on transport?
- Would it be cheaper to use the college mini-bus?

Activity 4.8

You have decided to hire a coach to take a group of children on a day outing. The coach will take up to 45 children. The total cost of hiring the coach is £126. Work out the cost that each child will have to pay for the day's outing

Can you think of any other things that you may need to know before you decide which kind of transport to use?

Activity 4.9

You have been allocated the individual task of arranging for the design and printing of invitations to a party for elderly people. You have limited money and cannot go to a private printers. You are a student in a college which has a large number of students doing art and design courses.

What questions would you need to ask yourself to make the best use of the resources available to you?

Did your list of questions include any of the following:
- Who is the best group or person to do the printing?
  – College reprographics?
  – Art/design students?
  – Private printers?
- Who is the best group or person to design the invitation?
  – Myself?
  – Art students?

It would possibly be the cheapest and best use of available resources if the art and design students designed and printed the invitation cards.

Review of the team activity

When you have completed the activity, you will need to review the team's and your own individual performance against the tasks that the team and you agreed to do in the action plans. To review the activity you will first need to look at whether you carried out the agreed tasks as a team and as individual. You should look at:

- whether or not resources were used effectively
- whether you dealt with any problems effectively
- whether you maintained the health and safety of those you were looking after and also your colleagues.

Your tutor will also observe your performance in the team and also review your individual performance on a one-to-one basis.

Review of the team's performance

To do this, you will need to look back at your original team action plan. For example, if the team activity was to design and print a health promotion booklet to give advice on the effects of smoking, the review could consider some of the following points:

- Were there any spelling or grammatical errors?
- Did the contents make sense to those for whom it was meant?
- Was the paper it was printed on the most appropriate type?
- Were the illustrations appropriate?
- Was the print size the most appropriate for your audience?
- Was the whole activity carried out within the time scale that was given to you?
- Did you raise enough money to pay for the booklet?
- Did it cost what the team agreed upon?

Answers to the above questions should be recorded only after a thorough discussion and agreement between all the team members. See the example below.

```
Review of illustrations: Were the illustrations appropriate?

We decided to illustrate the booklet with drawings - some colour and
some black and white line drawing. As the booklet was aimed at
teenagers we thought that some colour drawings would catch their
attention. Jack was given the job of asking students on the art course
to do some drawings illustrating some of our ideas. When this was done
we selected the ones we thought would be best. We had a lot of discus-
sion on this as it took a long time for us  to come to an agreement.
When Mary talked to some of the teenagers that we had given the book-
let to, they said that the illustrations were very good and  made them
think of the dangers of smoking.

We all agreed that the illustrations were appropriate.
```

An example of a review

When reviewing what you have done, it often a very good idea to ask the people you did the activity for what they thought about it. In the example above, the teenagers were asked about the illustrations. If you had organised a party you could ask the people you organised it for what they thought of it. One way of doing this could be by asking them to fill in a questionnaire or you could ask members of the team to interview some of those attending the party. For example:

Party for people over 65 years of age	Yes	No
Questions		
1 Was the time suitable for you?	☐	☐
2 Was the transport suitable?	☐	☐
3 Was the venue appropriate?	☐	☐
4 Did you like the food?	☐	☐
5 Was there enough food?	☐	☐

An example of a questionnaire

The information, or data, that you collect in the questionnaires can be presented in a number of ways. One way is to present it in the form of a chart, for example:

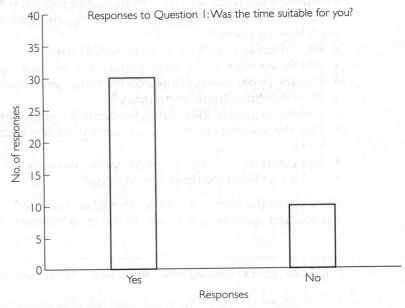

Responses to Question 1: Was the time suitable for you?

Review of an individual's performance

You can use the same methods to review your individual performance. You can ask people what they thought about what you did. However, you must also evaluate your individual action plan yourself, such as any letters you may have written.

Activity 4.10

Read the letter opposite that Mark has written to the manager of the local leisure centre.

Do you think that this is a good letter?

a Is it clear what Mark wants the centre manager to do?

b Does the centre manager know which days Mark wants the use of the swimming pool and for how many people?

c Is it clear whether Mark wants to pay for the session or is he asking for a free session?

> *The team agreed that I should write a letter to the local*
> *leisure centre asking if we could book a swimming*
> *session for a group of children with physical disabilities.*

Seaforth College
Seaforth
SF1 2PP

16 January 199-

Manager
Seaforth Leisure Centre
Seaforth

Dear Mrs Atkinson

Me and my friends want to organise a swimming session for some
people with physical disabilities. how much would it cost?
Can you let me know as soon as possible because we want to bring
the people along next week.

Yours sincerely

mark smith

d If you were the manager would you know how to answer Mark's letter.

e Is it a courteous letter?

f Is the grammar and punctuation correct?

g Has Mark used capital letters in the appropriate places?

This is Mark's own review of his letter:

> *I can see now that I did not write a very clear letter. I did*
> *not enclose a stamped addressed envelope, my English was not*
> *so good and I did not use capital letters to start all my*
> *sentences or when I signed my name. I feel that I should also*
> *have made it clearer when I wanted to use the centre.*

Can you think of any other suggestions you might offer to Mark to help him
write a more appropriate letter?

Health and safety

Health and safety is a very important aspect of any activity that we carry out.
Reviewing the health and safety factors of what you have done may prove a
little more difficult than some of the other tasks that the team or you as an

individual carried out. Read Chapter 5 before you review the health and safety factors of your activity.

Activity 4.11

The team agreed to organise a summer playgroup for children on a housing estate. The local housing department has agreed to let the team have the use of a ground floor flat with a garden to use for the summer months.

What basic health and safety factors would the team need to consider before it could open the playgroup?

Did your answers include any of the following:
- safe electrical plugs and wires?
- appropriate door locks?
- no access to kitchen for children?
- toilet and washing facilities?
- is the garden safe?
- can the children get out of the garden?
- are the toys safe?
- appropriate number of staff and volunteers?
- number of children?

Can you think of any more things that the team should consider as far as health and safety is concerned?

Activity 4.12

The team has asked you measure the height of every door handle in a local day centre which they are going to use for a local playgroup.

Measure each door handle and display your results on a graph.

Feedback

It is important to provide clear and CONSTRUCTIVE FEEDBACK to you colleagues on their performance and respond appropriately to feedback from others.

To help people in a sensitive and caring manner, we have to pay constant attention to the effectiveness of our communication skills. You will need to develop your communication skills and this team activity will help you to begin to do this.

All caring work involves good interpersonal skills. Telling people what you are doing will put them at ease. By explaining things, people will understand what you are doing and the reasons for your actions.

- Always maintain a friendly, welcoming approach.
- Always show an interest and understanding of other people's needs.
- Try to be helpful and supportive.
- Be ready to respond to others' conversation with a laugh, a smile or a word of support.

Providing feedback to people is also an important interpersonal skill that you will need to develop. But before you can provide feedback to your colleagues, you must listen to what they are saying.

How do you listen?
- The person speaking should be the focus of your attention.
- Listen to what is been said even if you do not agree with what the other person is saying.
- Do not disrupt the speaker by talking to others.
- Do not move around or fiddle with paper or pencils, etc.
- Ask questions of the speaker and react to them.
- Encourage your colleagues to talk and explain their ideas and feelings. Find out what are the main threads of their argument or ideas.
- Keep eye contact with the person who is speaking.

When you have listened to other people in the team and you understand what they are talking about then you may be in a position provide positive (fair) feedback. Positive feedback means that you should:
- acknowledge what people say or do
- praise them as appropriate and compliment them
- let them know how they are getting on – how clearly they have expressed their ideas, whether you think, for example, their suggestion or ideas could work.

Giving feedback is not just talking, it can also be done **non-verbally** (without talking). We can let others know what we think or feel about them by the expression on our face. You can have a bored expression or a happy one. By keeping eye contact with others, you also show that you are interested in what they are saying.

Activity 4.13

Work in pairs.

a Sit opposite each other. One person should talk to the other. You can say anything, perhaps how you arrived at college this morning or the last film you saw. The person listening should not look at the face of the person speaking (do not make eye contact). Change roles after about five minutes.

b Each of you should explain what your feelings were when you were talking to the person who was not keeping eye contact.
  • Did it make you feel uncomfortable?
  • Did you feel angry?

The person speaking should be the focus of your attention. By keeping eye contact, you show that you are interested in what they are saying

People like to work with those who give positive or good feedback. Such people are usually cheerful, friendly and helpful. However, you do not have to agree with everything everyone says. Responding to feedback positively does not mean agreeing with the other person. It means giving them a fair hearing and not reacting angrily to their suggestions or ideas. You may not agree with the feedback that a member of the team gives you, and they may not agree with your ideas. However the important thing is that you can listen to each other and discuss your ideas without getting angry with each other.

You must show that you value your team members as people and you do this by:
- listening to them
- allowing them to put their ideas forward without fear of undue criticism.

Aim to:
- Listen and respond to communications from other team members.
- Use good eye contact and keep smiling.
- Be sincere, sympathetic and understanding.
- Be kind, gentle and tactful.
- Be willing to allow other members of the group to do as much as possible for themselves. Encourage others to be as independent as possible.

Writing up the report of the team activity

Although you will have done many tasks as part of the team, each member will have to write a report describing:
- what the team has done
- what you have done individually – your individual contribution to the activity.

Your report must include all of the following:
- Team performance
  - Why you chose the specific activity
  - Why as a team you agreed to do particular things
  - Why you made the contributions you did
- Team action plan
  - The aims of the activity – what you intended to do
  - The actions the team and individual members took
  - A list of available resources
  - The resources used and why
  - Any problems the team encountered and what you did about them
- Your individual action plan
  - How you followed the individual action plan
  - How you made the best use of available resources
- How you maintained health and safety
- How you co-operated with your team members
- Review of the activity
  - The resources used
  - Your responses to any problems encountered
  - Health and safety
  - Your feedback to colleagues and how you responded to any feedback from other team members
- Your suggestions for improvements in the way you would tackle a similar activity in the future
- Evidence of core skills you obtained while doing the activity.

Test yourself

1 Why do people form groups?

2 What does it mean for a group to brainstorm?

3 What is time management?

4 What should you consider before you contact people?

5 What is the purpose of note-taking?

6 What is a team action plan?

7 What things may stop people from communicating?

8 What are the two parts of reviewing team activity?

9 What does it mean to provide feedback to your team members?

10 What does non-verbal communication mean?

Please note

No separate assignment has been included for this unit, as the chapter as a whole has been written as a team activity assignment

---

Key words

After reading this chapter you should be able to understand the following words and phrases. If you do not, go back through the chapter and find out, or look them up in the Glossary.

Mutual exchange	*Brainstorming*
Time management	*Note-taking*
Team action plan	*Recording*
Interpersonal communication	*Constructive feedback*

CHAPTER 5

Investigating Common Health Emergencies

What is covered in this chapter

- Key health and safety factors in care settings
- Common health emergencies and care procedures

These are the resources you will need for your Investigating Common Health Emergencies portfolio:
- health and safety procedure documents you have collected
- information about the roles of health and social care workers in common emergencies
- health and safety codes of practice
- your written answers to each of the activities in this chapter
- your written answers to the Test Yourself questions at the end of this chapter
- your completed assignments: A5.1 and A5.2.

Introduction

In health and care settings every attempt should be made to reduce the risks of accidents to both staff and clients. It is essential, therefore, that every carer is aware of potential hazards in any situation in which they support clients. If an emergency does arise it is also important that you know what to do.

This chapter:
- describes the main hazards that you might come across in care settings
- describes how to reduce the risk of accidents by following the most important health and safety regulations
- outlines what you should do when a common health emergency occurs.

Key health and safety factors in care settings

Going to work for the first time, or going to your first real work experience, can be exciting and a bit strange. It can also be dangerous. Every year over 500 people die at work and several hundred thousand have to stay off work because of injury.

Some hazards cannot be seen, such as:
- stress
- radiation
- inadequate information as to the handling and lifting of clients.

Some health hazards may often affect workers slowly over many years.

Heath and Safety at Work Act 1974

This is the law that controls health and safety in the workplace. Both employers and employees (you) have responsibilities under this law to protect the health and safety of yourselves and other people.

Responsibilities of the employer

An employer must provide a workplace that is safe from hazards and which does not harm an employee's health. This includes:

- having a safety policy
- hygiene and welfare
- comfort
- cleanliness.

Safety policy

Employers must tell their staff how they are going to ensure their health and safety. This is called a **safety policy**. It should tell you:

- who your key managers are, so that you can report any unsafe situation
- how they intend to protect you at work, including rules for safe procedures when carrying out particular tasks. The rules cover, for example:
  - the control of infection
  - the wearing of protective clothing
  - using correct lifting procedures
  - training in the use of equipment.

The safety policy will in many cases be in the form of a booklet, or it may perhaps be a notice on a notice board. The document should also be published in a number of languages to make it accessible to all staff.

A manager of a residential home for the elderly people, for example, or of a day centre for children must ensure that all staff know their duties so that they pay appropriate attention to health and safety when they carry out their work.

The maintenance of a safe environment and the practice of safe procedures (see page 141) enables the client to feel secure and confident. That is one of the necessities of good social care. **Make sure you know the safety rules and obey them.**

Important rules
- Learn how to work safely.
- Obey safety rules.
- Ask your supervisor or tutor if you don't understand any instruction or rule.
- Report to your supervisor, manager or tutor anything that seems dangerous, damaged or faulty.

Activity 5.1

Find out what the safety policy is at your work placement. Obtain a copy, if possible, and compare it with others your class colleagues will have obtained from their work placements.

Hygiene and welfare

This includes:

- separate marked toilets for each sex
- toilets kept clean and in working order and ventilated
- wash basin with hot and cold running water
- soap, dryers and nail brushes where appropriate
- waste bins, regularly emptied
- facilities for taking food and drink
- safe methods for handling, storing and transporting materials. For example, drugs must be stored and used in a way as to minimise risk to health. If a new cleaning product is introduced, an employer is obliged to tell employees of any possible harmful effects.

Comfort

The employer should consider the comfort of employees, including:

- furniture placed so that sharp corners do not present a danger to staff or residents
- good ventilation in bathrooms, toilets, bedrooms
- thermometer in each work room so that staff can check temperature. This is important in areas where elderly people are cared for and also for babies and young children
- good lighting.

Cleanliness

The employer should ensure that:

- workplace, furniture and fittings are kept clean
- all rubbish and waste food are regularly removed
- all spillages are cleaned up immediately
- dirty linen is stored appropriately
- dressings and medicines are disposed of according to instructions.

PROHIBITION

Don't do
(red circle and red
cross bar, for example
'No Smoking')

MANDATORY

Must do
(blue circle, for
example 'Wash
your hands')

SAFE CONDITION

The safe way
(green rectangle,
for example
'First aid room')

WARNING

Risk of danger
(yellow triangle with
black outline, for example
'Risk of electric shock')

Safety signs to take notice of in the workplace

Responsibilities of the employee

What are your responsibilities in the workplace? You have a duty to take 'reasonable care' to avoid:

- **injury to yourself** For example, a nurse or care assistant who injures their back by not using the correct lifting procedures, when they were aware of them, would probably not be successful in claiming any compensation for their injury.

- **injury to others** For example, if you injure a client by not using the correct lifting procedure (after you have been trained) or by not using lifting aids, you may be liable to prosecution (that is, you may be taken to court). You must report any hazards or accidents to your employers.

> It is your duty:
> - to take care of yourself and anyone else – that means the clients, customers, their families and anyone who may be affected by your working activities
> - to co-operate with your employer helping in any way that you can to carry out his duties under the Act.
> - not to tamper with or misuse anything provided by the employer.

For example, it would be the duty of a care worker looking after people in their own homes to take care of themselves and anyone else, the clients, their families and friends. The care worker has a responsibility not to tamper with or use any equipment such as washing machines, irons, electric kettles or gas fires, that they may feel is faulty or may cause harm to anyone.

As a care worker you should be prepared:
- by being dressed appropriately for work. Wear any protective clothing you have been given by your employer, such as overalls or rubber gloves. Also remember to wear well-fitting, comfortable shoes.
- be always on the look-out for SAFETY HAZARDS
- report any hazards or accidents to your supervisor immediately
- use only safe methods of working.

Never:
- cut corners for the sake of speed
- try to move or lift clients without appropriate help.

If you have any questions or worries about safety, talk to your tutor or supervisor in the workplace.

What should you do if you are injured at work?
If you are injured at work:
- report the accident to your immediate supervisor or tutor
- record it in writing (it is usually recorded in an accident book)
- see a doctor – a medical examination should be carried after the accident and the result recorded.

Activity 5.2

A member of your class has fallen down the stairs. Find out how you can report accidents that happen on the college premises. What procedures are in operation?

Your tutor or Student Union colleagues will help you with this.

Safe procedures of work

Systems of work can affect your health and the clients' health. For example, do you know what would happen to your work clothes if they were splashed by a chemical you were using to clean a floor? Could poor design of working areas like bathrooms lead to backache?

Are you aware of any potential safety hazard? Is there any risk of clients or patients transmitting disease? If you were working with old, unchecked electrical appliances in a client's home, would you know of the dangers or who to report your concerns to? Are all students and staff aware of the procedures for staff who are vulnerable to physical violence?

Safe systems – A checklist

- Do you know who your supervisor is? Who do you report accidents and hazards to?
- Do you know the safe ways of doing the job?
- Are you are using equipment? Have you been instructed in its use and limitations?
- Has anyone assessed whether the equipment you are using is safe for the job?
- If things go wrong, do you know what to do?
- Are you aware of a system for checking that jobs are done safely in the way intended?

Case study

A health authority ignores its responsibilities

One woman who had worked at a hospital for two years part-time had an unpleasant attack of irritant dermatitis (skin disease). Her duties included cleaning mop heads with a carbolic soap. The attack coincided with the introduction of a new brand. She experienced tingling and itchiness, and her hand blistered. She had only been given overalls – no gloves, glove liners or barrier cream.

Her employer, the health authority, was taken to court and was found to have failed in its responsibilities under the Health and Safety at Work Act. This was because it didn't supply proper protection (rubber gloves) for staff to use when they were exposed to common toxic materials while cleaning hospital corridors.

Activity 5.3

a List as many potential hazards that you can observe in:
- your work placement
- your classroom or laboratory.

b How could you make them safer?

How do you report a hazard?

Large organisations (such as factories, colleges, hospitals) will usually have:
- a health and safety officer who will have the overall responsibility for health and safety policy

- a system for reporting defects in equipment
- an accident book for recording accidents.

If you suspect that equipment is faulty do not use it. Report your suspicions as soon as possible.

Activity 5.4

You are working in a day centre looking after elderly people. You overhear a cleaner complaining to a care assistant about the lack of electrical power points in the TV room. She cannot find a free point in the TV room for her vacuum cleaner. The care assistant tells the cleaner to use a socket in the corridor. This will mean that there will be a long trailing wire extension across the corridor and TV room.

a What accidents do you think might occur?

b What action should you take?

Some examples of hazard warning signs

The Control of Substances Hazardous to Health Regulations 1988 (COSHH)

These regulations lay down the essential requirements and a sensible step-by-step approach for the control of hazardous substances and for protecting people who are exposed to them.

What is a substance hazardous to health?

Some substance used by carers are obviously dangerous. Others are not obviously hazardous until they are misused or used in the wrong place. For example, a bottle of bleach is not in itself harmful, but if it is left in a place where confused people or children could drink it, it would then become a hazard. Many substances can therefore be a hazard in one situation and not in another.

There is a wide range of substances capable of damaging health. Many are used for cleaning or decorating. The health of carers can be put at risk from these substances if the right precautions are not taken.

Many of these substances are labelled so that people know what they are dealing with. For example, labels indicate whether a substance is:

- very toxic
- toxic
- harmful
- irritant
- corrosive
- composed of any material, mixture or compound which can harm people's health

Radiation controlled area

CAUTION
Laser beam

CAUTION
Chemical store

Some examples of hazard labels

The possible TOXIC EFFECTS of chemicals
- Occupational dermatitis (skin disorder)
- Headaches
- Irritability
- Nausea and vomiting (sickness)
- Dizziness
- Nose and throat irritation
- Tiredness
- Sleeplessness
- Chest trouble
- Worsening of asthma (a lung condition)
- Reproductive hazards (may affect ability to have children)
- Heart, lung, liver disease
- Kidney damage
- Cancer

Activity 5.5

In your own home, examine cleaning substances. Record how they are labelled and the instructions for use.

Safe use of chemicals
Poor working practices when handling chemicals, cleaners and powders may have a serious effect upon your health. Before you use chemicals (for example in cleaning equipment, toilets, floors, etc.), **assess the risks:**
- read the label and the information supplied by the manufacturer
- find out how the substance affects the body if it is breathed in or absorbed through the skin
- find out what the signs and symptoms of over-exposure are.

Help yourself by:
- not keeping food near places where chemicals or cleaning materials are stored
- not putting pens, pencils or fingers in your mouth when handling these materials
- not storing substances in familiar containers such as milk bottles or jam jars
- never using anything that does not have a label on it
- always using rubber gloves or other protective clothing which should be supplied by your employer
- keeping cleaning materials, medicines and chemicals locked away
- knowing what first aid to do if an accident occurs with the substance.

Activity 5.6

Find out where the cleaning materials and medicines are kept in your work placement.

Smoking

What is the employer's responsibility towards people who do not smoke?
Non-smokers sharing the same work space as smokers cannot help but inhale some of the tobacco smoke. This is called PASSIVE SMOKING.

Smoking is one of the most important causes of disease and premature death. Tobacco smoke contains a substance known to cause cancer. Passive smoking can also cause cancer in non-smokers and also irritate the eyes, throat and lungs.

Employers have a duty to protect their employees from these hazards. To do this they should ensure that:
- non-smoking is regarded as the normal thing to do in the workplace
- smokers are segregated from non-smokers.

The European Union has issued instructions that smoking is prohibited (forbidden) in public buildings, such as schools, hospitals, colleges, except in places that are designated are smoking areas. However, the employer does not have to provide a place for smokers to smoke in.

Activity 5.7

Find out what provisions have been made for people who want to smoke in your college or workplace.

Fire hazards

The Fire Precautions Act 1971 is the main law controlling fire safety. It requires certain of types of establishments, such as homes for the elderly, hospitals, schools, colleges and hotels, to apply for a fire certificate from the fire service. This certificate must be obtained before the establishment can operate.

It is the management's responsibility to provide:
- adequate routes for escape
- a way of giving fire warning
- fire-fighting equipment
- written instructions for clients, workers, visitors displayed in prominent positions
- instructions and training for staff
- fire procedures and drills.

Maryland Home for Elderly People

FIRE RULES

If you discover a fire:

Raise the alarm by operating the nearest fire alarm and proceed to the assembly point at the nearest exit (outside the Day Room Exit).

Please go along the corridor through the Day Room and out the double-opening patio doors.

Close the door of your room as you leave and any others you may use.

Do not:
- use lifts as a means of escape
- shout or run.

Study this notice carefully so that you will know what to do in an emergency.

Do not re-enter the building until told to do so by an appropriate person.

A fire action notice

How could you help prevent fire?
The answers to all of the following questions should be 'yes'.

Are all parts of the premises clear of waste and rubbish, particularly:
- store rooms?
- attics and basements?
- boiler rooms and other equipment rooms?
- bottoms of lift shafts?
- staircases and under the stairs?

Smoking:
- Are enough ashtrays provided in all the areas where smoking is permitted?
- Are staff warned to use the ashtrays and not to throw cigarettes or matches into waste paper bins, through gratings or out of windows?

Electricity:
- Do all parts of the electrical installation comply with the Institute of Electrical Engineers (IEE) regulations for electrical installations?
- Is the electrical installation inspected and tested at least every five years?

- Are staff trained to report frayed leads and faulty equipment?

If you do not have central heating, are heating appliances:
- fixed rather than portable?
- provided with adequate and secure fireguards?

Are the staff warned to keep combustible materials away from heaters?

Activity 5.8

Locate the Fire Action notices in your college or school.

List where they are displayed and copy down what they say.

Fire fighting
- Are portable fire extinguishers and/or hose reels provided in clearly visible and readily accessible places throughout the premises?
- Are they maintained at regular intervals?
- Are staff familiar with their use?

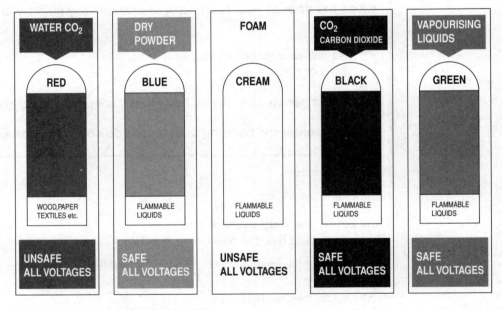

The different types of fire extinguisher

Activity 5.9

a Draw a plan of your college or school. Identify all the different fire extinguishers and water hoses in public places and mark them on the plan.

b Make notes of what types of fire the extinguishers are designed to deal with.

What should you do if you discover a fire?

You should notify a senior member of staff who should:

- ensure that the fire service has been called
- go to the scene of the fire and supervise the fire fighting until the fire service arrives
- clear everyone, except those actually engaged in the fire fighting, from the immediate vicinity of the fire
- order the evacuation of the building as soon as it becomes apparent that fire or smoke is spreading. Do not wait until the fire is out of control.
- take a roll call of all staff and residents or clients when the premises have been evacuated (a list of absentees from the building should be available).

Instructions should be given to caretakers and maintenance staff, setting out the action they should take in the event of fire. This should include:

- bringing all lifts to ground level and stopping them
- shutting down all services not essential to the escape of occupants or likely to be required by the fire brigade.

Lighting should be left on.

Activity 5.10

Find out what the fire evacuation procedure is in either your school, college or work placement.

First aid regulations in the workplace

Immediate and proper examination and treatment of a person who has suffered injuries may save life. This is known as **first aid**. First aid is also essential to reduce pain and help injured people make a quick recovery.

The Health and Safety (First Aid) Regulations 1981 state that employers must:

- provide adequate first aid for employees who are injured or fall ill at work
- provide sufficient numbers of first aiders
- appoint people to take charge of incidents
- appoint occupational first aiders whenever there are special hazards in the workplace.

Who is a FIRST AIDER?

A first aider is a trained person who has gained a first aid certificate. The certificate has to be renewed every three years.

Who is an occupational first aider?

An occupational first aider is a person holding an occupational first aid certificate issued within the past three years. The certificate must be from an organisation approved by the Health and Safety Executive, such as a college or other training organisation. Occupational first aiders are trained to deal with the effects the particular hazards of the workplace, such as working with chemicals or special machinery.

First aid boxes

A first aid box should be made of material designed to protect the contents from damp and dust. It should be clearly identified as a first aid box.

The following are the most common articles found in a first aid box:
- first aid guidance card
- individually-wrapped, sterile, adhesive dressings – various sizes
- sterile, unmedicated dressings with bandage attached
- eye pads
- triangular bandages
- safety pins
- individually-wrapped, moist cleaning wipes
- sterile water or saline in sealed containers.

Activity 5.11

Locate the first aid boxes in your college. Find out why each one is located in its particular position.

Lifting heavy loads

Lifting and carrying can, if not done properly, lead to ruptures, strains and back injuries. Safe lifting is a skill. It is easier to lift a heavy weight from the ground if the strain is taken by the leg and thigh muscles rather than by your back and abdomen.

> **Did you know that:**
> - at some time in their lives four out of five people will suffer from back pain?
> - 24 million working days are lost each year at a cost of over £1 billion per year?
> - approximately 5 per cent of people have to change the nature of their work completely because of back problems?
> - 80 000 nurses are off sick with back pain each year?

The European Community Manual Handling Regulations 1993 state that care staff are not obliged to lift anything or anybody that may damage their backs. Managers must examine every situation in which staff are expected to lift people or objects and ensure that staff are properly trained for any lifting that they do.

At present in health and social care over 50 per cent of all reported injuries are due to manual lifting of loads. Loads do not have to be heavy to be dangerous. In the health and social care, the 'load' is usually the client or patient. Many clients and patients are too heavy to be lifted bodily. Remember that people are more difficult to lift than boxes or sacks of corn. Most people may make unexpected movements when you are trying to lift them. Most difficulties arise when lifting people because of this.

Employers have the responsibility to make sure that staff do not put themselves at risk and must take all reasonable steps to protect them. In hospital and residential establishments, equipment, such as mobile hoists, should be available to move and lift dependent people.

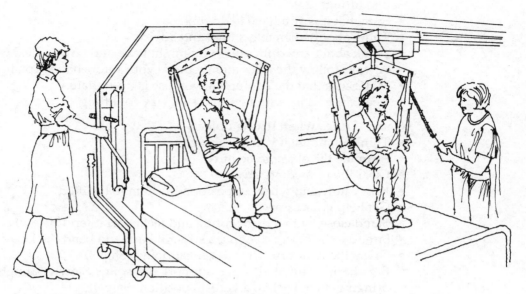

Mechanical lifts used in care situations

Working safely when moving and handling clients

Your back allows you to do everything – from sleeping to mountain climbing. People who experience back problems suffer pain and often have to take time off work. This can result in loss of earnings, inconvenience and even permanent disability.

Back pain and problems can be caused by:
- sprains due to faulty lifting
- disc trouble
- poor posture
- lack of exercise
- being overweight
- injuries
- diseases.

You can help yourself avoid back problems by ensuring that you maintain a good posture and making sure that you rest your muscles when you stand, sit and sleep. Follow the simple rules below.

Stand correctly with:
- your head high
- your chin in
- your chest forward
- your abdomen flat.

Sit correctly with:
- your knees higher than your hips
- your lower back firm against the backrest.

Sleep correctly with:
- a firm mattress
- a bed board
- your knees bent and lying on your side.

Before lifting:
- See what it is you have to do first.
- Think about when to get help and advice.
- Think about any difficulties you might have and how to deal with them.
- Always follow the rules and methods your tutors have explained to you.
- Make sure that the equipment you use is up-to-date.
- Keep up-to-date with new and safe ways of lifting.

General rules when lifting objects
- Think about what you are going to do.
- Examine the object to be lifted.
- Clear the immediate area.
- Know how and where to position the item to be lifted.
- Get help if necessary.
- Stand close, with a firm footing and feet apart (Step 1 below).
- Straddle the object, keeping a straight back and bend the knees (Step 2).
- Grasp the item firmly to prevent slipping (Step 3).
- Breathe in – inflated lungs support the spine. Slowly straighten your legs, bringing them back to a vertical position (Step 4).
- Hold the item firmly and close to the body (Step 5).
- Avoid sudden, jerky movements.
- Turn your feet not your back.

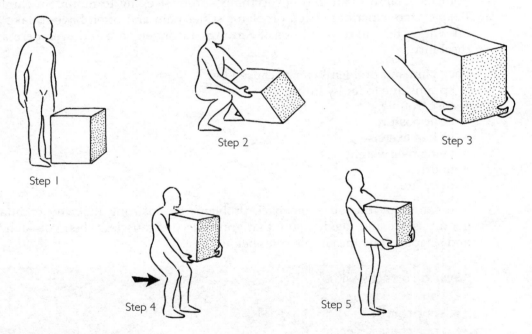

Step 1

Step 2

Step 3

Step 4

Step 5

Safe steps to lifting an object

Lifting or moving a client
When lifting or moving a client some important and specific rules apply:
- Always wear flat shoes.
- It is advisable to remove rings and watches. These may scratch the client or get caught in hair.
- Explain to the client what you are going to do.
- Clear the area.

- Where there is more than one lifter, co-operate to lift together.
- Do not rush the procedure.
- Do not drag the client.
- Apply all the general rules of lifting.

Remember
Always follow the rules.

Infectious disease

Infection means the passing of disease from one source (person, animal, soil) to another. This may occur in a number of different ways:
- by droplets or dust in the air
- by skin and mucus membranes
- by wounds
- by food and drink
- by soil, animals
- by infected articles.

Infections are caused by MICROBES (small living organisms or micro-organisms). These are so small that we need a microscope to see them. The main groups of microbes which are involved in infections are:
- **bacteria** – for example, cause TB
- **viruses** – for example, cause measles
- **fungi** – for example, cause ringworm
- **protozoa** – for example, cause dysentery.

When a person becomes contaminated by one of these organisms, they are said to be infected.

Activity 5.12

Make a list of diseases caused by the four main types of organisms.

Did your list include any of the following:
- bacteria: cholera?
- viruses: influenza?
- fungi: athlete's foot?
- protozoa: amoebic dysentery (tummy illness)?

Micro-organisms multiply very quickly under conditions of moisture, warmth and a food supply. In these conditions, they reproduce by splitting into two about every 20 minutes. One or two germs could, therefore, multiply into millions in a few days.

In the home, day centre, residential home, nursery or playgroup micro-organisms are to be found in warm, moist places with poor ventilation such as bathrooms, kitchens and bedrooms. They can also occur on food, face flannels, towels, floor coverings and mops. Micro-organisms can enter the body through:
- inhalation – breathing in through the nose and throat

- inoculation – through a break, cut or wound on the skin
- ingestion – through the mouth by swallowing.

The body has certain defences which protect against infection as shown below.

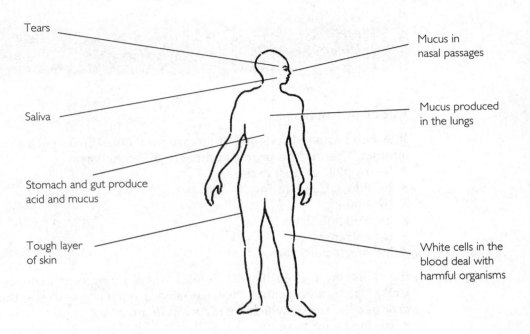

Tears

Mucus in
nasal passages

Saliva

Mucus produced
in the lungs

Stomach and gut produce
acid and mucus

Tough layer
of skin

White cells in the
blood deal with
harmful organisms

The body's defences

Carers should know how to prevent infection from spreading. If you use sensible hygiene practices, you should not be afraid of becoming infectious yourself. The following is a list of some of the ways in which the spread of infection can be prevented:

- adopting high standards of personal hygiene
- enforcing high standards of food hygiene
- providing good quality accommodation
- using disposable gloves, and washing hands before and after
- disinfecting or burning articles used by infected persons
- ensuring good ventilation
- making sure the establishment is clean throughout.

Simple routines to prevent the spread of infection

Avoiding contact with blood and body fluids
Always wear plastic gloves when in contact with blood or body fluids. If you are in contact with such matter, wash your hands thoroughly with soap and water.

Avoiding contact with cuts and abrasions
Cover open wounds with waterproof dressings. Blue plasters should always be provided for food handlers.

Disinfecting
- Wear plastic gloves and an apron when mopping up.

- Disinfect areas contaminated by blood and excreta with a bleach solution.
- Dispose of contaminated waste by using the appropriate bags and containers.

Carers must always be on the alert to the dangers of infection which may make a person seriously ill. In particular, babies, young children and elderly people have less resistance to germs.

Common health emergencies and care procedures

First aid

As we have already seen, first aid is assistance or treatment given to a casualty before a doctor or ambulance arrives. The aim of first aid is:
- to save life
- to prevent the injured person's condition deteriorating
- to aid recovery.

In an emergency situation, the priorities of a first aider must be to:
- Stay calm.
- Quickly assess the situation:
  – First make sure that you are safe.
  – Make sure the person injured is safe from further injury.
  – Find out what is wrong with the injured person.
- Get help.
- Move the injured person only if there is risk of further injury to them.
- Give essential first aid treatment:
  – Check the airway, breathing and circulation – A B C (see below).
  – Check for severe bleeding.
  – Check for unconsciousness.
- Make arrangements to send the injured person to a hospital, to a doctor, back to work or home.
- Pass on information about the injury and the casualty's condition to the doctor, ambulance personnel, etc.

How to get help
Find the nearest telephone and dial 999. Give as much information as necessary:
- service required – ambulance, fire or police
- your telephone number
- where you are located
- what has happened
- the number and type of casualties.

What is the A B C rule?

This is a very important rule for first aiders to remember. Thinking of the letters A B C will help you to remember the right order to do things in an emergency:

A = Airway Check that the airway is open. If not, open the airway (see page 154).
B = Breathing Check that the casualty is breathing. If not, resuscitation will be necessary (see page 155).
C = Circulation Check that the heart is beating by taking the pulse. If it is not, resuscitation and chest massage (CPR) will be necessary (see page 156).

If the airway, breathing and pulse are OK, you can then check for other injuries, such as fractures, cuts, wounds, etc. (These are described on pages 158–71.) Every few minutes you should check (monitor) A B C signs.

If the person is semi-conscious or unconscious you should also try and measure their level of consciousness.

Monitoring levels of consciousness

Unconsciousness can be caused by anything that interrupts the normal working of the brain. The most common causes are:
- suffocation
- shock
- heart attack
- head injuries
- poisoning
- epilepsy and diabetic emergencies.

Levels of consciousness
- **Fully conscious** – alert, responds to conversation in normal manner
- **Drowsiness** – easily responds, may give muddled or slow answers to questions
- **Semi-conscious** – aroused with difficulty, may only be able to carry out simple things like moving arm or leg or fingers, will be aware of pain
- **Unconscious** – no response, no reaction to questions, pain.

Keeping the airway open

Because a person's muscles are usually completely relaxed when they are unconscious they are at particular risk of choking. This is caused by the tongue falling backwards and blocking the air passage. This is one of the first things to look for in an unconscious person. So that air and oxygen can get to the brain, the first thing to do is to **make sure that the airway is open**.

How do you keep the airway open?
- Tilt the person's forehead backwards by placing one hand underneath the neck and the other hand on their forehead. This will ensure that the chin moves upwards.
- Remove your hand from under the person's neck and lift the chin upwards and forwards. The mouth will open slightly and the nostrils of the nose will be pointing upwards. In this position the tongue will move from the back of the throat and unblock the air passage.

Once you have unblocked the airway and the person is breathing, you must place them in either of these positions:
- **The prone position** 'Prone' means face downwards and the elbows bent, so that the forearms and hands are under the forehead.
- **The recovery position** The casualty is lying on their side, with the face turned towards the ground (see opposite). This position keeps the airway open and allows any fluid to drain from the mouth.

Activity 5.13

Practise placing a person in the recovery position with a class colleague.

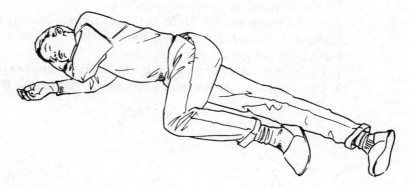

The recovery position

Resuscitation

Mouth-to-mouth resuscitation

The brain needs oxygen in order to function. The respiratory (breathing) system relies on our ribs, diaphragm, heart and lungs working together to transport oxygen from the air we breathe to the brain.

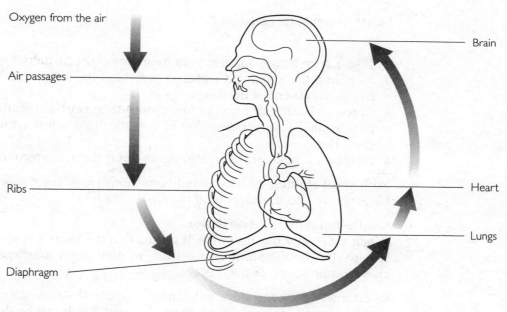

Oxygen from the air

Air passages

Ribs

Diaphragm

Brain

Heart

Lungs

Factors in respiration

A person who is not breathing, therefore, is being starved of oxygen. If the brain is starved of oxygen for more than four minutes it may be permanently damaged. One way to get air to someone's lungs is by breathing into their lungs. This is called **artificial respiration** or **mouth-to-mouth resuscitation**.

The air you breathe into the casualty's lungs will not be as rich in oxygen as the air they would normally breathe, but it will be enough to maintain life and avoid brain damage.

How to do mouth-to-mouth resuscitation

Artificial respiration will do the unconscious person no harm, so don't waste time on fetching help or dealing with other injuries. The casualty will die if the brain does not get oxygen immediately.

1 Lie the casualty flat on their back. Open the airway (see above).
2 Close the casualty's nose by pinching it, otherwise the air will escape through the nose.

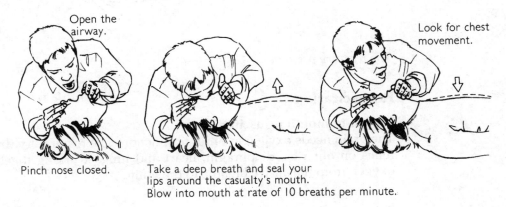

Open the airway.

Pinch nose closed.

Take a deep breath and seal your lips around the casualty's mouth. Blow into mouth at rate of 10 breaths per minute.

Look for chest movement.

Mouth-to-mouth resuscitation

3 Take a deep breath and put your mouth over the casualty's mouth.
4 Blow into the lungs and watch to observe if the lungs rise. The chest should rise as the air enters the lungs.
5 Carry on breathing into the lungs until they start to breathe again, or until professional help arrives. Don't blow too hard – just enough to make the chest rise.
6 As soon as they start to breathe again put them in the recovery position.

With small children or babies, put your mouth over their **nose and mouth** and blow gently into the lungs until the chest rises.

Cardio-pulmonary resuscitation

When a casualty has **no pulse**, it means that the heart has stopped beating. To restore the circulation, it is necessary to give **chest massage** (also known as chest compressions or heart massage).

Chest massage is best done combined with mouth-to-mouth resuscitation. This is called **cardio-pulmonary resuscitation** or **CPR**. It can be done either by one or two first aiders – one to give mouth-to-mouth ventilation and the other to do chest massage.

How to do chest massage

1 Lie the casualty flat on their back. Open the airway (see above).
2 Find the correct position for your hands (see opposite).
3 Leaning over the casualty, with your arms straight, press down vertically on the breastbone to depress it about 4–5 cm. Release the pressure without removing your hands.
4 Continue giving compressions at a rate of about 80 per minute. Check the pulse after every 10 compressions.

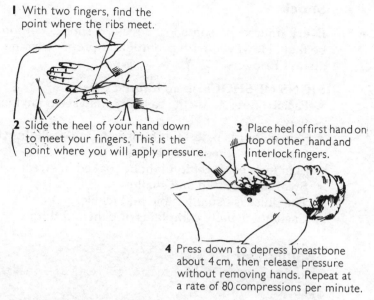

1 With two fingers, find the point where the ribs meet.

2 Slide the heel of your hand down to meet your fingers. This is the point where you will apply pressure.

3 Place heel of first hand on top of other hand and interlock fingers.

4 Press down to depress breastbone about 4 cm, then release pressure without removing hands. Repeat at a rate of 80 compressions per minute.

Position of the hands for chest massage

With babies, place the **tips of two fingers** in a position just below the mid-point of an imaginary line between the nipples. Give chest compressions of about 1.5–2.5 cm at a rate of 100 per minute.

With children under 5, put **one hand** in the same position as you would for an adult. Give compressions of about 2.5–3.5 cm at a rate of 100 per minute. For children over 5, use the method for adults.

How to combine mouth-to-mouth resuscitation and chest massage

Casualty	One first aider	Two first aiders
Adult	1 Give 2 lung inflations 2 Give 15 compressions to every 2 lung inflations	1 Give 2 lung inflations 2 Give 5 compressions to every lung inflation
Baby or child under 5	Give 5 compressions to every lung inflation	

Activity 5.14

a Practise mouth-to-mouth resuscitation on a first aid dummy.

b Practise chest massage on a first aid dummy.

c Practise CPR on a first aid dummy:
   • on your own
   • with a partner.

Your tutor will explain how you should do this.

Shock

Every injured person soon develops shock. Without proper treatment this can be fatal. However, with prompt and proper treatment the injured person nearly always recovers.

SIGNS OF SHOCK in an injured person

- Facial expression – the casualty may seem anxious and may stare in a vacant way.
- Skin colour is pale – white, ashen gray or slightly blue.
- Casualty is sometimes restless.
- Skin feels cold, yet it might be soaked in sweat.
- Breathing is rapid and shallow.
- The pulse is usually rapid and feeble.
- Casualty usually complains of pain and thirst.

Remember the signs of shock:
anxiety – pale – cold – sweating – restless – shallow breathing – rapid pulse – pain – much thirst

Treatment for shock

- Call an ambulance.
- Keep the casualty still.
- Cover wounds and stop external bleeding.
- Loosen clothing.
- Cover the casualty with a blanket or coat – do not over-heat.
- Comfort the casualty.
- Raise the casualty's legs to increase the blood flow to the brain.

Activity 5.15

You have been out rock climbing with your class. You come across a person who was climbing alone and has had an accident. You are the only member of the class who has had first aid training. The rest of the class think that the injured person has gone into shock.

a How could you tell if this is so? List the signs and symptoms of shock.

b What is the treatment for shock?

Asthma

What is asthma?

We usually do not think of how we breathe, it is a passive and effortless procedure. To understand asthma, we must first understand how we breathe.

When we breathe in, the lung tissue is stretched. The natural elasticity of the lungs then forces the air out and we breathe out. When someone has forced, wheezy and difficult breathing it is called **asthma**. The breathing tubes (bronchioles) become narrowed so that it is difficult to breath out naturally. Some people feel a great weight across their chest and have difficulty in breathing and they may make wheezing noises.

What causes asthma?
Asthma is often an ALLERGIC CONDITION. People may be allergic to:
- pollens
- smoke
- animals
- certain foods.

In Japan, for example, about half of the people who suffer from asthma are allergic to butterflies. Sometimes if a person is worried their asthma may be made worse. Attacks usually occur suddenly and at night or the early hours of the morning.

Who may suffer from asthma?
About one in twenty school children suffer from this disease. Many adults suffer. It is more common in men than women. Asthma also occurs later in life in individuals who suffer from chronic bronchitis (inflammation of the mucus membrane of the bronchial tubes).

How can you help someone who has an attack of asthma?
- If the person is lying down, sit them up (in bed or in a chair) in a comfortable position. In many cases, the person themselves will know which position is most comfortable. Sometimes the person suffering cannot bear to be touched and may want all their clothes loosened. Lean them slightly forward. In this position it is easier to use the chest muscles for breathing. Make sure that there is plenty of fresh air available.
- If this is a first attack, a doctor or ambulance should be called.
- If the casualty knows that they suffer from asthma, find out whether they have their inhaler with them. If so, help them to use it.
- Give plenty of reassurance until a doctor or ambulance arrives. The person will be very frightened, when they find difficulty in breathing. Young children may panic and will need lots of reassurance and emotional support.

Activity 5.16

You are travelling on a bus in town on a very foggy day. One of the passengers begins to have breathing problems. She manages to tell you she suffers from asthma.

a What causes asthma?

b When is it most likely to occur?

c What is the first aid treatment for the condition?

Epileptic fits

What is epilepsy?
Epilepsy is a nervous disorder characterised by a sudden loss of consciousness. Convulsions also occur. These can be frightening when seen for the first time, but they are not in themselves a medical emergency. Epilepsy can effect people of all ages.

Types of epilepsy

'Grand mal' or major fit

This type of fit can be very frightening when seen for the first time. The person may make a strange cry and fall suddenly. Muscles stiffen and then relax. Jerking or convulsions occur, and they can be quite vigorous. Saliva may appear about the mouth. The person may also pass water.

This type of fit may last several minutes. Then the person may recover consciousness, be dazed or confused. A 'grand mal' fit is not usually harmful unless it is followed by another fit.

'Petit mal'

This type of fit may pass unnoticed by others. The person may appear to daydream or stare blankly. There may be frequent blinking of the eyes. This type of fit may cause problems in children at nursery or school as the child may not learn or pay attention during the periods of fitting.

What causes epilepsy?

Epilepsy is **not** a disease or illness. It may be a symptom of some physical disorder, such as a disorder of brain activity. It may also occur after head or brain injury. In children, in particular, it may have no precise medical explanation.

Who may suffer from epilepsy?

Epilepsy can occur at any age. However, it is common in children. Over 100 000 children and young people have some form of epilepsy.

How can you help someone who has suffered an epileptic fit?

- Most fits stop spontaneously. All that needs to be done is to protect the person from asphyxiation by preventing inhalation of vomit or swallowing of the tongue.
- Don't try to hold the person down or stop them jerking or thrashing about. Loosen tight clothing.
- As soon as they stop jerking, wipe the froth from their mouth and place them in the **recovery position** (see page 155). Make sure that any vomit is cleared from the mouth.
- When the person regains consciousness, make sure that they have a change of clothes if they have wet or soiled themselves.
- Do not put anything between the teeth. **Do not** give anything to drink.

Activity 5.17

a How many types of epilepsy are there?

b What can you do to help someone who has just suffered a fit?

Concussion (head injuries)

Falls, blows and road accidents are the usual causes of head injuries. A blow to the head does not necessarily damage the brain, even if the skull is fractured. A crack in the skull will heal but a 'depressed' fracture (one which presses inwards on the brain) is serious and may produce symptoms of brain injury.

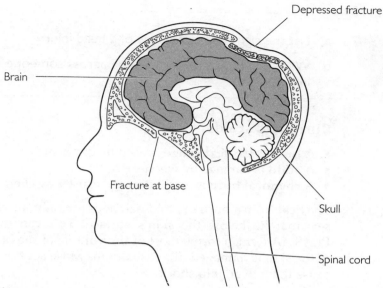

Skull fractures

Symptoms of head injury

- Unconsciousness. There may be immediate loss of consciousness after the fall or blow, or unconsciousness may follow after the casualty experiences extreme drowsiness.
- Flushed face. This happens because the body temperature may rise.
- Slow pulse.
- Noisy breathing or shallow breathing.
- Convulsions.
- Twitching of the limbs.
- Abnormal pupils.
- Muscle weakness or paralysis.

What do you do if you find a person with suspected head injuries?

With head injuries, the general condition of the person is important.

- Check the casualty's breathing – you or someone else may need to start artificial respiration (see page 156).
- Call for an ambulance.
- If the person is unconscious, place them in the recovery position (see page 155).
- Once you have placed the casualty in the recovery position, check for any wounds. If there is bleeding from the head, do not try to stop it. Put a pad (see page 164) on it and keep it in place with a bandage.
- If the casualty regains consciousness, make them rest and watch them carefully for any signs of brain injury.

Remember

Always make sure that you see your doctor if any of the following symptoms develop after a head injury:

- double vision
- continuous vomiting
- increasingly severe headache.

Activity 5.18

a List the signs and symptoms of a head injury.

b What would you do if you came across someone suffering from a head injury?

Burns and scalds

- A **burn** is tissue damage caused by dry heat.
- A **scald** is damage by wet heat.
- A **chemical burn** is tissue damage caused by chemicals.

The heat from a burn or scald damages not only the skin, but also the blood vessels that lie below the skin's surface. This causes a colourless fluid called PLASMA (which forms most of the volume of the blood) to leak. If a large part of the skin is damaged, the casualty may lose a lot of blood or plasma. This may cause them to go into shock.

Children and old people react badly to severe burns. They are also particularly liable to extensive accidental burns.

Activity 5.19

Mary, a care assistant, was preparing a bath for one of the elderly residents. She did not check the temperature of the water. When Joan, the resident, put her foot into the water, she was injured.

a Did Joan suffer a burn or scald?

b What is the difference between the two?

First aid treatment for burns and scalds

The aims of first aid treatment for burns and scalds are to:
- prevent shock
- avoid infection
- relieve pain.

Treatment
- Cool all burns and scalds as quickly as possible, by drenching the burn with cold water. Continue this for at least 10 minutes. If the burn is a small one hold it under a running tap
  Cooling relieves the pain and helps to stop plasma loss by closing up the damaged blood vessels.
- Remove any loose clothing near the burn.
- **Do not** remove clothing that has been burnt. Burnt clothing is sterile and will give some protection against infection.
- **Do** remove any clothing that is soaked in chemicals. Remember to protect your own hands when doing this.
- Remove rings, belts or anything tight from the burnt area. If the burnt part swells later, it may be then difficult to remove them.
- If the burn covers more than about the size of a 50 pence piece or if it is on the face, it needs medical treatment. Cover the area with a sterile dressing. In an emergency, you can use a clean cloth, such as a handkerchief or part of a

sheet. The dressing will keep the plasma from coming into contact with the air and forming a route for infection.

- Remember that a badly burnt person may suffer from shock. If they do, lie them down and keep them warm.
- If blisters form, **do not** burst them.

Activity 5.20

Make a list of the things you would do to help someone who has suffered a burn to their face.

Electric shock

What is an electric shock?
It is the body's reaction to the passage of an electric current. The electric current may cause sudden unconsciousness or just a slight tingling. An electric shock may cause the heart to stop beating and if the heart stops, breathing will also stop. The casualty may appear dead. However, a first aider must never presume that the casualty is dead.

The casualty may have severe burns at the point where the electric current entered and left the body.

What do you do if you find someone who has suffered an electric shock?
- Switch off the current at the mains.
- Switch off at the plug or try to pull out the plug.
- **Do not directly touch the casualty** – you will also get a shock.
- If you cannot switch of the electric current, break the electric contact by pulling the casualty away from it. Do this by putting a rope around their legs or arms. **Do this without touching the casualty**.
- When you are pulling the casualty away, stand or kneel on a dry rug, mackintosh, rubber mat or pile of newspapers.

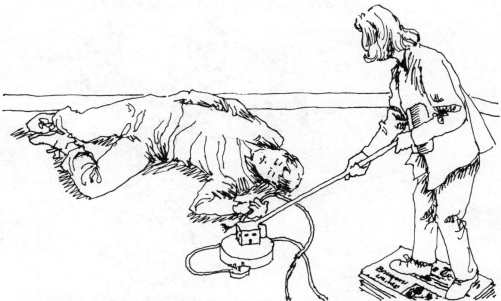

Use something non-metallic, such as a wooden broom handle, to push the appliance away from the casualty

- It may be easier to push the contact (wire or equipment) away from the casualty. Do this with a broom handle after insulating your hand with rubber gloves, a dry cloth or newspapers.

When you have removed the casualty from the electric current:
- Check for breathing and watch for signs that their heart may have stopped.
- If the heart has stopped, start chest massage (see page 156).
- If the heart is beating, but the casualty's breathing has stopped, start artificial respiration (see page 156).
- If the casualty is breathing, but unconscious, place them in the recovery position (see page 155).
- Report the accident to your manager or call an ambulance or a doctor.

Cuts

Cuts are a common occurrence. Small cuts will need little treatment – the bleeding will stop as the blood clots. If the wound continues bleeding after four or five minutes, a doctor should be seen as the wound may need stitching.

How do you control bleeding and dress wounds?
The body usually can stop bleeding itself but when there is serious injury the body is not able to cope. If the blood is flowing fast it does not get a chance to clot. Heavy blood loss can threaten life. For infants and children even a loss of half a pint can be dangerous.

How to stop bleeding
- Make the casualty lie down. This reduces the blood flow through the limb.
- Press hard on the wound, using a pad, folded handkerchief, bandage or dressing from a first aid kit.
- Maintain pressure for about ten minutes by which time a clot should have formed.
- As soon as bleeding stops pick out any obvious foreign bodies from the wound, glass, pebbles, etc. **Never remove foreign bodies embedded in a wound.**
- Apply a clean dressing. Bind it firmly with a bandage.

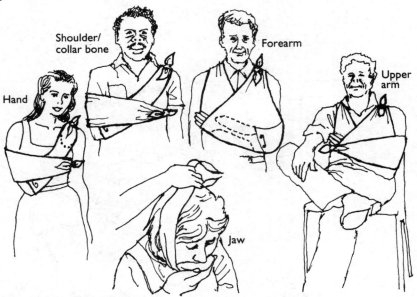

Different methods of bandaging

- If blood is oozing through the bandage, do not take it off but put another one on top of it.
- If the wound is serious, treat the casualty for shock.
- Elevate the limb or wound if possible.
- Rest and support the injury.

Activity 5.21

Practise different types of bandaging on a fellow student.

Points to remember

Minor cuts:
- clean with soap and water
- clean surrounding skin if dirty
- clean the wound
- apply clean or sterile dressing.

Major cuts and wounds:
- Examine cut.
- Control the bleeding by applying direct pressure on the wound.
- Remove any foreign bodies on the surface of the wound.
- Apply dressing.
- Elevate the limb or wound.
- Rest and support the injury.

With a major wound, many people may go into a state of shock. Treat them for shock (see page 158). Young children may go into a state of shock even with a minor cut. Reassure the casualty whatever the age.

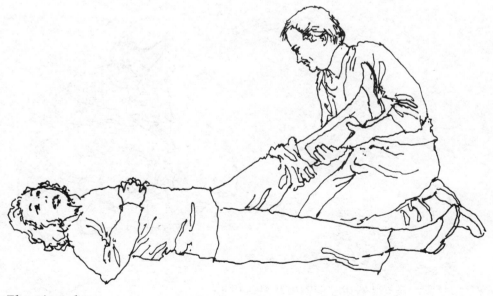

Elevating a leg

Remember
Always wear disposable plastic gloves when dealing with blood and wounds.

Activity 5.22

You are working in a playgroup and a child cuts their leg.

a What first aid would you give?

b What would you do to reassure the child?

Choking

Any foreign body (fishbone, piece of food) that lodges or sticks in the throat or in the windpipe will cause choking. With children or elderly people the most common cause is food or drink 'going down the wrong way'. With small children, choking is a particular hazard, because of their habit of putting everything into their mouths.

Symptoms of choking
- If the airway is not completely blocked, the casualty may be coughing.
- If the airway is completely blocked, they will be struggling for breath and their face will turn blue as the try to get air into their lungs.

Treatment for choking
1 Open the airway (see page 154).
2 Try to remove the obstruction with your finger.
3 If you cannot move the obstruction, give sharp blows with the heal of the hand between the shoulder-blades to try to dislodge it. Make sure that the casualty's head is lower than their chest.

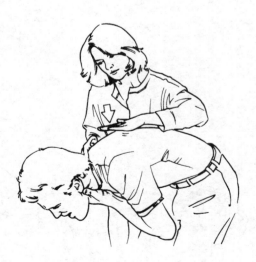

Dealing with a choking adult

The abdominal thrust

4 If you cannot clear the obstruction, give abdominal thrusts.
5 If this all fails, get the person to hospital as soon as possible.

If a baby or child is choking, use the techniques shown below.

Abdominal thrusts **may** be used on children over the age of 5.

Dealing with a choking baby or child

Broken bones

A break in a bone is called a **fracture**. There are three types of fracture:
- **open fracture** – the broken bone penetrates the skin. This is very serious because of the danger of infection getting into the open wound.
- **closed fracture** – no open wound

- **greenstick fracture** – a common fracture in children. The bones of a child are not so brittle and therefore more likely to bend rather than break. The bend causes a partial break.

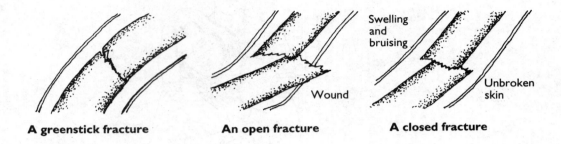

A greenstick fracture　　**An open fracture**　　**A closed fracture**

The three types of fracture

General signs of a fracture
- Crack of bone breaking.
- Difficulty or loss of movement.
- Pain.
- Swelling and later signs of bruising.
- The limb may be deformed.
- The person may suffer from shock.

What can you do?
- **Do not** move the person. By moving the casualty or the broken limb, you may cause more damage and much pain.
- If help is not immediately available:
  – Cover any open wound.
  – Try to stop any severe bleeding by applying pressure alongside the broken bone. Alternatively you can press the edges of the wound gently but firmly together.
  – Immobilise the injured part. Move the injured limb into the most comfortable position and bandage it to the casualty's body (see opposite).
  – Use lots of padding around the limb – blankets, folded clothes, pillows or towels.
  – Raise the injured part. This helps reduce pain and swelling.
  – Try to prevent shock. Loosen tight clothing, and cover the person with a blanket or coat.
  – **Do not** give anything to eat or drink

Activity 5.23

a List the three types of common fracture.

b Which of the three is mostly likely to occur in children and why?

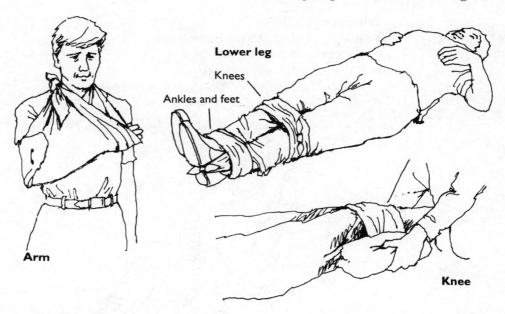

Ways of immobilising broken limbs

Heart attack

A heart attack is caused by a blood clot blocking a coronary artery. The blood clot prevents blood reaching the heart.

What are the signs and symptoms of a heart attack?

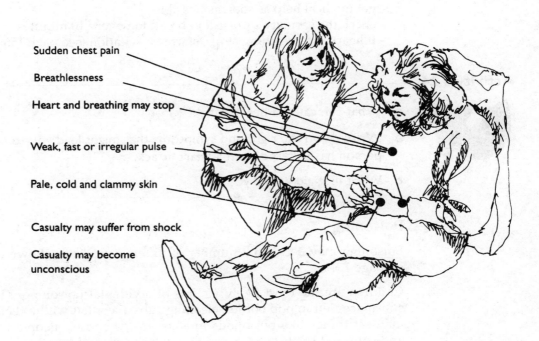

Sudden chest pain

Breathlessness

Heart and breathing may stop

Weak, fast or irregular pulse

Pale, cold and clammy skin

Casualty may suffer from shock

Casualty may become unconscious

Signs of a heart attack

What can you do?
- Telephone for a doctor or ambulance.
- Try not to move the casualty.
- If the casualty is conscious:
  – place then in the 'W' position (see below).

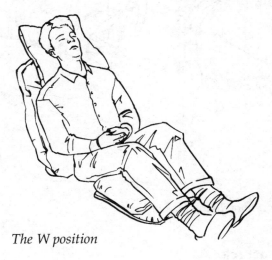

The W position

  – loosen any tight clothing
  – talk to the casualty and comfort them.
- If the person is unconscious:
  – place them in the recovery position (see page 155)
  – get medical help as soon as possible
  – check the casualty's pulse and breathing every 10 minutes.
  – if heart and breathing stops, start resuscitation (see page 156).

Activity 5.24

a What can cause a heart attack?

b Write down the signs and symptoms that might lead you to believe that a person has suffered from a heart attack.

c What first aid would you give?

Poisoning

Poisoning may occur in a number of different ways, as shown in the diagram on page 171.

Children are the most likely victims of accidental poisoning. They may drink substances left in pop bottles, cleaning substances left within their reach or they may eat things like poisonous mushrooms or berries. People who are elderly and confused or absent-minded may take accidental overdoses of pills or other drugs.

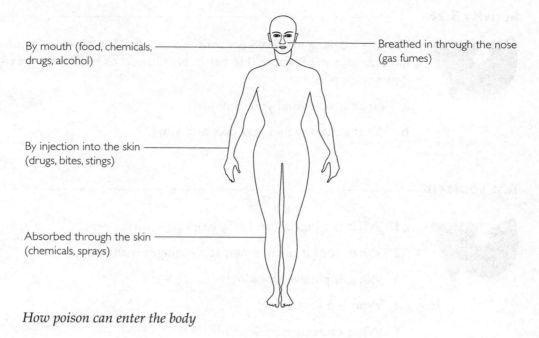

By mouth (food, chemicals, drugs, alcohol)

Breathed in through the nose (gas fumes)

By injection into the skin (drugs, bites, stings)

Absorbed through the skin (chemicals, sprays)

How poison can enter the body

Activity 5.25

List the kinds of things which are common in the home that would cause poisoning to a young child.

Signs and symptoms of poisoning
These will vary according to:
• the poison taken
• how it entered the body
• its effect on the person.

If a poison is swallowed, it may cause the person to be sick and vomit. This may mean that the body has rid itself of the poison. However, if the poison has been absorbed into the blood or inhaled, it can cause unconsciousness, stop breathing and eventually cause death.

What can you do if someone has been poisoned?
• Call an ambulance.
• Find out what the poison is – ask the person or look around.
• **Never** give salt or mustard and water to make them sick.
• If they have swallowed a corrosive substance that has burnt or may burn their lips (such as petrol, household cleaners, paint stripper), do not make them vomit. This will only cause more damage.
• If the person has taken a corrosive substance and if they are conscious, try to dilute the poison by getting them to drink one pint of tepid milk or water.
• Keep any evidence, such as vomit, pills or container, to show the doctor or ambulance personnel what the poison was.
• If the casualty loses consciousness, put them in the recovery position (see page 155).
• If they stop breathing, start artificial respiration (see page 156).

Activity 5.26

You are working in an old persons' home, You find an elderly confused man unconscious in his room. He has been allowed to look after his own anti-depressant pills.

a What signs would you look for?

b What action would you take and why?

Test yourself

1 What is a healthy and safe working environment?

2 What does it mean when something is mandatory?

3 What is passive smoking?

4 Who is a first aider?

5 What can cause back pain?

6 What are the signs of shock?

7 What is the first aid treatment for asthma?

8 What is the first aid treatment for choking?

9 Name the three types of fracture?

10 What does A B C mean?

Assignment A5.1
Key health and safety factors

You have just been appointed the manager of a care setting: an old persons' home, a playgroup, a nursery, a day centre or a hostel. The owner of the establishment wants you to prepare a report (preferably word-processed) outlining:

• the health and safety responsibilities of the employer and the employees

• what the common hazards might be

• what equipment and safe systems might be necessary to prevent risks to staff and clients

• what benefits the employer, staff and clients would get from a safe and healthy environment.

1 Select which type of establishment you wish to make the report on. You may wish to base your assignment on your work placement. Whatever you chose to do you will need to visit your chosen organisation and talk to the manager, staff and clients.

   a Select your establishment.

   b Make arrangements to visit the establishment.

   c Decide what questions you are going to ask the manager, staff and clients.

2 **a** Choose at least three common hazards from the following list:
   • fire
   • substances
   • unsafe equipment
   • unsafe working environment
   • infectious disease.

   b Explain and list the health and safety regulations that apply to each of the three selected hazards.

   c List the employer's responsibilities in relation to the three hazards.

   d List your responsibilities as an employee in relation to the three selected hazards.

   e Explain how you could reduce the risks to clients and staff presented by the three selected hazards in the workplace.

3 **a** Describe the safety equipment that the employer should provide to reduce the risks associated with the three selected hazards. For example, first aid equipment, alarms, emergency systems, fire doors, fire extinguishers, etc.

   b List the safety precautions and safe working practices, such as lifting regulations, that apply to each of the three hazards you have selected

4 **a** Visit the establishment of your choice and talk to:
   • the manager
   • staff
   • clients.
   Ask them what they think are the benefits of applying health and safety regulations and working and living in a safe environment.

   b List the benefits of a safe working environment for:
   • the employer
   • staff
   • clients.
   For example prevention of accidents, improved and safer service to clients, happy workforce.

Assignment A5.2
Health emergencies and care procedures

This assignment gives you the opportunity to look at four common health emergencies which require the attendance of the emergency services. You will be expected to describe the key signs and the care procedures. You will also describe how you would monitor the casualty's condition, safety requirements and the correct procedures to be followed. You may want to present evidence in the form of photographs or a video. Use a word-processor for your work, if you can.

Your tasks

1 a Choose four common health emergencies from the following list:
asthma
epileptic fit
concussion
burns
scalds
electric shock
cuts
choking
broken bones
heart attack
poisoning

   b Select a residential care setting (from the list below) in which you are going to describe each emergency:
   • an old persons' home
   • a nursery or playgroup
   • a hospital
   • a client's own home.
     For example: a fracture in an old persons' home; choking in a nursery; a head injury in a hospital; a burn in a client's own home.
     Remember the health emergency you describe **must** be serious enough to call the emergency services.

2 Describe and list the key signs of each of the four health emergencies you have chosen.

3 a Describe the care procedures for each of the four health emergencies you have selected. For example ABC, resuscitation, controlling bleeding, emotional support.

   b Describe how you would monitor the condition of the casualty.

   c List the safety requirements you would take into account. For example, how would you protect yourself from infection or injury?

4 a List the information you need to give the emergency services when you call them.

b Describe the information you should have available to give the ambulance personnel or doctor when they arrive.

Key words

After reading this chapter you should be able to understand the following words and phrases. If you do not, go back through the chapter and find out, or look them up in the Glossary.

Prohibition	*Warning*
Safe condition	*Mandatory*
Safety hazards	*Passive smoking*
First aider	*Toxic effects*
Microbes	*Signs of shock*
Allergic condition	*Plasma*

CHAPTER 6

Planning Diets

What is covered in this chapter

- The features of a healthy diet
- Balanced diets for people with different needs
- Planning and costing diets

These are the resources you will need for your Planning Diets portfolio:
- information and leaflets you have collected about food and diet from health education units, doctors' surgeries, shops, etc.
- your written answers to the activities in this chapter
- your written answers to the Test Yourself questions at the end of this chapter
- your completed assignments: A6.1, A6.2, A6.3.

Introduction

What you eat plays an important part in your health. In this chapter you will:
- look at your diet in terms of the amount you eat and the different food groups
- consider the importance of a well-balanced diet
- look at special diets and analyse them to see how they contain the balance of nutrients.

Having understood more about diets, you will then be able to plan and cost balanced diets to meet client needs.

The features of a healthy diet

I don't eat a diet, I eat food

It is often very confusing to think about the food you eat in terms of what it contains. When you eat a sandwich, for example, you are not thinking about the protein and starch in the wheat that forms the flour to make the bread. You are presumably more interested in the fact that it tastes good and stops you feeling hungry.

In this section, we are going to look in more detail at what food consists of and how your body uses it. We describe the content of food in terms of the NUTRIENTS it contains.

Types of nutrient

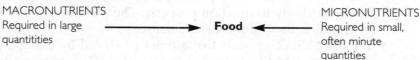

MACRONUTRIENTS
Required in large quantitities

Food

MICRONUTRIENTS
Required in small, often minute quantities

Macro means big and micro means small. All diets contain something of these major nutrient groups

177

The table below summarises the main nutrient groups.

The main nutrient groups

Macronutrients	Importance in the diet	Major sources
Proteins	Needed for growth and repair of cells within the body. They form a large part of muscle tissue.	Meat, fish, eggs, cheese, beans and grains (rice, wheat, etc.)
Fats	Needed to provide energy (calories, kJ) for all body activity. Also needed to maintain cell structures (cell membranes are largely fat).	Meat, cheese, eggs, oils, butter, margarine
Carbohydrates	a) Digestible sugars and starches provide energy (calories, kJ).	Sweets, drinks, potatoes, flour, rice
	b) Indigestible FIBRE (roughage) helps food to pass through the digestive system. It has a protective effect against some diseases.	Vegetables, wholemeal flour and bread, bran
Micronutrients		
Vitamins	A group of substances given letters to describe them (vitamin A, vitamin C, etc.). These are needed in small quantities to help take part in chemical reactions inside the body.	See table page 179.
Minerals	Chemicals that contribute to structures and reactions in the body, such as iron for carrying oxygen, calcium to build the skeleton and help muscles to work.	See table page 180.
Also		
Water	Many reactions take place inside the body in water. In fact your body consists of about 70 per cent water (figures for this vary depending upon how you measure it). Water is also important in helping get rid of poisons that we produce ourselves (such as getting rid of urea in urine).	

Macronutrients

There are three main macro nutrients:

- PROTEIN
- FAT
- CARBOHYDRATE.

Micronutrients

There are two important classes of micro nutrients:

- VITAMINS – chemicals produced by living organisms that are needed to help your body to function properly. The table on page 179 provides details of vitamins, their functions and sources.
- MINERALS – chemicals that are not produced by living organisms (in most cases they could be extracted from rocks). They perform important roles in body chemistry. The table on page 180 gives details of minerals and common dietary sources. (Note: Although they can come from rocks and soil, we normally obtain minerals from plants and animals as part of our food.)

The major vitamins

Vitamin	Deficiency disease	Functions	Major sources
Fat-soluble vitamins			
A (retinol)	Night blindness. Xerophthalmia (drying of the cornea)	Essential for light detection by eye	Carotene in plants, such as carrots, spinach, lettuce. Also liver.
D (calciferol)	Rickets in children Weakened bones in adults	Aids calcium and phosphorus absorption Aids bone formation	Fish, liver, egg yolk Formed by action of UV light (sunlight) on skin
E (Tocopherol)	Degeneration of gonads, only demonstrated in animals	Poorly understood	Lettuce, peanuts, egg yolk
K (Phyloquinone)	Extended clotting times	Required for blood clotting	Leafy vegetables
Water-soluble vitamins			
B_1 (Thiamine)	Beri-beri – muscle wastage and paralysis	Helps us use energy	Yeast, rice and most other plant and animal tissues
B_2 (Riboflavine)	Dermatitis and skin sores	Required for aerobic respiration	Leafy vegetables, fish, and eggs
B_5 (Pantothenic acid)	Poor muscle control Gastro-intestinal problems	Forms co-enzyme A which is important in fat metabolism	All animal and plant tissues.
B_6 (Pyridoxine)	Anaemia and vomiting	Helps make the best use of protein in the diet	All animal and plant tissues
B_{12} (Cobalamin)	Pernicious anaemia. Not treatable with iron.	Required for correct red blood cell formation	Beef, kidney, liver
C (Ascorbic acid)	Scurvy – breakdown of membranes	Required to help hold cells together	Citrus fruits, green vegetables

Water

There is one important part of everyone's diet that does not fall into the category of micro or macronutrient. This is **water**. We all need it to replace water lost from the body in sweat, urine, breathing and faeces.

Its role is to allow biochemical reactions to go on inside the body cells. It also forms an important part of blood and is needed to transport things around your body. More people in the world are ill or die because of the lack of clean water than die because of a lack of other nutrients.

A more detailed look at macronutrients

It is important to have a good understanding of macro nutrients. Let us look at them in more detail.

Protein

The word 'protein' describes a large group of chemicals that are made up of smaller building blocks called **amino acids**. There are about 20 different amino acids commonly found in proteins. A protein is made up of several hundred of the building blocks, each of which is one of the 20.

The major minerals

Mineral	Deficiency disease	Functions	Major sources
Calcium	Poor skeletal growth Delayed blood clotting Muscle spasms	Skeleton and teeth Blood clotting factor Muscle contraction	Milk, cheese, fish and hard water
Chlorine	Localised shortage linked to muscle cramp	Required for activity of nerve and muscle	Cooking salt, cheese
Cobalt	Pernicious anaemia	Part of vitamin B_{12}	Most foods
Fluorine	Weak tooth enamel	Helps to prevent dental caries	Drinking water, toothpaste (trace)
Iodine	Goitre (swollen thyroid)	Constituent of thyroxine (thyroid hormone)	Sea fish, shell fish (trace), iodised table salt
Iron	Anaemia	Constituent of haem – oxygen binding part of haemoglobin	Liver, eggs, cocoa powder Not easily absorbed from plants, such as spinach
Magnesium	Rare/not known	Constituent part of skeleton Co-factor in energy transfer	Most foods
Phosphorus	Rare/not known	Skeletal formation Energy transfer Membrane structure	Most foods
Potassium	Rare/not known	Required for activity of nerve and muscle	Leafy vegetables, liver
Sodium	Localised deficiency causes muscle cramp	Required for activity of nerve and muscle	Cooking salt, bacon, most foods
Zinc	Rare/not known	Enzyme co-factor Constituent of insulin (see page 204)	Most foods (trace)

We can make some of the 20 amino acids ourselves. Those that we cannot make have to be obtained from food. It is important to understand that, while we eat protein-containing foods, what we really need is to get a good balance of amino acids.

What happens to the protein you eat?
It is first digested to break it down into the individual building blocks (amino acids). These are then absorbed from the digestive system into your blood and transported around your body. They are used to make your own body proteins.

Proteins in your body are used for:
- structural things like tendons ligaments and cartilage
- movement – they are a key part of muscles
- chemical reactions – the chemistry of your body is controlled by a large group of proteins called enzymes.

Protein in your diet is used to build and repair cells and tissues. As such, it can be described as being used for growth and repair. If you eat more than you need, it cannot be stored and so is broken down to form urea (a waste product in urine) with the rest being a source of energy.

Sources of protein
In your diet you need to eat a balance of protein to provide all the amino acids

(particularly the essential ones) that you need to make your own proteins. There are two sources of protein:

- **sources of first-class protein** These are foods that are rich in proteins that contain the essential amino acids. Meat contains the right proportions of amino acids to make muscle. Other animal sources that are very good are fish, milk (and products like cheese) and eggs. Milk and eggs naturally provide the nutrients required for the growing animal.
- **sources of second-class protein** These foods that contain protein but not all of the essential amino acids. Second-class protein is found in vegetables (particularly beans, lentils, rice and grains, such as wheat). It is, therefore, important to eat different types to obtain all the essential amino acids. This is particularly important for people who eat no animal protein (meat, milk or eggs).

Sources of first-class protein

Sources of second-class protein

Essential amino acids

Your body is able to convert many of the amino acids from one to another amino acid. There are about seven that you cannot make in this way. These seven are called **essential amino acids** and you must eat a balance of proteins to supply these.

Fats

Like protein, the term 'fat' describes a broad group of chemicals. These are particularly important in two areas:
- providing energy within the body
- as part of membranes within and around cells.

Fats in the diet can largely be described as:
- saturated

- mono-unsaturated
- poly-unsaturated.

The names refer to the chemical structure and the form of some chemical bonds.

There are some essential fatty acids (smaller molecules that form part of a fat molecule) that are a necessary part of your diet. These are required in small amounts and are important in membrane structure. It is unlikely that these fatty acids will be missing from your diet.

All fats can be used as an energy source. This means that they are broken down inside your body to provide the energy needed to keep you warm, alive and moving. However, any excess fat in your diet can be stored to provide for future energy needs. This stored fat is largely found in a layer of fat underneath your skin, called subcutaneous fat. This fat layer also acts as an insulating layer to help to keep you warm.

Sources of fat
Sources of fat in the diet can be from:
- **animals** Most animal fats are solid at room temperature and contain a high proportion of saturated fats.
- **plants** Fats from plant sources are often liquid at room temperature and are usually called oils. These are normally found in seeds and fruits, such as corn, olives, avocadoes, and often contain a high proportion of unsaturated fats.

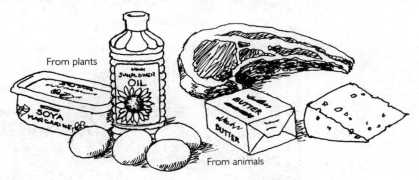

Sources of fat

Carbohydrates

This is a group of chemicals made up from simple sugars. These are sweet-tasting chemicals such as glucose and sucrose. The most familiar sugar is the one sold as white or brown sugar made from sugar beet or sugar cane. This sugar is called sucrose.

Sugar molecules can be joined together to produce different carbohydrate molecules. As the number of sugar molecules joined together increases, the molecule becomes less sweet and eventually takes on one of two basic forms:
- **digestible starch** Starch molecules are complex carbohydrate molecules which we can digest and absorb as simple sugars. They are found in potatoes and grains (like wheat and rice) in particular. The bulk of flour is starch. Starches and sugars are used by the body as an energy source. Any excess is converted to fat and stored under the skin.
- **indigestible cellulose**, which is one of the things that makes up dietary fibre.

Dietary fibre
Fibre is indigestible material, mainly from plants. It consists of carbohydrates

Digestible sugars and starches

Indigestible fibre

Sources of carbohydrate

like cellulose and other more complex chemicals that help support plants. Its most noticeable effects are:

- speeding the passage of food through the digestive system
- increasing the bulk of faeces
- making faeces softer (stopping constipation)
- reducing hunger between meals
- slowing the absorption of nutrients.

The benefits of these effects are:

- toxic materials are not retained in the digestive system, particularly the bowel where they are associated with cancer.
- going to the toilet (defecation) involves less physical strain and so there is less damage to the lining of the lower gut
- digested nutrients are absorbed over a longer period of time which reduces the work of internal control mechanisms (see Diabetes, page 201).

There is some evidence that soluble fibre found in things like oats may affect blood cholesterol levels and reduce the risk of heart attacks. We do not fully understand the link and how it may work.

> **Nutrients are important for:**
> - Body building and repair – protein in particular.
> - Energy and warmth – carbohydrate, fat and some protein. Some vitamins and minerals are also important.
> - Healthy development and body maintenance – vitamins and minerals in particular.

A BALANCED DIET

The important aspect of your diet is balancing what your body needs for it to work as you want it to, with what you eat and drink. In doing this you supply all that is needed for the body to function without building up too much stored fat or causing any deficiency disorder.

> **What is a balanced diet?**
> A balanced diet is one that provides you with enough of the various types of nutrient to meet your needs. It does not have excesses (too much) or deficiencies (too little) of anything.

It would be easy to provide a balanced diet if all the food you ate was made up of specific amounts of the required nutrients. This is the basis of many of the foods used by astronauts. However, no one food that you eat contains all the nutrients in the correct proportions.

If you are going to eat a balanced diet, you need to know:
• what your body needs – this depends upon your age, sex, and activity level
• what nutrients are contained in the foods you eat.

REFERENCE NUTRIENT INTAKES
The table on page 185 shows some daily requirements for different groups of people – the reference nutrient intakes. You will see that carbohydrate is not included (other than fibre). This is because it is part of the energy intake (see page 194) and the amount required varies according to the amount of fat and excess protein in the diet. Throughout this chapter we will not expect you to calculate carbohydrate intake unless you choose to find information for a diabetic diet.

Food tables
To know what nutrients different foods contain, you can use food tables which give the **composition of foods** per 100g. You may also be able to use one of the many computer programmes that help you to analyse your diet. However, the tables do not always give details of all possible foods.

Activity 6.1 ————————————————————————————————

Food tables are not the easiest things to understand and so it is worthwhile taking a little time to look at them. Obtain a copy of up-to-date food tables (see page 303).

a Write a diary of what you eat for a day.

b Carry out an analysis of the macro nutrients you ate on that day. Use food tables to divide the foods into three groups:
• those that contain more protein than fat or carbohydrate
• those that contain more fat than protein or carbohydrate

Reference nutrient intakes of selected nutrients, per day

Age range	Protein (g)	Calcium (mg)	Iron (mg)	Zinc (mg)	Vitamin A (µg)	Thiamin (mg)	Vitamin B₆ (mg)	Folic acid (µg)	Vitamin C (mg)
0–3 months (formula fed)	12.5	525	1.7	4.0	350	0.2	0.2	50	25
4–6 months	12.7	525	4.3	4.0	350	0.2	0.2	50	25
7–9 months	13.7	525	7.8	5.0	350	0.2	0.3	50	25
10–12 months	14.9	525	7.8	5.0	350	0.3	0.4	50	25
1–3 years	14.5	350	6.9	5.0	400	0.5	0.7	70	30
4–6 years	19.7	450	6.1	6.5	500	0.7	0.9	100	30
7–10 years	28.3	550	8.7	7.0	500	0.7	1.0	150	30
Males									
11–14 years	42.1	1000	11.3	9.0	600	0.9	1.2	200	35
15–18 years	55.2	1000	11.3	9.5	700	1.1	1.5	200	40
19–50 years	55.5	700	8.7	9.5	700	1.0	1.4	200	40
50+ years	53.3	700	8.7	9.5	700	0.9	1.4	200	40
Females									
11–14 years	41.2	800	14.8	9.0	600	0.7	1.0	200	35
15–18 years	45.0	800	14.8	7.0	600	0.8	1.2	200	40
19–50 years	45.0	700	14.8	7.0	600	0.8	1.2	200	40
50+ years	46.5	700	8.7	7.0	600	0.8	1.2	200	40
Pregnant*	+6.0	–	–	–	+100	+0.1	–	+100	+10
Lactating*									
0–4 months	+11.0	+550	–	+6.0	+350	+0.2	–	+60	+30
over 4 months	+8.0	+550	–	+2.5	+350	+0.2	–	+60	+30

* For pregnant and lactating women, the figures given are to be added to the amount for the woman's age range.

Source: Table 25 from MAFF, *Manual of nutrition* (HMSO, 1995)

- those that contain more carbohydrate than protein or fat.

c   Look at the lists in each group and check the food tables again. This time note down which nutrient (fat, protein or carbohydrate) is the second largest amount for each food.

You will now have an indication of which foods are important in your diet, in terms of the main nutrient. You will also know which other main nutrient they contain. This will be very useful if you want to identify ways of changing your diet.

Note Keep your food list because you will use it for a later analysis.

But I don't want to have to carry a book of nutrients around with me!
Fortunately there is no need to carry round a book of nutrients. For most people it is sufficient to sort foods into different classes and eat samples from each class. This is the basis of the Balance of Good Health *National Food Guide*. In the *Guide*, foods are divided into five groups:

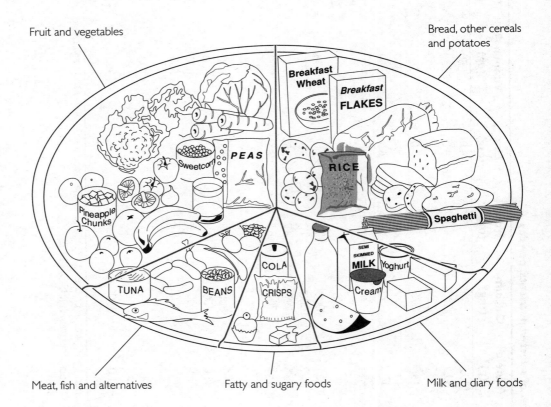

Fruit and vegetables

Bread, other cereals and potatoes

Meat, fish and alternatives

Fatty and sugary foods

Milk and diary foods

Benefits of a balanced diet
- By matching your diet to your needs, you give your body the opportunity to function at its best efficiency. In such a situation you are also more likely to be physically fit. This does not mean that you are athletic. It means that your heart, lungs and the rest of your body are in balance and little stress is being caused to any part.
- Monitoring and maintaining a balanced diet means that your weight should be correct for your height (see page 188). This again means that your muscles

and skeleton are in balance and are not being damaged by too much weight.

- A balanced diet can help prevent disease. Clearly you will not suffer any deficiency diseases or diseases of excess. General health and resistance to infection is also improved. This is because a balanced diet assists all the body systems to be in balance. This includes those which are involved in preventing and fighting disease.

Detrimental effects of an unbalanced diet

Looking at the tables of minerals and vitamins you will see that the deficiency diseases are listed. These are the diseases that are caused by not having enough of the vitamin or mineral in the diet. If you have not heard of most of them it is not surprising. Deficiency diseases are very rare in the UK.

There are three major areas in which your diet may be unbalanced:
- your energy (calorie/kJ) intake
- too little fibre
- a specific lack of a mineral (most commonly this is iron).

Unbalanced energy intake
The way to detect whether your energy intake is regularly too great or too little is to look at your weight in relation to your height. You can plot your height and weight on the graph on page 188 to find out if you are taking in too much (overweight) or too little (underweight).

As you have already read, excess quantities of the macro nutrients are stored in the form of body fat. In fact, every 38 kJ (9 calories) that is taken in and not used is enough to add about a gram of body fat.

This system of storing energy evolved as a way of preparing for times when food is scarce. However, in the UK it is unlikely that you will go through periods of starvation (unless they are self-imposed!). The overall effect is that many people are storing too much energy and as a result their bodies are heavier than ideal.

Too little fibre
The fibre (or roughage) content of your diet seems to be an odd thing to consider. Why should something that passes through the digestive system be so important? To a large extent this is difficult to answer as we have only a limited understanding of how dietary fibre has the effects it does.

What we do know is that a lack of fibre in the diet is linked to cancer of the bowel. This is thought to be related to the amount of time food spends passing through the bowel. High-fibre diets mean that the food passes through quickly and so any cancer-producing chemicals pass out before they can do any harm. With a low-fibre diet, food may take more than twice as long to pass through

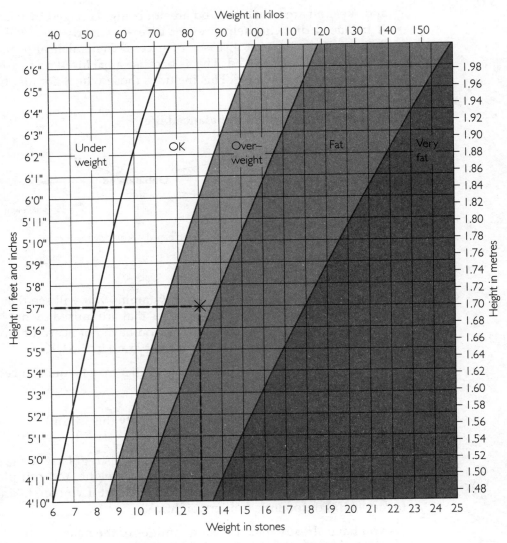

— — — For example, a person who is 5'7" tall and weighs 13 stones is overweight

To find out whether you need to lose or gain weight, draw a line up from your weight and across from your height. Put a cross where the two lines meet.

the digestive system and so there is more opportunity for cancer-causing chemicals to have an effect.

Vitamin and mineral deficiencies

Having said that deficiencies are unusual, there are some which do occur in the UK. In particular the intake of iron, calcium and vitamin D need to be monitored in some groups of people who are at risk.

- **Iron** (see the table on page 180). One particular group at risk from lack of iron is VEGETARIAN women going through, and just after, puberty. Menstruation has started with its associated loss of blood. There is also a growth spurt. Both of these cause an increased demand for iron to replace and make haemoglobin.

  The limited uptake of iron from vegetables can mean that vegetarians do not absorb sufficient to cope with the extra demands. This lack of iron gives rise to anaemia which means the blood's ability to carry oxygen is reduced.

People today are more aware of the food they eat. Food manufacturers, health charities and health authorities produce leaflets about healthy eating

This shows up as increased tiredness, particularly with even mild exercise.

- **Vitamin D and calcium** (see the tables on pages 187 and 188). These two are linked, as vitamin D helps us to absorb calcium. There are two groups at risk: the first because of a lack of vitamin D (and hence calcium), the second because of changes in the way our bodies use calcium.

  - When a growing child has too little vitamin D (and/or calcium) in his or her diet, the bones fail to form properly. This deficiency disease is called **rickets**. The disease is associated with poverty in the UK and was, until recently, very rare.

    The increase in poverty in the UK has led to an increased number of cases of rickets in the poorest communities. This can be linked to the lack of vitamin D but the effect of poverty cannot be ignored. The incidence of rickets in people of similar ethnic origins, but who do not live in poverty, is much lower.

  - Our reduced ability to absorb calcium in middle and old age means that some may be lost from the skeleton and not replaced. This makes the skeleton more liable to wear or break. It also means breaks take longer to heal. This condition is **osteoporosis**.

    Women, during and after the menopause, are most at risk. During the menopause the ovaries stop producing hormones as well as stopping egg production. This change in the body's hormone balance means that calcium loss increases. To compensate, women often increase vitamin D and calcium in their diet. Many also use hormone replacement therapy to help control calcium losses.

Activity 6.2

Select five of your favourite foods from the list that you prepared for Activity 6.1. For each these foods, do a micro nutrient analysis. To do this, calculate what percentage of your reference nutrient intake of vitamin C, vitamin D, iron, and calcium is provided by 100 g.

So far, we have identified that a lack of specific vitamins and minerals can lead to deficiency diseases. We have identified some factors relating to energy intake and also to dietary fibre. Let us now look at some of the less specific issues of an unbalanced diet. In 1983 the National Advisory Committee on Nutrition Education (NACNE) identified some issues.

THE NACNE REPORT

In 1983 the National Advisory Committee on Nutrition Education (NACNE) produced some proposals for nutritional guidelines for health education.
The proposals concentrated on body-weight and health. They also looked at issues relating to carbohydrate, fat and coronary heart disease. The relationship between salt and high blood pressure was investigated.

The recommendations of the report

The Report concentrated on health education aspects of nutrition. It set targets for health education to meet in terms of changing people's attitudes and diets. In summary it recommended a dietary energy intake of:

Protein	11%	(no change)
Fat	34%	(a reduction)*
Carbohydrate	50%	(an increase)*
Alcohol	5%	(a reduction)
Total	**100%**	

* The types of fat and carbohydrate were recommended to be changed (see below). This would lead to a change in the types of food consumed and to an increase in minerals, vitamins and essential fatty acids.

The report concluded that even being mildly overweight increased health risks.

Why did NACNE reach these conclusions?

Fats
There were two important parts to the recommendation:

- **to reduce the total fat intake.** As fat is high in energy, this would help reduce weight. Also, evidence from the medical profession stated that death rates from from heart disease in the UK are amongst the highest in the world and that this is related to fat intake.
- **to increase the ratio of polyunsaturated fatty acids to saturated fatty acids.** This followed evidence that a diet with most of the fat as polyunsaturated fatty acids could reduce the incidence of heart disease. This is partly because the body makes cholesterol predominantly from saturated fats. Cholesterol has been linked to heart attacks.

Research has also identified certain types of polyunsaturated fatty acids as being particularly beneficial. For example, there is a very low incidence of heart disease in people who consume a large quantity of oily fish. The fats in oily fish have a lot of omega-3 fatty acids. This is linked to reduced blood cholesterol levels and fewer heart attacks.

Carbohydrates

The recommendations were to:

- **reduce sucrose (sugar) intake.** This would help to reduce weight. Sugar is also a linked with dental caries (tooth decay). But the proposed reduction in sugar intake would have little effect on this.
- **increase the intake of complex carbohydrates as fibre.** This would have the effect of slowing down absorption. This means that blood sugar levels do not change rapidly. Most complex carbohydrate is also associated with vitamins, minerals and indigestible fibre.

Fibre

As we have already seen (pages 182 and 187), low levels of dietary fibre are linked to large bowel disease, including irritable bowel syndrome, constipation, diverticulitis and colon cancer. The effect of an increase in dietary fibre is to increase the bulk of faeces and reduce the time material stays in the colon. We have also already mentioned the possible link with blood cholesterol levels.

Salt

Very high intakes of sodium as salt may lead to high blood pressure (hypertension). Some people tend to have high blood pressure and for them above average levels of salt can be dangerous. The recommendation to reduce salt intake follows these results. It is not easy recognise people at risk.

Alcohol

Alcohol and diet were not studied in detail. Alcohol supplies energy and so should be reduced as part of the move towards weight reduction. Alcohol causes liver damage and for this reason also it should be reduced. It should not necessarily be cut out altogether as moderate alcohol consumption (a glass of wine per day) may reduce the risk of heart attacks.

Protein

No recommendations were made about protein intake although a suggestion was made that people should eat a little less protein as current intake was greater than required.

So why is my diet so important?

The saying 'You are what you eat' is in many ways very true. The material that enters your body is used by you to make your body tissues. If your diet is wrong then your body becomes out of balance. An unbalanced diet can lead to:

- overweight – associated with heart disease and damage to joints
- underweight – giving rise to tiredness, reduced resistance to infection and, in extreme circumstances, starvation
- nutritional deficiencies, most commonly anaemia, and specific diseases, such as the consumption of too much refined sugar being linked to tooth decay.

The problems of being overweight
One of the basic problems is having to carry around the excess weight. This:
- puts a stress on the heart because it has to pump more blood per minute to provide for the extra energy needed
- means that the lungs have to work harder to provide the oxygen
- puts the joints under greater strain.

What tends to happen is that an overweight person does less, walks more slowly and reduces the amount of exercise taken. This reduces the energy being used and increases the risk of becoming even more overweight.

Lack of exercise contributes to a lack of physical fitness. This means that the individual is less ready to respond to any extra physical demands. Eventually the weight of an overweight person tends to stabilise at a point where the extra energy required to move the extra bulk balances the excess energy intake. At this point the person is effectively constantly working harder than necessary without getting physically fitter. The resulting strain and wear and tear leads to heart disease and joint damage.

For many overweight people their lack of physical fitness makes many tasks harder. Feelings of apathy or not being bothered become common. There may be an intention to lose weight or increase exercise, but the effort of doing so becomes a barrier in itself.

Poor self-image
Apathy also leads people to become unconcerned about the impression they make on others which, in turn, leads to a poor self-image as friendships fail to develop because of lack of effort.

Many overweight people have an image of themselves that they do not look or feel good. This can be reflected in their ability to make friends and can also lead to them being depressed. A cycle can develop of being unhappy and eating for comfort. This leads to greater overweight or guilt about eating. The extreme effects of this on mental health can be clinical depression.

An illness that appears to be linked to an image of overweight is anorexia nervosa. People suffering from this often have an image of themselves that they are overweight and the wrong shape. They effectively starve themselves (sometimes to death) while still feeling that they are overweight.

Problems of underweight
Many people do not recognise underweight as a problem unless it is at the extreme of starvation or anorexia. Taking in too little energy means that the person cannot do everything because of a lack of energy. This leads to tiredness and, like overweight, a level of apathy and feelings of 'I can't be bothered'. The energy required to exercise is not available and physical fitness suffers.

Taking in too little energy to meet your daily needs causes the stored fat to be utilised. This is the basis of weight reduction diets. However, if the intake is not monitored, protein (in the form of the person's own muscles) is used, as well as fat. In the long term, this means that muscles become weaker. It is important to monitor the balance of foods even when going through a period of self-imposed starvation.

Ill-health and an unbalanced diet
You have seen that lack of nutrients can lead to ill-health. Did you realise that eating an unbalanced diet can make you more prone to disease?

Too much energy in the UK diet

Another problem of taking in too much energy is the type of food being eaten in excess. In the UK, sugar and saturated fat consumption is high. This means that most of the fat in the body is saturated and that most of the fat circulating in the blood is saturated. This has been linked by many people to an increased risk of heart disease.

The fat in circulation becomes attached to artery walls and has the effect of reducing blood flow and also putting a strain on the elastic structure of the walls. To overcome the reduced blood flow the heart has to work harder to push the blood around. Arteries can become blocked so that they starve the area that they supply of oxygen. If the artery is one that supplies the heart with oxygen then a heart attack occurs.

People who are significantly overweight or underweight tend to be ill more. It is thought that the immune system that helps fight disease does not work well when the body is under stress. Overweight and underweight are both examples of physical stress and so they increase the risk of ill-health.

Balancing diets for different groups of people

From what we have said so far, it is clear that a balanced diet is one that matches food intake with nutritional needs. However, it is not possible to specify a single diet that will provide for the needs of all people.

A quick look at the table of reference nutrient intakes on page 185 gives you an idea of some of the basic categories into which people are placed when considering a balanced diet. Let's look at some of these in more detail.

Activity 6.3

a   Using the table of reference nutrient intakes (on page 185), identify the amount of protein recommended (in grams) for:
  • children aged 10–12 months
  • children aged 8 years
  • boys aged 12 years
  • girls aged 12 years
  • men aged 30
  • women aged 30
  • men aged 60 years
  • women aged 60 years
  • a pregnant woman aged 25 years
  • a breast-feeding woman aged 30 with a 2-month-old baby

b   Look back at your diary for activity 6.1 (page 184). Using food tables calculate the amount of protein in your diet. Comment on how close you are to the daily reference nutrient intake for your age and sex (page 185).

c   Use the table on page 194 to determine how much energy (MJ) you need per day. Weigh yourself (in kg) and calculate how much energy per kg of body weight you might need. Compare your results with people from a different age range and/or sex. Do you notice any trends?

Identify the average requirements for energy for the people listed in task (a).

Estimated average requirements for energy in the UK (per day)

Age range	Males		Females	
	MJ	**kcal**	**MJ**	**kcal**
0–3 months (formula fed)	2.28	545	2.16	515
4–6 months	2.89	690	2.69	645
7–9 months	3.44	825	3.20	765
10–12 months	3.85	920	3.61	865
1–3 years	5.15	1230	4.86	1165
4–6 years	7.16	1715	6.46	1545
7–10 years	8.24	1970	7.28	1740
11–14 years	9.27	2220	7.92	1845
15–18 years	11.51	2755	8.83	2110
19–50 years	10.60	2550	8.10	1940
51–59 years	10.60	2550	8.00	1900
60–64 years	9.93	2380	7.99	1900
65–74 years	9.71	2330	7.96	1900
75+ years	8.77	2100	7.61	1810
Pregnant			+0.80	+200
Lactating:				
1 month			+1.90	+450
2 months			+2.20	+530
3 months			+2.40	+570
4–6 months			+2.00	+480
>6 months			+1.00	+240

Source: Table 24 from MAFF, *Manual of nutrition* (HMSO, 1995)

d How would energy requirements change for very active and very inactive (sedentary) people? Why do you think this is?

Children

Children have a range of dietary requirements, as you will have discovered from the activity above. If we ignore infants who obtain their balanced diet

You and I need to select from a bigger range of foods than this baby to achieve a balanced diet

from breast milk or formula baby milks, it is still clear that requirements change between 1 year old and 8 years old.

Protein requirements

Children grow rapidly in the first three years of life and then slow down. This is reflected in protein intake. Energy requirements in part reflect this growth but also changes in physical activity.

A 1-year-old child may be just starting to walk, while an 8-year-old is likely to be moving about a lot more. The 8-year-old needs more energy in the diet to support this increased activity. Balancing this, a 1-year-old child loses heat faster than an 8-year-old. This is because of the younger child's size. In the small child, there is a large area of skin in relation to body weight. Heat does not have to travel far before it reaches the skin and is lost to the air. Relatively more energy from food is needed to keep a 1-year-old warm compared to an 8-year-old.

Vitamin requirements

These are fairly constant throughout childhood or reflect growth rates. The exception is the recommended intake of vitamin D for under-fives which is significantly higher than for older children. This in part is because of the rate of bone growth, but is also to prevent rickets.

Adolescence

Protein requirements

The period of puberty is a time of rapid growth and great physical activity. These are reflected in increased requirements for protein and energy.

Mineral requirements

Menarche, the first menstrual flow, is the start of a cycle of regular loss of blood. Iron is a key component of blood and so there is an increased requirement for iron in the diet compared with men until menstruation ceases during the menopause.

Adulthood

Throughout adulthood differences in dietary requirements are largely related to physical activity and differences in size. If you carry out the calculations for different nutrient requirements per kilogram of body weight you will find that there is very little difference between men and women. The differences in the daily requirements are related to the fact that the average adult woman is smaller than the average adult man.

To a lesser extent, there are sex differences with regard to requirements for specific nutrients. The male hormone testosterone affects protein requirements and so men require slightly more than women for equivalent physically active lifestyles. As we have already mentioned, women have a greater requirement for iron.

Pregnant women

It is often said that a pregnant woman needs to eat for two. This may be true, but in the early stages of pregnancy the growing foetus is so small that its requirements are very small. What is important is for the woman to eat a balanced diet, avoiding some of dangers associated with alcohol, drugs and smoking (see Chapter 1).

As the foetus grows, there are increased requirements for nutrients – for both the mother's needs and those of the growing baby. Protein is required for growth of the foetus. Energy is required by the foetus as well as the mother who is using more energy than normal because of the extra weight being carried. Towards the end of pregnancy the woman is carrying extra weight equivalent to several bags of sugar.

Vitamin and mineral requirements increase to provide for the growing foetus:
- Calcium levels in the diet need to increase to provide for the developing skeleton and also for the growth of the mother's skeleton to cope with the increased weight.
- Iron requirements increase as the foetal blood forms with its need for iron. Pregnancy is a time when a woman becomes slightly anaemic (reduced iron levels in the blood). This is natural and allows the foetus to obtain oxygen more easily. It is important not to try to correct this mild anaemia with too much iron as this can damage the foetus.

Elders

As people get older they tend to become less physically active. This is reflected in a reduced energy requirement. Growth ceases and repair process become slower and less efficient with age. The protein requirement in the diet reflects this.

There is good evidence that levels of calcium and vitamin D need to be increased to prevent or delay the process of calcium loss from the bones. This particularly affects women after the menopause but it also affects men.

FOODWISE HINTS FOR SENIOR CITIZENS

Good Nutrition is important, no matter what your age. This guide is to give you some guidelines on eating for health and enjoyment, with minimum fuss and expense.

Activity 6.4

The details given above and tables of recommended daily allowances are for typical or average people.

What things do you think also need to be considered when planning a balanced diet for a specific person? Remember that the tables list nutrients and we eat food!

Factors influencing dietary patterns

We all have different likes and dislikes in terms of food. We also all have different lifestyles. What you eat and when you eat is determined by a variety of things. These include:

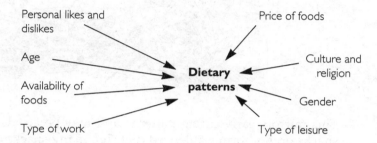

Personal likes and dislikes

Age

Availability of foods

Type of work

Dietary patterns

Price of foods

Culture and religion

Gender

Type of leisure

Eating patterns

The pattern of meals for very young babies involves small intakes of food about every four hours. This pattern has evolved to provide the required nutrients without putting a great strain on the digestive system. It is thought that early people had a feeding pattern of frequent small meals with occasional large ones. This reflected the hunter-gatherer lifestyle.

Our current eating patterns are often governed by the requirements of work, school or college. Traditionally in the UK, there is a pattern of three meals a day: breakfast, lunch and dinner/tea. This means that a person's diet is based around these three meals with associated between-meal snacks. These snacks form a very important aspect of the diet.

If we take the three-meals-a-day model, it is possible to identify common variations:

I never eat breakfast – I'm always in too much of a hurry !

This pattern is fairly common but it puts a strain on the digestive system. Breakfast is, as its name indicates, a time for breaking a fast. Most people will not have eaten much for up to 12 hours before breakfast. Breakfast is an important meal enabling people to start the day with an energy intake.

This mirrors early eating patterns and may be an ideal. The risks are that the snacks do not form a balanced diet. Too many snacks are high in fat and carbohydrate with few of the micro nutrients. People who 'snack feed' tend to be those in a hurry who grab food when they can. Being in a hurry is a stressful behaviour and so there are also risks associated with this.

Many people do need to ensure they eat sufficient to meet the needs of their work. Those involved in physically strenuous work will need to ensure that they have a high energy diet. There are a lot of people who are expected, or are tempted, to eat as part of their work. Included in this category are those involved in food preparation and those who have 'working lunches'. It is often difficult for these people to accurately monitor and control their food intake.

I always eat when I'm watching T.V, having a cup of tea or out with friends

These people have developed a reflex to eat in certain situations. Often the foods are snacks and it is difficult to monitor the food intake.

Activity 6.5

a The eating patterns described above are stereotypes. Identify people or occupations that may lead to each of the eating patterns.

b For each group, identify ways they might maintain a balanced diet without altering the eating pattern. Examples might involve planning healthier option snacks or changing the content of main meals.

Eating patterns and elders

Many elders adopt an eating pattern that mimics that of young babies. They eat small amounts throughout the day. This reduces the strain on the digestive system and supplies the nutrients in a more consistent manner.

It follows the pattern for many other activities. Many elders punctuate their day with naps and continue this pattern through the night. It is important to identify such activities when planning meals for these people. It is also important to ensure that the small meals provide a balanced diet and do not over-emphasise the high-energy foods.

What influences diet choice?

Three factors have a major effect on diet choice, other than likes and dislikes. They are:
• availability of the food
• price of the food
• religious and cultural factors.

Availability of food

In the past the availability of food was controlled by the seasons. For example, strawberries were only available for a short season during the summer. Now it is possible to obtain most foods at any time of the year. However, the fact that the foods are available does not mean that everyone can have them. Even though they are available, strawberries are very expensive at Christmas!

In planning a diet it is useful to use the foods in season for two reasons:

South African Granny Smith 49p

Chilean Grapes 88p

Tomatoes Spain 45p

70p

Spring Onions Mexico Class 1 48p

King Edward Potatoes 22p

Parsnips 20p

Carrots Class 1 UK Loose Per lb

32p

Strawberries Spain Class 78p

Good transport systems mean that foods are much less seasonal than they were. Transport costs, however, increase the prices.

- If they are in season, they cost less than out of season.
- They may have a greater nutritional content because they are fresher. Nutrients such as the vitamins may be lost as a result of storage while foods are transported across the world.

The latter can be an important factor in considering different foods. For example, potatoes are a source of vitamin C. Freshly dug potatoes have a higher vitamin C content than those that have been stored. As freshly dug potatoes are not available through the winter and they cannot be seen as an important source of vitamin C.

Similar comments can be made about many fresh vegetables compared with those that have been frozen or tinned. It is important to note the word 'fresh' is open to interpretation and many 'fresh' foods lose important nutrients if they are stored incorrectly for even a short period.

Cost of food
As we have already indicated, the cost of food can have seasonal variations. More important here is a person's ability to buy the food to produce a balanced diet. People living on low incomes or benefits may struggle to provide a balanced diet from the available income.

There are regular articles in the press from people suggesting that it is possible to provide a balanced diet on a low income. This may be true, but the choice of foods becomes limited and the diet, while nutritious, could become boring and monotonous.

Religious and cultural factors
It is only possible here to touch briefly upon some issues relating to diet in religion and culture. It is important that you recognise this and use it only as a guideline if you are planning a diet for someone from a cultural or religious group other than your own. (If you are planning to do this, then it is important to ask about foods that should not be eaten.)

Some people will refuse to eat specific foods because of their religious beliefs. They may also require that the food that they eat is prepared in a special way.

Neither orthodox Muslims or Jews will eat pork. Both groups also require that their meat comes from animals that have been slaughtered or butchered in particular ways. These restrictions present few problems in providing a balanced diet as the nutrients required can be provided from other sources.

Orthodox Jews also have dietary restrictions on combinations of food served in a meal. For example, it is not acceptable to serve beef in a meal that also contains milk products. Therefore, roast beef and yorkshire pudding are clearly unacceptable, as would be a meal containing beef and a final course of cheese and biscuits or coffee with milk. Again awareness of this enables well-balanced diets to be devised.

There are some areas where dietary restrictions and cultural factors restrict the choice of foods. There are some people whose religion requires that the women cover their skin. (Remember that Vitamin D is produced by the action of sunlight on skin.) For the large majority of the population this restriction would be no problem as vitamin D is also found in butter and milk and added to margarine. But this culture also requires its members to follow a largely vegetarian diet. There is a risk that these women could have a diet deficient in vitamin D because their culture and food preferences do not include those foods that are good sources of the vitamin.

Special diets

In the last section, we began to see that not all people have access to the same foods. In this section we will consider how people following special diets may have to plan their diet carefully.

Weight-reduction diets
It must be amazing that in the whole of this chapter, this is the first time we have described diets in the way that many people think of them – we think of 'being on a diet' as meaning trying to lose weight.

The simplest way to lose weight is to ensure that your energy intake is less than the amount of energy you use. As soon as you do this you will start to use up the fat stored under your skin and so start to lose weight. It would be so easy but for two things:
* The first is the will-power needed.
* The second is that you do not eat energy, you eat food.

Planning a weight-reduction diet
* First of all, it is important to have an idea of how much energy you need. An estimate of this figure can be obtained from the table of reference nutrient intakes on page 185.
* It is also important to identify a target weight from the graph of ideal weights and heights on page 188.
* The next step is to identify how to cut down the energy intake while maintaining a balanced diet.

It is easy to cut out the energy from sugar as there are no other significant nutrients. Cutting down on margarine or butter reduces the vitamin D content of the diet. Clearly a weight-reducing diet needs to be planned to include all the nutrient requirements of a balanced diet with the exception of the energy intake. In the UK, many people eat more protein in the form of meat and dairy products than is necessary and so it may be possible to reduce the intake of these, while

Organisations such as Weight Watchers advise on balanced, weight-reducing diets and support for their members by holding regular meetings

increasing the amounts of vegetables which provide fibre, reduce the hunger pangs and are good sources of many vitamins and minerals.

One further factor relating to diet that needs to be considered was mentioned earlier in the chapter. Starvation (weight-reducing diets are a controlled form of this) can lead to apathy. What is actually happening is that the body reduces its energy requirements and slows down. In doing so the anticipated weight reduction does not work. To counter the apathy effect, it is important to increase exercise levels at the same time as dieting.

Diets for people with diabetes

Diabetes is a disorder of the body's internal control of blood glucose levels. Insulin is produced by the pancreas and the mechanism is controlled by the level of blood glucose. Diabetics either produce:

- no insulin, or
- too little insulin.

Diabetics who produce no insulin

This people usually have to inject a mixture of slow and fast action insulin designed to match their sugar intake and needs. The aim in controlling diabetes is to keep blood sugar levels within acceptable norms and as steady as possible.

The skill in planning a diet for a diabetic is to provide the carbohydrate in forms that allow sugar to pass into the blood stream in a way that mirrors the available insulin. The diabetic person has to space out meals and eat carbohydrate between meals to match the energy requirements. This means that a diabetic planning to undertake vigorous exercise may prepare by eating a sweet biscuit to balance the sugar required for the exercise.

A high-fibre diet is useful for insulin-injecting diabetics as it helps reduce the swings in blood sugar levels and balances the fast- and slow-acting insulin that is injected.

Diabetics who produce some insulin

These people need to try to balance their carbohydrate (starches and sugars) intake with the amount of insulin produced. One important way of doing this is to have a diet that is high in fibre. This has the effect of slowing the digestion of the starches and so releasing sugars at a reasonably steady rate. These are absorbed from the intestines into the blood stream at a similar steady rate. The limited amount of insulin produced is sufficient to cope with this steady intake of sugar. Without the fibre the digested sugars would be absorbed rapidly and overwhelm the limited supply of insulin.

Key things to monitor in diets for diabetics are:
- sugar content (glucose and sucrose)
- complex carbohydrates (starches and fibre).

Vegetarian diets

Vegetarians are people who do not eat meat. There are a wide variety of preferences within this but we will use the term vegetarian to indicate those people who eat no meat or fish, but who do eat eggs, milk and milk products. Those people who eat no animal products are called vegans (see below).

There are few problems in vegetarian diets as all nutrients are available. Milk and eggs are first-class protein sources (see page 18). However, their protein contents need to be monitored as these foods also contain a lot of saturated fat. Beans and grains provide second-class protein sources. It is important, therefore, for the diet to contain a mixture of beans and grains to provide all the essential amino acids.

The vitamin and mineral content of the diet is normally reasonable as the cheese, milk and eggs are good sources of the B and D vitamins that are commonly provided by meat.

Vegan diets

This much stricter form of vegetarianism requires a closer attention to balancing the diet. Because protein has to come from plant sources, it means that at least two different sources are required to provide the correct balance of amino acids.

There are two micro nutrients that are difficult to provide in a vegan diet:
- Calcium is available in small amounts from green vegetables and flour that is fortified with calcium carbonate. It is a legal requirement for some flours to contain added calcium.
- Vitamin B_{12} is more difficult to provide. It is almost always from animal sources which are unacceptable for vegans. One natural source is yeast extract which contains less than 0.4 per cent of the amount from the best animal source. Most people on a vegan diet therefore take supplements of vitamin B_{12} extracted from bacterial sources.

Planning and costing diets

Element 6.3 of Unit 6 requires you to plan and cost a diet. It is not possible for us to do this for you as you need to research the information yourself. What we can do is give you some guidelines on how to undertake your task in Activity 6.6.

Activity 6.6

Initial research

Identify your client's dietary needs
To achieve this element, you will need to identify a client for whom you are going to plan the diet. If this client is a real person, it would be useful to find out what foods he or she likes and how much money would normally be spent on food for a week. If you are not working with a real person, make up the details of your client. Base the money available on things like state benefits.

Obtain a copy of the most up-to-date reference nutrient intakes that you can and also a copy of food tables. These may be available in the form of a computer program that will help you to analyse the diet.

Use the table of reference nutrient intakes to identify your client's needs.

Research the cost of foods
This can be carried out with the help of your colleagues. Make a list of all of the foods you are likely to want to provide. This list should cover all of your ideas and those of your colleagues. Divide the list up and each of you take one part and find the prices from your local shops. (Hint: Many supermarkets include on their price labels a price per unit, such as the price for 100 g.)

Get together and produce a computer database or spreadsheet that lists the foods and their prices.

Plan the menus for seven days

For this part you need to take into account your client's preferences and requirements. You will also need to work out what a standard serving is for each of the foods

a Food tables normally give nutritional details per 100 g of each item of food, but your client may like two tablespoons of peas! For as many things as possible, weigh or estimate the weight of a standard serving. Use this figure to calculate the nutrient content of the serving.

Many packaged foods give details of the nutrient content. If they are not listed in the standard tables try to get a copy of the information on the label.

b Write out your proposed menu for seven days. Then produce your own food table with the following headings for each item of food in the meal:
   • energy per serving
   • protein per serving

- fat per serving
- fibre per serving
- iron per serving
- calcium per serving
- vitamin C per serving
- vitamin D per serving
- cost of the food.

At the bottom of each column add up all the values to get the total figure for that meal.

c   When you have done this try to put together daily meals that provide the average daily requirement for energy, adjusted to suit your client's needs. You may need to change the meals for different days to help you to get the balance. You may also need to change the foods to get the costs to meet your target.

d   Once you are satisfied that you have the daily energy requirements and costs right, you can then work out the daily intake of protein and fat.

e   Calculate how much of each of the micro nutrients (vitamins and minerals) the week's diet contains. For each micro nutrient divide the number by seven to calculate the average daily intake.

Check to see that the average daily intake for each of the micro nutrients equals or is bigger than the reference nutrient intake.

Present the menu to your client

When you are satisfied that your menus for the week meet the dietary requirements and that the costs are acceptable, you should prepare a written menu for your client. This should include:
- details of each meal
- the cost of each meal and the total cost
- a description of how the meal meets the needs of your client
- an outline of the roles of each of the nutrients you have analysed in the diet.

Remember this menu is for your client and so it should be produced so that he or she can understand it. If it is for a very young child, it should be written so that the parent or carer can understand it. If the menu is for a real person, ask for his or her views on the menu you have planned.

Suggestions for clients (remember you can adapt these for vegetarians):
- A 6-year-old child who takes a packed lunch to school.
- Your teacher who never has time to cook a big meal other than at weekends.
- An elderly relative who likes to have breakfast, lunch, tea and supper.
- A new friend who has just moved to your town who is a Sikh, Muslim or Jew.
- An 8-year-old child who is violently ill if he has milk or milk products (including yoghurt, cream, butter and cheese).

Unless you are particularly interested, we would not suggest that you look at any very specialist diets like those for diabetics.

Test yourself

1 What are the seven types of nutrient?

2 Which of the seven types are:

  a macro nutrients?

  b micro nutrients?

3 What is the function of protein in the diet?

4 What is the main vitamin found in oranges?

5 How can fibre in the diet help to maintain health?

6 Why does the nutritional requirement for a young child differ from an adolescent person?

7 Using the Balance of Good Health guidelines, which foods should you eat lots of?

8 What types of food does a vegan not eat?

9 Name two religious groups who do not eat pork.

10 What are the detrimental effects of being overweight?

Assignment A6.1
The features of a healthy diet

In this assignment you will be asked to produce a booklet about healthy eating.

The headteacher of the local junior/middle school is very worried that the children in their final year at the school are not eating a healthy diet. He plans to open a 'healthy tuck shop' and review the meal choices for school lunches. You have been asked to prepare an information booklet about nutrients which will help the children to understand more about foods, nutrients and healthy eating.

The leaflet must have sections that:
- identify and give examples of macro and micro nutrients
- identify and give examples of five good sources of the major groups of macro and micro nutrients.
- describe what the nutrient groups are used for in the body
- describe what constitutes a well-balanced diet
- describe the effects of an unbalanced diet
- give guidance about foods that should be selected from the 'healthy tuck shop' and also foods that should be available for lunches.

The assignment can be carried out as a group activity (see Chapter 4).

Your tasks

In order to do all of this you will need to plan each step carefully.

1   First you will need to gather together the information you need. Some will come from this book. Some may come from leaflets available from, for example, doctors' surgeries, health education units and supermarkets.

2   Think about foods that might be liked by junior/middle school children and that fit into the needs for promoting healthy eating. Any examples of foods that you use should be ones that the pupils are likely want to eat.

    You might consider conducting a small survey of school children to do this.

3   Plan what information you want to put into the booklet. It should:
    * not be too long
    * be written so that the children can understand it
    * be interesting and eye-catching, using illustrations wherever possible to communicate information.

    If you can, it is always useful to try out the booklet an people from your target audience.

4   You could produce the booklet using a word processor or desk-top publishing software if you wish.

Assignment A6.2
Balanced diets for people with different needs

In this assignment you will be asked to research the dietary needs of individuals in a residential establishment.

You have been offered work assisting with the running of a week-long residential for foster parents and their foster children at a seaside town. The person running the residential is concerned that many of the people involved will have different dietary needs. You have been told that there will be at least one person on a weight-reducing diet, one with diabetes, several vegetarians and a vegan in the group of 30 people. The ages range from 1 to 60 years old.

The residential leader has asked you to research the different dietary needs of individuals.

Your tasks

1   Research and describe the nutritional needs for one of the adults and one of the children in the holiday group. You may decide the age and sex of the person that you are going to describe. Produce a table that indicates the amount of nutrient each person will require in a day.

The table should indicate the age and sex of the person you have identified.

2 The holiday leader is uncertain about how much activity any individual will undertake.

   a Add to your table details of the nutrient requirements if the individuals:
   • are to be very active
   • spend most of their time reading in the holiday home.

   b Add a paragraph at the end of the table to explain why nutrient needs vary for different people and the factors (age, sex, activity, etc.) that need to be considered. Describe the effects of each of the factors on the amounts of nutrients needed.

   (This should be a general description and not just relate to your two chosen people.)

3 As you were informed by the group leader, there are several people who have restricted diets:
   • weight-reducing
   • vegetarian
   • vegan
   • diabetic.

   a Choose three of these and research their special dietary needs.

   b Write a short report for the group leader to explain the different dietary requirements of the three people. You should describe any potential nutritional weaknesses in each type of diet and describe ways that these can be overcome.

Assignment A6.3
Planning and costing diets

In this assignment you will be asked to devise a plan, with costs, for one person for one week.

Your tasks

For one of the people you have identified in Assignment A6.2, plan and cost a balanced diet for a week.
• You must give the age, sex and any special dietary requirements at the start of your plan.
• The plan should be written so that it can be given to the cook to show what meals will be eaten.
• You should also have a shopping list for the cook with the price of the different foods on the list.

You will need to explain how the plan meets the client's dietary needs.

The budget that you are allowed is £25. (You may need to work out the price of individual portions from bulk packs to help you keep the costs down.)

Re-read Activity 6.6 to remind you how to carry out this assignment.

Key words

After reading this chapter you should be able to understand the following words and phrases. If you do not, go back through the chapter and find out, or look them up in the Glossary.

Balanced diet	*Minerals*
Carbohydrate	*Nutrients*
Fat	*Protein*
Fibre	*Vegetarian*
Macro nutrients	*Vitamins*
Micro nutrients	*Reference nutrient intake*

Exploring Health and Recreational Activities

What is covered in this chapter

- Recreational activities
- Surveying local recreational activities
- Activities for people with specific needs

These are the resources that you will need for your Health and Recreation portfolio:
- information you have collected about recreational facilities in your area
- your written answers to the activities in this chapter
- your written answers to the Test Yourself questions at the end of this chapter
- your completed assignment A7.1

Introduction

Recreation covers a broad range of activities. In this chapter you will look at the role of recreation in supporting:
- physical development
- intellectual development
- social development.

You will not only be considering your own recreation, but also looking at appropriate recreation for a wide range of people.

Recreational activities

Recreational activities are important for health and well-being. You will already be familiar with the ideas of keeping fit to maintain health, but recreation helps to maintain more than just physical health. The role of recreational activities in maintaining intellectual and social well-being is also important. It is useful to consider recreational activities in three areas:

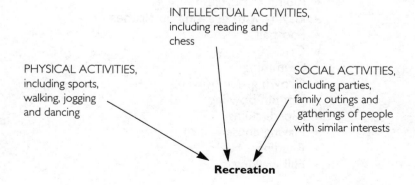

INTELLECTUAL ACTIVITIES, including reading and chess

PHYSICAL ACTIVITIES, including sports, walking, jogging and dancing

SOCIAL ACTIVITIES, including parties, family outings and gatherings of people with similar interests

Recreation

Recreation can be taken to mean anything that is done as a leisure pursuit. Hobbies are recreational. For some people their paid work may also be an enjoyable recreation. However, for this chapter, we will limit recreation to leisure activities. In some cases these may also form part of a therapy. That is, they may be part of a programme to maintain health and well-being – many occupational therapy activities are recreational.

Recreation can take many forms. Some activities appeal to different groups of people.

Activity 7.1

a For each of the following activities write down the type of person most suited to it. Give reasons for your choices.
  • Disco dancing
  • Ballroom dancing
  • Riding a tricycle
  • Playing with dressing up clothes
  • Football
  • Cricket
  • Swimming
  • Crown green bowling
  • Ten pin bowling
  • Alpine skiing
  • Playing chess
  • Reading
  • Hill walking

- Playing pool
- Listening to jazz music
- Drawing and painting
- Model making
- Knitting

b What might stop someone from undertaking any of the activities?

In the activity you will have identified some recreational activities that are associated with different client groups. For example, disco dancing is seen as an activity for young people. Crown green bowling may be seen as a pastime for older men. The stereotypes are not accurate, but they do help us to consider some issues about different recreational activities.

The suitability of an activity

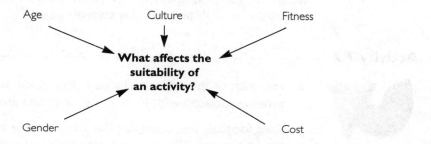

Age

From Activity 7.1 it is clear that the age of a person can be very important in identifying recreational activities. This can be because the activity is one that can be dated as to when it became popular.

Many recreational activities become popular for a short time and then another takes its place. This may be related to something new being made available or it may be that someone has popularised the activity. For example, ice skating became very popular after Torvill and Dean won several competitions. Chess increased in popularity with television coverage of the world championships.

The age of a person can almost be determined by the books he or she reads. The books of J.R.R. Tolkein, for example, were very popular in the 1960s and 1970s. Popular books in the early 1990s have been adventure books that allow the reader to make decisions and solve problems.

Age has an effect on physical recreation. Some activities require skills and strength to be developed and are most appropriate for people when they are at their fittest as adolescents and young adults. Such activities may be inappropriate for elders where speed of reaction is reduced. The risks of injury in such situations may be of importance in choosing recreational activities.

Some activities are inappropriate recreation for different groups because of their age, for example:
- Young children would find games with complex rules or requiring good hand-eye co-ordination difficult. Team games involving the use of a ball fit into this category. The children have difficulty understanding the idea of

rules and are not physically developed to cope with the moving ball.
- Elders could well find physical recreation requiring rapid reactions difficult. Bones and joints become weaker with age and so physical activities that put these under strain need careful checking. As with children, but for different reasons, many games like hockey, netball and tennis become less accessible.

It is important to recognise that these are generalisations and individuals do not always fit into the stereotype for their age.

Fitness

Fitness is often linked to age. This is a combination of strength, suppleness and efficiency of the heart, lungs and circulation. It is unwise for anyone to undertake physical activity without considering personal fitness. Most of us would not expect to be able to run a marathon. However, many people of all ages do develop fitness over time to enable them to do so.

Gender

Many recreational activities are considered to be suitable for just males or just females – we call these **gender stereotypes**.

Activity 7.2

a For each of the activities listed below, note down the sex of people most often associated with it. In some cases the answer may be 'both'.

Take football, for example. We know that women and girls do play football, but it is generally associated with being a male sport.
- Squash
- Badminton
- Netball
- Aerobics
- Hockey
- Swimming
- Disco dancing
- Ballet
- Chess
- Reading
- Snooker and pool

b How would you react if you were asked to be involved in activity that was considered not for your gender?

c How would other people react to you?

The issue of gender is not just that only men or only women are able to do certain things. Difficulties may arise because of:
- stereotypes. In many cases it is less easy for one sex to get access to an activity.
- a person's socialisation. For example, some women may feel uncomfortable in mixed sex swimming.

There are gender differences in many team activities. Where physical strength is involved it is unusual to find mixed sex teams of people beyond their early

The designers of this club didn't think women would be using it!

teens. This does not mean that the activities are not enjoyed by both sexes and it is often the case that the club involved has separate teams for men and women.

Culture

When considering suitable activities, a person's culture may affect the choice. Culture refers to beliefs, values and religion. For example, there are religions that have dress codes that make some physical activities less accessible. Muslim women would not be expected to show their legs in mixed company. Swimming would therefore have to be in single sex swimming sessions.

Cost

One of the biggest factors to suitability of activities is related to the amount of money available. Even a free activity may have hidden costs related to equipment. Often organised activities involve costs that put them outside the reach of many people. Even where costs are low, they may be too great for some people. Access to a playgroup may be a benefit to both parent and child. The cost, including travel, may make it an infrequent luxury.

There are often hidden costs that reduce access to some recreational activities

Cost also needs to be considered for the different groups:

- Children and adolescents may pay from their limited amount of pocket money. Immediately, they have to balance the value of the recreation to them with the value of other demands on their money. Many activities are available to children at a reduced cost to reflect this.
- Similar considerations need to be made for elders. Many elders have a low income and the cost of activities needs to be balanced against their need for other things. Again this is recognised in price reductions for pensioners.
- For families, the cost of any activity needs to be balanced against the already high costs of running the family. If the family undertakes recreational activities together, the cost may be several times the cost for an individual. There are of course many activities where the purchase of family tickets reduces the cost.

With all of these groups the cost of any specialist equipment is not reduced because of age or family size.

When considering suitability of any activity, the amount of money available becomes an important consideration. Not only the daily costs of undertaking the activity, but also the costs of any materials, equipment and travel.

Activity 7.3

The original list of activities in Activity 7.1 can be analysed to identify suitability for different client groups. We will return to the list of activities again. You are free to add to the list any other recreational activities that you think of.

a Look at the list of activities again (page 212) and sort them into the following categories:
- Physical – those that involve some level of exercise
- Social – those that involve other people in a non-competitive way
- Intellectual – those that involve a lot of thought and problem-solving.

Some of the activities will fall into more than one group.

b Identify those recreational activities that would be suitable for people with a low budget. Take into account any costs for materials or equipment.

c From those that you identified in (b), select three that you consider would provide for physical, intellectual and social recreation for adolescent people on a low budget. Write a few sentences to explain your choice.

Activities beneficial for different client groups

From the last activity, you will have the tools to help you to consider aspects of recreational activities that affect choice. Broadly speaking, the different groups of people to consider are:
- children
- adolescents
- elders
- families.

For activities to be beneficial they need to match the needs and abilities of the individuals. There should also be a balance in terms of physical, social and intellectual pursuits.

Children

Most of us would consider the major recreational activity for children to be play. Play provides physical, intellectual and social benefits. The type of play will depend upon the stage of development that the child is at (see Chapter 2). Some physical activities, such as swimming, are appropriate for all ages of child. Other activities such as team games (football, hockey, netball, etc.) require physical, intellectual and social development before they are appropriate. Young children may not have:

- the physical co-ordination to catch or hit a ball
- the intellectual development to understand rules
- the social development to play co-operatively in a team.

What recreational activities are suitable for children?

Young children For young children, much of their recreation occurs in and around the home. Often it involves supervision and co-operation from an adult. Typical activities and the areas that they address might include:

- drawing painting and colouring – physical and intellectual
- looking at books – intellectual
- playing with dolls – social and intellectual
- dressing up – intellectual and social
- pretend cooking – intellectual, social and physical.

The list could, of course, be extended. Most toys for young children support their need for physical, social and intellectual activities.

For most children, recreation involving social interaction with other children takes place with friends in the home or in organised groups. Organised groups include playgroups, creches and nurseries. These groups also provide recreational activities that clearly support physical and intellectual needs.

Some organised physical recreational activities are available for young children. Most swimming pools have specific times for parents and young children. Gymnastic activities are also available in association with national gymnastic associations. Both of these clearly provide for physical recreation.

Many local authorities provide playgrounds for children with climbing frames, swings and slides. These offer opportunities for recreation, particularly physical but also involve social interaction. Fantasy play, for example by turning the climbing frame into a fortress, is a form of intellectual recreation.

Activity 7.4

This activity can take place anywhere that children play. It is important that any adults present know what you are doing. It would be a suitable activity for a work placement.

Observe a young child playing. List the different activities being undertaken in a period of 15 minutes.

Next to each activity write down the areas it benefits (physical, intellectual or social).

*Examples of young children
undertaking social and
intellectual recreation*

Older children As children get older the availability of organised recreational activities increases. The child's development makes organised team games possible. Parental involvement may become less and the child may undertake some recreation away from home and parental supervision. Growing independence can make playgrounds and parks more available.

There are many organisations that provide supported recreation for children They include national provision through organisations like the Scouts, Guides and Woodcraft Folk. Each of these supports recreational activities across a wide age range.

Physical recreation through team sports, swimming and gymnastics are frequently organised by schools, sports or leisure centres. Many areas also have frequently organised discos for children providing both social and physical recreation.

Normally, as children get older they learn to read. Reading becomes available as a form of recreation. It also makes games with written rules available for recreational activities.

Childhood is also a time when hobbies develop. Often these involve:
- model-making in some form
- collecting
- developing skills in dance or playing a musical instrument.

All of these provide an intellectual side to recreation. They also offer opportunities of meeting people with similar interests and so bringing in the social aspects.

The Guide Association provides opportunities for social, intellectual and physical recreation (such as rock climbing) that might not otherwise be available

Adolescents

This follows on from the developments in childhood. Again, as people get older, their independence increases. Recreation outside the home may be more easy to access. The range of activities includes social gatherings in youth clubs and other organised functions.

For many people this is a time of peak physical fitness. It is also a time when recreation patterns become established and are maintained throughout the rest of life. Access to and availability of recreation facilities can be very important.

The social aspect of recreational activities now becomes very important. It is a time where relationships are being explored and many recreational activities involve social groupings.

Adolescence is a time when gangs may form. The term 'gang' describes a group of people who behave in ways that are unacceptable to other people. A gang may form partly because there are no other facilities available for recreational activities.

Social and physical recreation are important aspects of being at a disco

Elders

A common stereotype of elders implies that physical recreation has to be limited. This view is incorrect. What must be taken into account is the need to ensure the physical recreation is *appropriate*. Care needs to be taken to ensure that the activities help maintain the body, rather than damage it. Activities can be physically demanding without causing damage.

Elders are not at a peak of physical fitness:
• Reaction speeds reduce with age.
• Bones become more fragile and injuries take longer to heal.
• Heart, lungs and circulation are less efficient than when they were much younger.

All of these will affect the choice of activity. Often recreation that is physical and also has a social focus is appropriate.

The stereotypical game for older people is often considered to be bowls. It meets the needs on many counts. It involves some physical activity. There is a very strong social element of meeting with other people and having time to talk. The skill of controlling the ball and playing to win involves an intellectual challenge.

Activity 7.5

Go back to Activity 7.1. Identify how those activities that you identified for older people meet their needs for intellectual, social and physical recreation.

Families

Potentially a family includes all the groups of people already mentioned (children, adolescents and elders) together with adults. Suitable activities ideally meet the needs of all members. This is difficult, but not impossible. Certainly it is possible for all members of a family to benefit from swimming, for example.

There are difficulties and shared activities have to involve co-operation from all members of the family. An adult can transfer an enthusiasm for reading by reading to younger children. The enthusiasm can also be transmitted by being together while reading separate books.

Some recreational activities have been designed with families in mind. Theme parks often attempt to provide recreation for all members of the family. In these situations a variety of activities are available for people of different ages.

Reading is a shared recreation which provides intellectual stimulation. Parents can communicate an enthusiasm for reading to their children

The benefits of recreation

Activity 7.6

a What recreational activities do you do?

b Why do you do these activities?

c Analyse the activities in terms of the three types of recreation (physical, social and intellectual).

Write a few sentences about your analysis.

The answers to the questions in Activity 7.6 most probably have a very strong theme of liking what you do. Recreation normally has the **emotional benefit** that you enjoy doing it. This is a very positive benefit as it fits in with the idea of recreation bringing a balance back to your life. Where work, school or college may be stressful, recreation provides activities that, while being demanding, are also relaxing.

Physical benefits

Physical activity contributes to fitness in several ways:

- **strength** – the ability of muscles to work over short periods of time. It is required for lifting or in the act of jumping.
- **stamina** – the ability for muscles to continue working without fatigue (becoming tired)
- **suppleness** – the flexibility of the joints. Exercise to develop suppleness is part of warming up and avoids strains to muscles and joints.
- **speed of reaction** – the ability to respond rapidly to changes. This is linked to things like hand–eye co-ordination. Linked to these are improved balance and agility.
- **heart and lung efficiency** – Regular physical recreation makes the heart, lungs and circulation work. The exercise improves their abilities to provide oxygen to the body. This has the benefit of reducing risks of heart disease.
- **determination** – Regular physical activity has a knock-on effect in providing the determination to follow tasks through to a finish.

Problem-solving provides mental stimulation for people of all ages

Different physical activities develop different aspects of fitness. Jogging and dancing develop stamina. Gymnastics improves suppleness. Badminton improves strength, suppleness and stamina.

Clearly activities need to be balanced with ability and age. Well-thought-out physical recreation provide benefits to physical health. It is also important to recognise that there are many activities which are not considered to be sports, but which also contribute to physical health, such as recreational dancing and walking for pleasure.

Intellectual benefits

You may think that all your mental activity should be confined to school or college. Recreation should be relaxing. Intellectual activity can, however, provide a stimulating, satisfying and, at the same time, relaxing recreation. The types of activity often involve problem-solving in some way. This may be in terms of strategies in games like chess.

Reading also provides an intellectual stimulus. Reading for relaxation can involve stories that stimulate your imagination. Using your imagination stimulates mental activity and satisfaction in the enjoyment of the story. Many books also involve problem-solving as part of the enjoyment. Mysteries and detective stories often give sufficient information to enable you to solve the problem before the main characters.

Problem-solving activities and using your imagination both lead to a more active mind. You can use your experiences from reading to help make connections and solve problems for yourself in your life. Strategy games or books that involve thinking about choices help to make you analyse questions, such as 'What would happen if . . .?' This can carry over into your daily activities where you start to think further about the consequences of your actions.

Many hobbies that involve collecting, learning new skills (such as playing musical instruments) or making objects (models or pottery) involve intellectual skills. Meeting with others with similar likes in clubs and societies provides some of the social benefits of recreation.

Social benefits

People are naturally social animals. One of the worst possible tortures is to deprive a person of contact with other people. To be social animals we need to know how to interact with other people.

Young children often appear to be very selfish. They do not know how to share. They always want things for themselves and their needs are most important. Many recreational activities for young children help them to learn about playing with other children and sharing. A major importance of pre-school activities is in learning these social skills. A second important aspect is to see many different children acting in different ways. These different role models help the child to learn how to interact with other people.

The need for social contact is recognised in most caring systems. For older people, there is a risk of isolation. Where a husband or wife dies the surviving partner may be left to live in a house with little contact with other people. This isolation can be worsened by difficulties in moving out of the house. Many social services departments recognise this and organise day centres to support people by coming together for social interaction. Other recreational activities are often provided to support this. Dances, bingo and special swimming sessions for pensioners, for example, can all be provided to help maintain social interaction.

Any social interaction helps people to understand each other. For adolescents, the social interaction may be in situations where individuals can start to explore relationships. Many youth clubs, discos and youth organisations are offered to provide an opportunity for individuals to meet and learn about each other. In some cases, these relationships may develop further into friendship or, in some cases, marriage.

Shared recreational activities imply shared interests. This is the first step towards friendship. The benefits of recreational activities are normally a mixture of physical, intellectual and social. The mixture contributes to a balanced personality and a balanced lifestyle.

Barriers to recreational activities

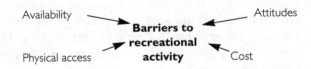

Availability

One common complaint is that there are not enough facilities available to meet the needs of everyone. For example, the availability of golf courses does not meet demand and so there is often a long waiting list for membership. The same complaint can be levelled at the provision of almost any recreational activity. It would be impractical to provide facilities for everyone who wanted them. There will always be some level of rationing.

The facility may be available locally, but bookings may mean that it is not available at convenient times. Many local authority-owned swimming pools, for example, have limited access for the general public because they are booked for clubs or school swimming lessons. There are also times when the pool is booked for specific groups, such as elders or parents and toddlers.

Availability affects activities like reading, just as much as physical activities. Often you may wish to borrow the latest best-seller from the library and it is already on loan. The only answers are either to buy the book (too expensive) or to reserve it and wait until it is returned!

Social recreation is often controlled by the availability of the activity. Rooms may only be available for dancing at certain times. Organisations such as the scouts or youth clubs normally have regular meeting times during the week. There may also be irregular meetings at other times. Many leisure centres and libraries offer rooms for hire, but these are often booked well in advance so to organise a leisure activity may require planning.

Activity 7.7

a Go to a recreational facility close to your home and find what activities are available. Obtain a timetable of the activities, if this is appropriate.

b Find out whether you would need to book a room, a court or a pitch, and how you would do so. Also find how far in advance you would need to book to get the facility you would like.

c Check whether any organisations have regular bookings that reduce your freedom of choice in the time that you could use the facility.

d Find out any costs involved.

Improving availabililty

The availability of recreational resources is a difficult problem to address. It is possible to campaign for a new sports and leisure centre to be built in your locality. However, it is unlikely, though not impossible, to be successful. Even if successful, it would not solve the problem of availability for several months or years ahead.

What is more useful is to press for improved availability of existing facilities. For example, opening times may be extended. Schools and colleges may be prepared to make facilities available outside normal opening hours if there is sufficient demand. Improving availability often involves groups of people getting together to demonstrate a need.

Physical access

Access to a recreational activity can be affected by:

- **the ability of different people to get to the necessary facilities.** Easy-to-identify problems, such as lack of wheelchair access, can stop some people from being able to participate in the recreation.
- **availability of the activity in a specific locality**. It would be difficult for a rock climber to spend an evening after work climbing if he or she lived in an area like the Fens of Lincolnshire, for example. The area is flat and there are no natural rock faces. Someone living in the Peak District of Derbyshire would be much more able to have an evening climb.
- **travelling times.** Even in areas where the facilities are available, travelling times can create problems. For example, a long journey to spend 40 minutes playing badminton may become unacceptable to a player. A difficult bus journey for someone with arthritis may stop attendance at a bingo session.

Improving physical access

Problems of physical access to any facility should be easy to identify. Barriers produced by closed minds are more difficult. Many people stereotype disabled people and assume that some recreational activities should not be available to them. They may also limit access just to specific times when support can be given. For such situations, improved access to facilities can often be negotiated with support coming from volunteers.

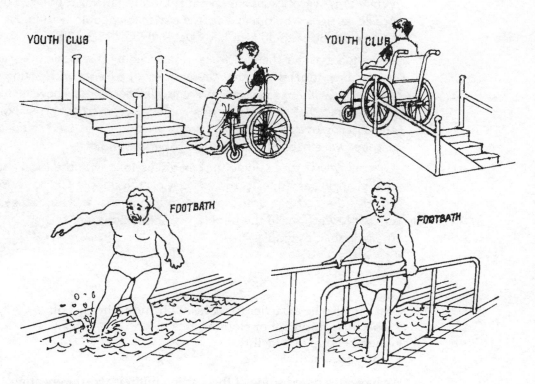

Some thought and simple changes can remove barriers to physical access

Case study

Swimming is an excellent physical recreation that provides exercise for almost all groups of people. Many swimming pools have barriers to some potential swimmers.

Jane has multiple sclerosis. She is able to walk, but very unsteadily. She was beginning to find it increasingly difficult to go swimming. Getting to the changing rooms was no problem. However, the pool had large baskets for clothes which had to be taken to an attendant for safe keeping. Jane could not safely carry the basket.

Going from the changing room to the pool involved walking through a foot-bath. Jane was very concerned that she would slip over. The same was true for her journey to the side of the pool.

Once in the pool, Jane was able to swim and enjoy the ability to move around. The water supported her and made it possible to move much more freely than on land.

Getting out of the pool was a problem. All of the ladders were vertical and climbing out proved almost impossible.

The local authority, who owned the pool, were sympathetic to Jane's problems. Together they worked out what could be done. Hand rails were fixed in the changing rooms, the foot bath and to the side of the pool. Steps were fitted that had a slope more like stairs. Immediately Jane was able to move about much more safely.

While they were discussing the adaptations, Jane also pointed out that adding Braille to signs would make access easier for people with impaired sight. The side of the pool could also have water depths in Braille.

The effects of the changes were monitored by the local authority. One of the things they noticed was that the number of parents with young babies attending swimming sessions dramatically increased. They started to ask why and realised that people carrying babies also have concerns about balance and slipping over. The rails and steps provided increased safety and more parents were happy to bring their babies swimming.

One thing that Jane said about her discussions with the local authority was that changing attitudes is the hardest part. If people talk to those with disabilities then change does no have to be expensive. The changes introduced do not have to make the people with disabilities feel singled out by having their disabilities emphasised.

Cost

Cost can also be a barrier to access. It includes the cost of:

- specific equipment or clothing
- membership of a facility
- entry to a facility.

We have discussed some of this earlier, but it is worth repeating.

Where an activity is scarce then the cost may be high. Membership fees for golf clubs can seem exorbitant. Private sports facilities often have membership fees that provide a barrier. Local authority-run facilities often have reduced rates for different groups of people, but these are often only available at specific times – another barrier to access.

Costs may not be obvious. Walking as a recreational activity often means that different routes are used for variety. The cost of transport to the start and finish of a walk may be a barrier. To be limited in the number of routes available can lead to boredom and becoming less enthusiastic about the activity.

Many social activities have implied costs. Most youth clubs, cinemas or theatres have food and drinks available. Expectations of friends may be that an individual spends money on food and drink. This adds to the cost of the activity and may make it too expensive for some people with low incomes.

Overcoming problems of cost

This can be approached in two main ways:

- **by looking for recreation which involves little or no cost.** Many physical activities do not need specialist equipment or facilities. Walking and jogging only require the roads and paths that are readily available. Reading does not mean that expensive books have to be bought. Public libraries are able to obtain copies of almost any book you wish to ask for. There may be a small charge but it is less than the cost of the book.
- **by trying to reduce costs.** This can be done in a number of ways, such as:
  - Sharing transport costs often makes it possible to get to activities that would otherwise be too expensive. This has the knock-on effect of increasing the social nature of the recreation.

- Many recreational facilities have special rates for groups. They may also have discounts for groups of people on low incomes. It is not unusual to find discounts for students, unwaged people and elders. It is also possible to find discounts offered for times when fewer people want to use a facility. For example, early afternoon in the cinema is often cheaper than the evening.
- Expensive equipment does not always need to be purchased. Many organisations offer to hire the equipment necessary to participate in an activity. This can extend to the hire of specific uniform items. A local Scout or Guide group may loan equipment to help members participate fully.

Attitudes

As we mentioned in the case study of Jane, attitude can be a barrier to access. This may be the prejudice of adults with regard to children. Statements like those below need to be challenged:

'Children wouldn't want to . . .'

'Children only mess around so we are not prepared to . . .'

'It wouldn't be safe for blind people/people with cerebral palsy/disabled people to . . .'

Where there *appears* to be no demand for something, then consider what the real barrier to access might be.

Surveying local recreational activities

A major task for Unit 7 of the Foundation GNVQ is for you to identify what recreational facilities are available locally and look at their use. This can best be done as a series of tasks in the following activity. You will need to work in cooperation with your colleagues.

Activity 7.8 _____

For this activity you will need:
- a map of the area you are considering
- a *Phone Book*, *Yellow Pages* and a *Thomson Directory* of the area.

a Use the directories and your own knowledge to find out what is available and where it is available. You may also find that your public library has a list of recreational organisations and clubs.
As a guide, look for:
- sports centres
- swimming pools
- leisure centres
- outdoor pursuits centres
- cinemas
- theatres
- sports clubs, such as squash, bowls, athletics, archery
- societies and clubs, such as rambling associations, chess clubs, groups for collectors of items

- public libraries
- creches, pre-school playgroups and nurseries.

You will probably be able to add to this list.

b Mark on your map the location of the different facilities. For each facility, identify:
- the activities available
- the client groups catered for.

Devise a key for your map to identify the client groups and the type of recreation available.

c In your group, decide the facilities to be investigated. Each person should take two facilities which cater for different client groups. If the facility offers many activities, select only one or two that represent activities for the different client groups.

Visit your chosen facilities and find out:
- the recreational activities available
- the opening hours and costs of activities. Are there any days when it is not open, such as Sundays or Christmas?
- the main groups of clients who use the facility
- the nature of the client groups – age, physical condition (for example, are they expected to be fit), any special needs they may have (for example, a social recreation club for physically-disabled and able-bodied people)
- how often the facility is used and when it is used
- how long people spend on the chosen activity (for example, some people may play squash for 40 minutes or a chess club may involve people for three hours in their activity)
- what the physical, social and intellectual benefits are. Which benefit might the people involved in the activity identify?
- what the barriers to access are, if any – physical barriers, attitudes, costs, specialist equipment, clothing, location or transport. Is there easy public transport? Do people attend from all over the district or are they very local? Are there times when the facility is not available because it is booked on a regular basis by one group of people? Where there are barriers, try to suggest ways that they can be overcome.

Some of the information may be obtained using a questionnaire. If you design a questionnaire that you all use, the next part will be easier.

d The purpose of you all identifying different facilities and activities is that you should now be able to produce a guide to what is available.

To do this well, you will need to sort the different activities and facilities into groups. This may be according to:
- the main users – children, adolescents, families and elders
- the benefits – physical, social and intellectual
- the cost.

It is for you to decide. Once you have decided how to group the facilities, you should agree a simple structure for your guide. The guide will need to give information about the facility in a way that readers can easily find the information they need. They may want to know the opening times, the costs, the groups catered for and any barriers to access.

Agree the structure of the reports on each facility and then each person should write a guide for the facilities he or she has investigated. Bring the individual guides together to make a booklet or display.

If you have access to a word processor or desk-top publishing software, you should make use of it in producing this booklet. Use appropriate illustrations to make it interesting.

Recreational activities for people with specific needs

So far we have considered recreational activities in general. There are many people who, for a variety of reasons, may have specific recreational needs. For example:

- People living alone need to be able to take part in social activities.
- People with disabilities may need support to take part in some forms of recreation.
- Elderly people may have a variety of specific needs for recreation that reflect age, mobility or living alone.
- Other people may have needs because of their concerns about their own obesity (overweight).

In all of these cases, the choice of recreation has to be made to provide for the need. To suggest that a person living alone undertakes solitary recreation, such as jogging, does not meet the need for social recreation. To encourage an obese person to take up physical activities involving strenuous exercise would be dangerous to his or her health. You would also need to consider the feelings of an obese person who may be embarrassed to exercise where others may laugh at the obesity.

Many of the issues associated with specific needs can be addressed by increasing awareness of the issues. In the case study of Jane (page 227) we saw how awareness enabled a person with disabilities to participate in recreational activities. Let us consider specific groups in more detail.

People with physical disabilities

This covers a wide range of disabilities and may include people who:
- are visually impaired
- are hearing impaired
- are in wheelchairs
- have a limited range of movements (such as severe arthritis)
- have poor muscle control (such as cerebral palsy, Parkinson's disease, multiple sclerosis).

All of these people have one thing in common – they suffer from the attitudes of others. Many well-meaning people try to take control of their lives and tell them what they *ought* to do in terms of recreation.

While some people with disabilities may feel unable to participate in some recreational activities, most will be able to identify activities they would like to undertake. In many cases, the recreational activity can be developed to support the specific need.

People with disabilities have the same needs for recreation as everyone else:

- physical recreation
- social recreation
- intellectual recreation.

Physical activities may have an important health-related role in improving mobility, but that is also true for everyone else.

One aspect of physical disability that creates issues for able-bodied people is social recreation. There is a tendency for activities to be organised for people with similar disabilities. These can be very useful as self-help groups, but they do tend to limit contact with others. The reactions of able-bodied people to those with disabilities provides a barrier to many activities in general. This can cause feelings of isolation from society with social links only developing with other people with similar disabilities.

Recreational activities for people with disabilities should cover all of those available in general. Allowances may need to be made for disability. After all, if marathon races were not segregated then few of the runners would have any contact with the competitors in wheelchairs.

It may be necessary to allocate facilities and times specifically for people with disabilities. This goes against much that we have said, but in competitive activities where the disability is significant then it would be reasonable. Other situations should encourage participation of all. As we saw in the case study of Jane, adaptations to the environment are more important than providing separate activities.

Many recreational facilities are made available to people who find access difficult

People with specific health-related problems

In this category would be obese people and those with heart and circulation problems. There are two issues involved in selecting recreational activities. These are related to:
- self-esteem
- health and safety.

Self-esteem

Any recreational activity that exposes a person to embarrassment will lower his or her self-esteem. An obese person may feel unable to participate in an activity because of the possible comments of others. This is a case where self-help groups can be important.

In health terms, an obese person needs to lose weight. Recreation may be directed to this with physical activity and diet contributing. If the physical activity is carried out with others who are obese, the embarrassment factor can be reduced. There is also an element of understanding and pressure from colleagues which helps a person to continue in the activity. This social aspect of the recreation is important.

Health and safety

An obese person should undertake physical activity under guidance from a health practitioner. The strain of exercise on joints, muscles and the heart need to be monitored carefully.

General advice is to work up gradually to a high level of physical activity. This enables the body develop the strength necessary and also encourages weight loss. For this purpose, there are many groups that offer recreation (associated with weight loss) for obese people. For many of these, there is also a cost in money terms that needs to be considered.

Health and safety is also a consideration for people with heart and circulatory problems. Physical recreation needs to be supervised and monitored.

Providers of facilities are concerned about health and safety. Notices and lifeguards remind people of hazards

Swimming is a very appropriate activity for both obese people and those with heart and circulatory disorders. The buoyancy provided by the water reduces the stresses on joints and the exercise can be tailored to meet needs. Swimming provides exercise that improves muscle tone and joint flexibility. It improves breathing and increases the heart rate. Both benefit the respiratory and circulatory systems.

Recreation for elders

Many elders maintain a healthy independent lifestyle. They organise their lives to meet their recreational needs. It is not this group that we will consider.

For some elders, specific recreational support is needed. Those living alone may need support in maintaining social activities. Others may have very little mobility and need assistance in physical activity. There are also needs to provide intellectual stimulation.

Facilities available that provide recreation specifically for elders include day centres and residential homes. Some leisure centres also run specific sessions to support the recreation needs of elders.

Day centres and residential homes provide a variety of activities:
* They provide a place where people meet socially. They offer opportunities for conversation and other forms of social recreation.

A day centre provides a place for social and intellectual recreation for elderly people

- They provide intellectual recreation in a variety of ways.
  - It may be associated with playing games. These may be group games, such as bingo, or individual challenges, such as chess and draughts.
  - With some people the intellectual stimulation has to be organised on a one-to-one basis by the care workers. Conversation with care workers involving talking about things that have happened in the past is important. Using photographs and things from the past to stimulate memories also enables people to think about the present.
  - Intellectual recreation can also include activities related to occupational therapy. Intellectual activity may come from concentrating on painting, sewing or knitting. It may come from practising a skill like cooking. All of these also have benefits in physical activity. They do not provide exercise like swimming, but they support fine movements and help maintain hand and finger mobility.

Factors influencing activities

So far we have only been able to touch on some of the factors relating to recreation for people with specific needs. Some (cost, accessibility, the time, requirements of health and safety and physical access) affect everyone, not just those with specific needs.

The major difference is that specific needs may require support. It may be to:
- **help a person gain independent access to recreation**. An example of this would be the provision of grab rails around a swimming pool to allow people with mobility difficulties to use the pool safely. Your survey of local facilities should have identified some similar examples.
- **provide the support of another person.** For example, a visually disabled runner may need a companion to run alongside. At a riding school for disabled people, each rider is accompanied by a helper. Without the support of the helper the individual would not be able to undertake and enjoy the activity.

Activity 7.9

This activity may be part of an investigation carried out on work placement or it may require support from your lecture/teacher in arranging for people to come in to college or school.

Your task is to identify recreational activities for two client groups with different specific needs. To do this we do not expect you to devise something totally new.

Part 1: The investigation

a Identify the two client groups that you wish to study. Use your previous activities to see whether there is any local provision for the groups. It may be that you are working with (or have worked with) one of the groups while on work experience.

b Arrange to talk to someone involved with the provision of the recreational activities for your client groups.

c Write out a series of questions that you would like the person to answer. These might include questions about:
- the activities that are appropriate and available
- the needs, in terms of physical, social and intellectual activities
- factors such as cost, time, health and safety, access and physical ability that affect the types of activity
- any risks involved with the activity.

d If you are allowed to, you should observe or participate in the activities with your client groups.

Part 2: The reports

From the information you have gathered, write a short report on each client group identifying:
- the client group
- the specific needs
- the activity
- factors that affect the choice of activity
- any hazards or health and safety issues (precautions needed, specific safety requirements)
- the benefits to the clients (intellectual, physical and social).

You should produce one report for each client group you study.

Test yourself

1 What are the three broad classes into which recreation can be divided?

2 Playing chess and reading are examples of what type of recreational activity?

3 Swimming with a group of friends falls into which recreational categories?

4 Give two examples of social recreational activities.

5 What factors might affect a person's choice of recreational activity?

6 What factors might be a barrier to a child playing golf?

7 What might put an obese person off physical recreation?

8 What benefits are gained by recreational activities?

9 Suggest a suitable physical activity for an active elderly person.

10 What safety issues might you need to consider for an elderly person undertaking strenuous physical activity?

Assignment A7.1
Exploring health and recreational activities

For this assignment you will need to:
- carry out a survey of local facilities
- prepare information sheets about two different recreational activities.

This is a group activity. The tasks will need to be shared amongst the members of your group. Chapter 4 will tell you all about organising a group activity. If you have chosen Unit 4 as an optional unit, this assignment will provide you with some evidence for it.

A recent revolution in Foundasia has meant that many refugees have come to the UK. A group of 30 have come to live in your district. The group consists of two families with elderly grandparents, parents and children aged three, nine and fifteen. There are also some single adults, one of whom has multiple sclerosis and is very unsteady in walking, although he does not use a wheelchair. One of the family members is very obese. (You can add your own details to this outline description of the refugees.)

You and the rest of your group are working with the local Council for Voluntary Services. Your group has been asked to produce some information sheets about the various recreational activities available locally.

Each sheet should include:
- type of activity and where it takes place
- the opening hours
- the results of your survey – who uses the facilities and when they use them (when are popular times for different groups?)
- a brief description of the activities
- an assessment of the suitability for the different refugees (this must include those refugees with more specific needs)
- the benefits to the people of the different activities
- any barriers to access (such as cost, distance, specialist equipment)
- suggestions of ways to overcome the barriers
- identification of any health and safety issues associated with the activity and how they are dealt with.

Your tasks

1 As a group, carry out a survey of the recreational facilities available in your area. (You will find the work you did for Activity 7.8 useful here.) Check back through the list of things that should be on the information sheets and devise a recording sheet to note down all the information you will need.

Remember to plan carefully to obtain all the information you will need.

2 a Come together and make a database of all of the information you have gathered. (This may be a paper-based database rather than one on a computer.)

b Evaluate the information you now have. Do you have enough to start writing the information sheets, or is more work necessary?

3 Each person will then need to look at two different activities and prepare the information sheets about those activities. Consider the following:
- write clearly and organise the information with headings to break it up
- illustrate the sheet with relevant results from your survey (use graphs, pie charts or diagrams – produced on a computer if possible)
- think about the appearance of the sheets – use a word processor or desk-top publishing software to produce the sheets if you can.

Key words

After reading this chapter you should be able to understand the following words and phrases. If you do not, go back through the chapter and find out, or look them up in the Glossary.

Intellectual recreational activities

Social recreational activities

Physical recreational activities

CHAPTER 8

Exploring Physical Care

What is covered in this chapter

- The provision of physical assistance
- The use of aids to physical care
- Maintaining independence using assistive equipment

These are the resources you will need for your Exploring Physical Care portfolio:

- documents and leaflets you have collected relating to assistive equipment
- your written answers to the activities in this chapter
- your written answers to the Test Yourself questions at the end of this chapter
- your completed assignments: A8.1, A8.2, A8.3.

Introduction

Many people need physical help with a number of activities that they do every day. Any assistance offered to dependent people must be provided in a manner that will not harm the client or the carer. This chapter sets out to show how physical assistance can be offered in a way that is safe and that maintains the client's independence and dignity.

The provision of physical assistance

The quality of life of a client will depend to some extent on their being able to move around freely without pain, discomfort or danger. We all take mobility for granted from the time we first learn to walk.

If a person's mobility is reduced, the scope of their daily lives can become severely limited. A number of clients will need physical assistance with DAILY LIVING ACTIVITIES, such as eating, walking, hearing or seeing. This support and assistance has to be provided safely and using equipment such as wheelchairs, walking frames and hearing aids where necessary.

Many factors contribute to loss of, or reduced, mobility in elderly people:
- arthritis
- strokes
- breathing problems
- heart conditions
- foot problems.

Many of these problems can be alleviated by assistive aids to mobility.

One important aspect of providing support to any client is to do so in a way that maintains the client's independence and dignity.

A caring attitude

You have chosen to do this Foundation GNVQ course because you want to work in social care, you have a caring personality and you want to help people. Your most important assets are your personality and your attitude towards the people you are caring for.

Your attitude is most important when working with people with disabilities. They may, for example, have no control over movement, they may be unable to speak or may have impaired sight or hearing. While you are in college you are the focus and attention of the tutors and other staff, but when you are working with clients you become part of a caring team. The clients are then the focus of your attention.

Activity 8.1

a In pairs, ask your partner to assist you to blow you nose (use clean, disposable tissues only).

b How does it feel to be dependent on another person? Discuss you feelings with the rest of your group.

c Discuss situations when an elderly client might find dependency upsetting.

To help people in a sensitive and caring manner, remember that you will need to pay constant attention to the way you talk to them. Be polite and respectful when talking to them and talk in a clear voice. Always talk to the person about what you are doing and why. This will help them to feel at ease and understand.

Aim to:
- Listen and respond to communications from clients.
- Use good eye contact and keep smiling.
- Be sincere, sympathetic and understanding.
- Be kind, gentle and tactful.
- Be willing to assist, but always allow the elderly person to do as much as possible for themselves. Encourage them to be as independent as practical.

When working with people with disabilities we must be careful not to oppress them. We could do this by exercising power over their lives, by doing things for them or making decisions for them. The language we use to describe elderly dependent people can be oppressive. For example, labelling everyone over 65 as 'elderly' can be damaging to their self-esteem or self-confidence.

Activity 8.2

Write down what you feel when you hear people say 'Oh, it's students again, all of them are into drugs, sex and drink.'

Do you think that statement describes you or any of your student friends?

Old age

When we discuss services for elderly people we are usually referring to people who are past retirement age. In men this is at 65 years and for women it is at 60 years at present (it may change to 65 years in the near future).

Percentage of elderly people in population, 1900–2001

Year	Percentage
1900	4.7
1930	9.0
1950	10.8
1970	16.0
1981	17.4
2001	16.0 (estimated)

Old age can be divided into two categories:
* early old age (up to 75 years old)
* late old age (over 75 years).

It's a fact

People are living even longer now than ever before.
* In 1900, less than 1 in 20 people were over 65 years of age.
* By 1990 approximately 1 in 7 were over 65.
* Between 1995 and the year 2001, the number of elderly people over 85 years of age is expected to double and most of these will be women.

Number of people over retirement age in Britain

Year	Number of people over retirement age	Percentage of retired people over 85 years
1991	10 000 000	8
2021	12 000 000	10 (estimated)
2051	12 000 000	15 (estimated)

Activity 8.3

a Find out how many people there are over retirement age in your locality. To do this, go to your college or local library and ask to look at the population statistics for your local authority area. Look for the numbers of elderly people in each 'ward' (sub-division) in the area.

b Is there a difference in the number and percentage of elderly people in each ward?

Old age and disease

Old age is not necessarily a time of problems. Many elderly people will not require assistance from carers. There is no 'standard model' elderly person. Elderly people differ widely in needs, lifestyles and expectations. They have the same emotional and human needs as young people.

While age cannot be equated automatically with dependency, many people, as they grow older, find themselves generally slowing down. Some of their faculties may start to decline or certain disabilities may develop.

It's a fact
- About 65 per cent of all disabled people are over 65 years of age.
- At the age of 75 and above, the proportion of people with some degree of disability rises sharply.

The ageing body is increasingly subject to DEGENERATIVE DISEASES. These are diseases which gradually worsen over time and can be any of the following:
- **Atheroma** This is a gradual build-up of fatty deposits on the walls of the arteries giving rise to coronary heart disease and strokes.

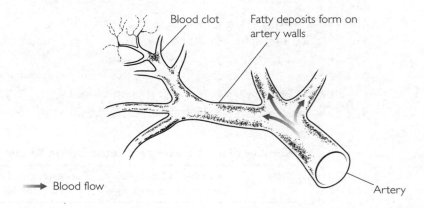

Atheroma restricts the flow of blood through the arteries. Clots may form and block small blood vessels.

- **Osteo-arthritis** Changes occur in the joints giving rise to pain and loss of mobility.
- **Brain degeneration** There are two main causes of this:
  – Alzheimer's disease, which is the excessive degeneration of the nerve cells
  – atheroma of the arteries supplying the brain.
  Both these conditions can lead to gradual loss of intellectual power and ability.
- **Cancer** There is an increase in the incidence of many cancers with advancing age.

The onset of one of these diseases can seriously affect an elderly person's ability to carry out daily living functions without assistance.

Activity 8.4

a Obtain a copy of your local social service department's annual Community Care Plan.

b Find out what plans they have for providing services for elderly people who live in their own homes.

c Make a list of the services offered.

People involved in the provision of physical assistance

In Chapter 3 the roles and responsibilities of many of the people involved in supporting and providing physical assistance to clients were discussed. We looked at the support that the occupational therapist, the physiotherapist, the social worker, the GP and nurses could provide. The diagram below shows all the services that could be involved in delivering physical assistance or emotional support to an elderly person with a disability.

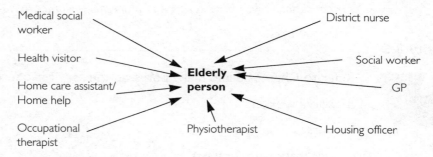

Professional support workers

As you can see, there are many people involved in providing services and assistance to an elderly person with a disability. All of these people must work together to provide the best service possible. It is also important that they co-operate very closely with relatives and friends of the client.

However, **most important** of all is that everyone, professional workers and carers, **must** take into account, and act upon, the wishes of the client. What the client wants is the most important thing, not what is available to offer them or what we as carers might think is the best thing for them. The elderly person themselves must have the final say in what services and support they want.

So that the client can make a meaningful decisions, we should:
• explain what process they are involved in
• let the client put forward their own views
• agree with the client what services they would wish
• talk through with the client how the services can be delivered
• involve the client fully in reviewing the situation as appropriate.

The diagram on page 244 shows the different organisations which may be involved in offering support.

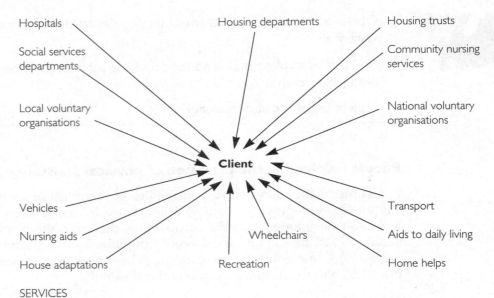

ORGANISATIONS

Hospitals

Social services departments

Local voluntary organisations

Housing departments

Housing trusts

Community nursing services

National voluntary organisations

Client

Vehicles

Nursing aids

House adaptations

Wheelchairs

Recreation

Transport

Aids to daily living

Home helps

SERVICES

Organisations who offer support and physical assistance to elderly dependent clients

Activity 8.5

Refer to Chapter 3 and make notes on the services offered by:

a social workers

b nurses

c occupational therapists

d physiotherapists.

Elderly clients with restricted mobility

Case study

Mrs Jackson is 90 years of age. She was a nurse all her working life and, by the time she retired 30 years ago, she was a matron of a large hospital.

Her family all live overseas and she sees them infrequently. She lives alone in a small house with one room, a kitchen and bathroom and toilet downstairs and one bedroom upstairs. She suffers from glaucoma and arthritis of the hand, wrists and hips. She has difficulty in using cooking appliances and getting upstairs. She cannot get into the bath. She also has difficulty in writing letters because of the pain in her fingers from the arthritis.

Mrs Jackson has very restricted mobility and will need much physical assistance to allow her to live as normal a life as possible in her own home.

The first step to helping Mrs Jackson is to talk to her about how she feels and what she wants. One other important consideration is Mrs Jackson's cultural background. We have not mentioned her ethnic background. Would

you give Mrs Jackson different consideration if she was of Asian background? After the social worker had talked to Mrs Jackson and obtained her permission, she asked a number of professionals to assess her needs.

Activity 8.6

a What services and physical aids do you think Mrs Jackson might need?

b Explain what each one you recommend is for.

Did your answers include any of the following?

Physical aids	Reason for aid
Stair lift	To allow Mrs Jackson to get up and down stairs
Bathroom hoist	This will assist the nurse or carer to help Mrs Jackson in and out of her bath
Bath aids	Rubber grip mats to stop Mrs Jackson slipping in the bath
Bed comfort	Aids such as adjustable back rests, triangular pillows and cushions to help her sleep and rest.
Feeding aids	Specially-designed knives, forks and plates to help with eating
Kitchen aids	Special taps to allow her to turn sink and bath taps on or off
Walking aids	Walking stick or zimmer frame for mobility
Sight aids	A magnifying glass to help her read

Personal support:

Nursing service	To help her in and out of bed
Home help	Cleaning and cooking, shopping
Friend	Reading and writing letters

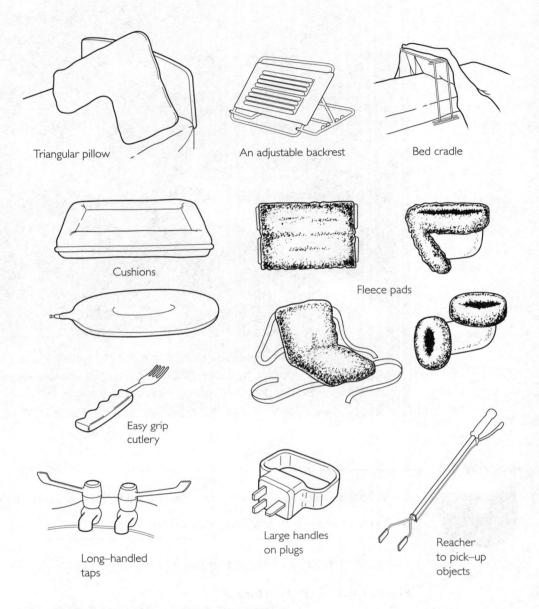

Triangular pillow   An adjustable backrest   Bed cradle

Cushions

Fleece pads

Easy grip
cutlery

Long–handled
taps

Large handles
on plugs

Reacher
to pick–up
objects

Some aids that might be useful for Mrs Jackson

Case study
Mr Butterfield worked as gardener for all his working life. He loved working outdoors but, four years after he retired at 65, he had a serious stroke. This left him with restricted mobility in one leg and arm. He finds difficulty in feeding himself as he cannot keep the plate from moving and slipping when he eats. He also finds that he cannot grasp the knives and forks as he cannot grip the utensils. He is also depressed at having to stay indoors all the time.

Activity 8.7

a How would you help Mr Butterfield? What assistive equipment would you recommend to him?

b What other steps would you take to make him more mobile?

Did you answer include any of the following?

Physical aids	Reason for aid
Special non-slip plates	To allow him to feed himself
Knives/forks/spoons with thick handles to allow better grip	To allow him to grip feeding utensils and feed himself
Walking stick	To allow him to get about the house

Did you also give some thought to the fact that as Mr Butterfield was a very active man in his working life and liked the outdoors, he might improve his spirits if he could get out of the house? It could be arranged for a volunteer to take him out in car a few days a week or the Social Service Department could be asked to arrange for Mr Butterfield could go to a DAY CENTRE.

MOVING AND HANDLING TECHNIQUES

Sometimes as a care worker you will be asked to lift or move clients. You may have to move them from a bed to a chair, into a bath or onto the toilet. Lifting techniques in general are described in Chapter 5. In this chapter moving and handling techniques relating specifically to clients will be discussed.

Lifting or moving a client

When lifting or moving a client some important and specific rules apply:

- Always wear flat comfortable shoes.
- It is advisable to remove rings and watches. These may scratch the client or get caught in hair.
- Explain what you are going to do to the client.
- Clear the area.
- Where there is more than one lifter, co-operate to lift together.
- Do not rush the procedure.
- Do not drag the client.
- Apply all the general rules of lifting.

> **Remember**
> Always follow the rules

The European Handling Regulations came into effect on 1 January 1993. They place the responsibility for the safety of workers on the management of the organisation you are working for. **All** employers must ensure the safety of their workers:

- All manual-handling tasks that might injure anyone should be avoided where possible.
- If it is not possible to avoid a hazardous manual-handling task, it must be assessed first to decide how it is to be done.

- Once the task has been assessed, action must be taken to reduce the risk of injury.
- The employer must ensure that they have a safe manual-handling policy and must give training before staff begin lifting.

As a care worker, you too should always be aware of the appropriate and safe way to carry out a manual-handling task. You should also **call for assistance** when you think it is necessary.

There are some special difficulties lifting clients:
- Many clients are too heavy to be lifted bodily.
- Clients are unwieldy and difficult to grasp.
- Many dependent or injured clients will make unexpected movements.
- Most injuries occur to care staff because of the physical behaviour of the client.

Things to look for when assessing whether a lifting task is necessary

The lifting task
- Does the client need to be lifted?
- Could the client move themselves?
- Could a lifting aid be used?
- How long will it take to lift the client?

The client
- What is wrong with the client? Remember that if a client has suffered a fall or other injury, you should not lift them until either you, a qualified first aider or a doctor is satisfied that it is safe to move them.
- The weight, height and shape of the client
- How much can the client assist you?
- How is the client going to behave? A confused client or one in great pain may make sudden movements.

Where is the lifting to be done?
- Are there any potentially dangerous objects about, such as furniture, equipment, etc?
- How much space have you to carry out the lift? Is the client in a confined space such as a toilet, bath or in their bed?
- Is the floor safe? Is there water, loose carpets, rugs, clothing or other hazards on it?

What lifting techniques will you use?
- Will you use a lifting aid or hoist?
- Will you be lifting manually? If so, how many staff are required to do the lift safely?

Those who will lift the client
- Are they trained? How much experience have they of lifting this type of client?
- How skilled are they at communicating with clients?

There are many different ways of lifting a client. Your teachers will show you how safe lifting is carried out. You can only learn how to lift safely by practising under supervision. **Never** practise without supervision.

Remember when lifting from the floor:
- Keep your back straight.

- Bend your knees and hips.
- Use your stomach and thigh muscles.
- Keep your feet apart.
- Avoid twisting your back.
- Let the person you are moving help you as much as possible.
- **Be careful**.

Remember
It is unsafe to:
- lift at arm's length
- lift at a distance from the body
- lift in front, or to one side of, the knees.

How can you maintain the client's independence and dignity?

One of the ways in which we can support clients to maintain their dignity and independence is to give them choice and allow them to make decisions that affect their lives.

Client choice is central to the quality of care. It takes the power and control from the worker and places it where it belongs, with the client. Society, that is us, tends not to listen to people who have disabilities. However, by offering choice to people we EMPOWER them. This gives them a sense of dignity and worth.

We can empower elderly people with disabilities by:
- being sensitive to their needs
- listening to what they are saying
- not 'talking down' to them
- not labelling those elderly people with disabilities
- negotiating with the client, carer and any other professionals
- giving appropriate support as necessary.

Case study
Jack Rudd was bereaved by the loss of his wife, upon whom he depended a great deal. A few weeks later he suffered a stroke which restricted his mobility and physical competence.

‘I felt helpless and lonely at home and I think I was getting depressed. I wanted to go into an old persons' home, but the social worker and home help kept telling me that I was better-off in my own home. I got very angry, but was afraid to argue in case they wouldn't give me any help.’

Activity 8.8

a Do you think that the social worker and the home help were empowering Jack?

b How could they have made him feel better and worth listening to? Discuss your ideas with your colleagues.

Did your answer include any of the following?
- Ask Jack what he wanted.
- Explain to him what is available to help his mobility.
- Ask him if he would not mind been visited by an occupational therapist or physiotherapist.
- Discuss with him the results of any assessment.
- Let him make the final choice.

People such as Jack should be encouraged to make their own decisions and to be involved as much as possible in making decisions about their own lives. In this way we empower people and allow them to keep their dignity and self-respect.

We show respect people by trying to find out what they really want. We do this by observing them and listening to what they are saying. We don't just listen to what they are saying verbally, we also have to 'read' their BODY LANGUAGE (or **non-verbal communication**).

When we talk to people with disabilities, we should choose the words we use very carefully and the body language we use should re-enforce what we are saying. When talking to people who are anxious, we should give them enough time to absorb what we are saying and give them time to respond.

Body language
We use body language to communicate with people. It is unavoidable. We send messages by the way we use our face, the way we stand, sit or gesture. Body language indicates a person's mood, feelings and attitudes. If you recognise some of these methods of communicating, you become more sensitive to other people and their needs.

What are these signs that we make to show how we feel? If you have done something well, we may communicate it by the thumbs-up sign, for example. This non-verbal communication indicates that we are happy.

Activity 8.9

List as many signs, or non-verbal communications, as you can that would indicate you were happy or unhappy.

Did your list include: Smiling?
                           Frowning?
                           Turning your back on the person?
                           Bored face?
                           Angry gestures?

Facial expressions

Facial expressions are probably the most important aspect of non-verbal communication. Your face is very flexible and capable of showing your innermost feeling to others. Smiles are one of the most obvious signs we use to communicate. Smiles indicate warmth and openness. Smiles make other people react positively to you.

Eye contact

Eye contact is an other important way that we communicate. When we communicate with clients, we normally have eye-to-eye contact. A strong gaze shows that you are paying attention. Breaking eye contact can indicate embarrassment. A lack of eye contact could indicate that you do not like the client and therefore do not wish to enter into meaningful conversation.

Do you feel at ease with those who keep eye contact with you? Do you remember when you told white lies to one of your parents? Did you look your parent straight in the eyes when telling an untruth? Have you heard the expression they 'have shifty eyes'?

Posture

How you move your body, the way you sit or stand reflects your attitudes and feelings towards other people. How you use your posture can effect the way a client reacts to you. When you sit with a client, you can make them feel important by leaning towards them or sitting with your arms unfolded. Sitting with yours arms folded may indicate that you are not willing to listen.

Height

If you sit in a higher position than your client, you can make a them feel inferior. For example, when talking to someone in bed or in a wheelchair, it may be important to sit down so that you can maintain good eye contact with the client. People feel that they are been told off when someone stands over them.

Activity 8.10

a List the non-verbal communications that would make you think that people were listening to you.

Did your list include:
- rubbing their hands together?
- sitting or leaning forward?
- looking directly at you?
- nodding in agreement with you?

b Make a list of the ways that people could indicate friendliness by using non-verbal communication.

Did your list include:
- smiling?
- non-threatening gestures, handshakes, pat on back?
- using eye contact?
- sitting or standing with unfolded arms?

How can you recognise clients who might be feeling threatened?

How do *you* behave when you feel under threat? Do you fold your arms or cross your legs? Do you withdraw eye contact, become verbally aggressive or do you stand your ground?

Listen to them. Listening is more than hearing. It is **paying attention** to what people say as well as to their non-verbal communication. You show that you are listening by keeping eye contact or perhaps nodding. There is very little point in trying to listen seriously to a client when you are clearing away the tables or writing a report.

We show respect to clients by listening to them and treating them as individuals. To do this you must find out what is important to the client, how they dress, what their interests are, their religion and ethnic customs. Do not judge other people's actions.

Case study

After some effort, Jack Rudd managed to get himself admitted to the residential home of his choice. However, he became very unhappy after living there for some months.

‘I was really happy when I found that I was to be given a place at Hill Edge Home. It is only half a mile away from my old home and I could keep in touch with my old friends.

253

> The day I was admitted to the home, they said they were short-staffed and I was left waiting around in the TV room. I felt very embarrassed as I knew no one. I also found that I was not allowed to bring in any of my furniture or personal effects.
>
> I was given a room, but when I asked for a key the staff said "What would happen if you became sick in the night?" I did not understand what they meant. I do not like the way I am always accompanied to the bathroom by a member of staff when I am having a bath.
>
> I also have to be in bed at the same time as everyone else – that is 11 o'clock. Breakfast is at eight in the morning, lunch is at noon and evening meal is at five o'clock. I am allowed to make a drink at nine in the evening if I wish. I do not smoke and I did not like watching TV because everyone smoked and it made my eyes and throat sore and my clothes smell.'

Activity 8.11

How would you have organised things to show respect for Jack's individuality and to empower him in this situation?

Did you list any of the following points?
- The staff should have explained what was happening during the admission process.
- Staff should have introduced Jack to other residents in the TV lounge.
- Jack should have been able to bring his personal possessions into the home. These would have made him feel more at ease.
- What Jack wanted at bath time should have been discussed with him.
- If staff had fears for his safety, they should have discussed this with him and a system worked out to the agreement of each person.
- Jack's dignity and self-respect were affected by not having any privacy in his own room.
- A non-smoking client should not have to share the same facilities as smokers.
- Jack does not smoke. He should not have to be subjected to the problems caused by passive smoking.

If we are to show respect for Jack, value his individual identity and respect his choice, all of the above points should have been taken into consideration. Jack lost his dignity and individuality when he was not allowed to do things for himself. Clients, such as Jack, with such personal care needs should to be treated with great respect so that they can maintain their dignity. For example, they should be allowed as much privacy as possible when performing personal tasks such as bathing.

Confidentiality
People have a right to privacy. Confidentiality is of the greatest importance. You have no right to intrude into client's lives.

In your work as a carer you are likely to obtain information about clients. Any information, of whatever nature, **must** remain confidential to you and the appropriate staff. You may wish to use situations you have experienced or observed in your work experience to put in your portfolio. If you do this, you must maintain the confidentiality of the client and the staff of the work placement.

Health and social care organisations need to keep records of patients and clients. These records are kept in personal files or on computer. In most care settings, only certain people will have access to personal information. However, clients may tell you things about themselves or relatives, this information should remain confidential to you. This will help the client maintain trust in you. You must respect the client's right to confidentiality.

If you think that a client has told you something that you should pass on to another member of staff, talk to the client and see if you can get their permission. If you cannot, then in most situations you should not pass on the information. Remember to respect the client's wishes.

The key to the practice of confidentiality is respect for the client. A breach of confidentiality is a breach of trust between the carer and the client.

People now have a right to see their records whether they are held on computer or in manual records.

Activity 8.12

What would you do if a client said to you 'If I tell you something, will you promise not to tell the manager?'

Discuss your decision and your reasons for making it with your class colleagues.

The use of aids to physical care

Main types of ASSISTIVE EQUIPMENT

The use of assistive equipment can help an elderly, dependent person to live as independent a life as possible in their own home. Assistive equipment improves the client's ability to do certain tasks such as feeding, bathing or other personal tasks. It can also make life easier in residential establishments by helping with mobility and feeding and bathing for example.

The range of equipment available to the elderly person either in their own home or in residential care is vast. They range from knives and forks to large and very expensive pieces of equipment, such as hoists or stairlifts. However simple the aid, the purpose is to help the elderly disabled person to move about or carry out daily living tasks as best as they can.

Assistive equipment falls into the following categories:
• personal care support
• hoists and lifting equipment
• eating and drinking aids
• help with dressing and undressing
• mobility aids
• reading and hearing aids.

Personal care support

This includes such aids as rails in bathrooms, showers and toilets, also commodes, bed pans, urinals and waste disposal units.

Using a rubber mat in the bath can prevent the client from slipping. Hand rails allow the client to walk unaided in bathrooms or toilets. The rail also allows the elderly person to lower themselves onto the toilet. Sometimes a raised toilet seat also helps. A bath seat allows the person to swing themselves, on their own, into a bath or shower, thus not stripping them of their dignity or self-respect.

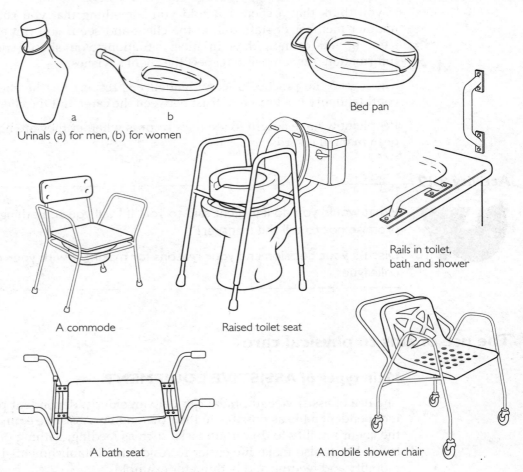

Urinals (a) for men, (b) for women

Bed pan

Rails in toilet, bath and shower

A commode

Raised toilet seat

A bath seat

A mobile shower chair

Examples of items for personal care

Hoists and lifting equipment

Hoists and lifting equipment not only help maintain the independence of the client, but they are also an enormous help to the carers. They make lifting safer and easier. Some hoists are fixed, perhaps beside a person's bed or bath, but most are portable. This means that they can be used in a number of situations in the home with safety. Some are manually operated, but other are electrically operated.

Case study
Mrs Patel is an 86-year-old Hindu lady who has only just been admitted to a residential home. She is the first person from an ethnic group to have been

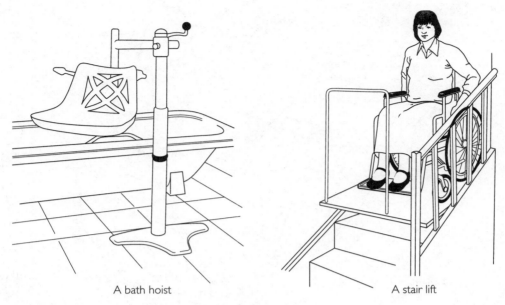

A bath hoist   A stair lift

Examples of a bath hoist and a stair lift (see also page 262)

admitted. She became incontinent and the female care worker took her to the bathroom, removed her clothes and, using the bath hoist, safely lowered her into the bath.

'I felt very embarrassed and hurt when the staff did not ask me if I needed a bath. No one talked to me about my culture or religious beliefs. Hindus prefer to wash with running water. I would have rather had a shower.'

Activity 8.13

Discuss this situation with your class colleagues. What would you have done?

Remember
Discuss with people what they want. Always ask about any religious, cultural or personal preferences.

Eating and drinking aids

To help people feed themselves, there are a number of aids available: cutlery, plates, trays, drinking aids. For example, clients with arthritis of the hand, which may cause poor grip, can have knives and forks with thick handles. Plates with rubber bases are useful for people with the use of only one hand. The rubber base stops the plate from slipping.

Help with dressing and undressing

Older people sometimes have problems with dressing and undressing. They are simple tasks, but can be made difficult by even the simplest disability, such as a broken finger or a muscle strain. Arthritic joints make it difficult to do up

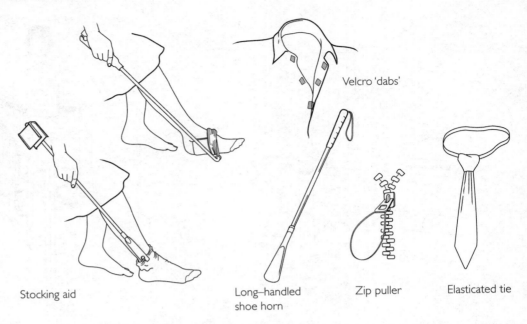

Velcro 'dabs'

Stocking aid

Long–handled
shoe horn

Zip puller

Elasticated tie

Examples of dressing aids

buttons or lift arms above the head. Clients can use Velcro instead of zips or buttons. A number of aids to dressing can be used as illustrated above.

Mobility aids

Getting around the house or residential home can cause problems for many elderly people. Help can be available in the form of a simple walking stick or walking frame.

Wheelchairs can be either electrically or manually propelled.

Buildings can be adapted to help people. For example, kitchen worktops can be lowered to allow wheelchair-bound people use them. Ramps can be installed so that people can get in and out of buildings.

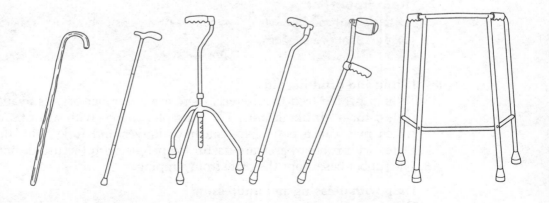

A selection of sticks, crutches and a zimmer frame

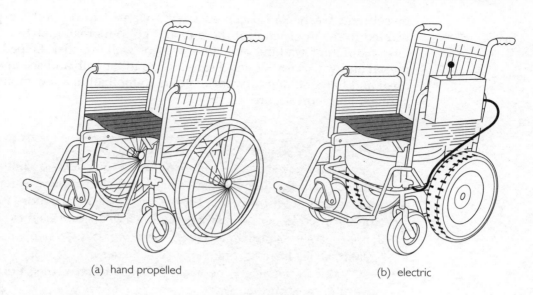

(a) hand propelled   (b) electric

Examples of (a) a hand-propelled wheelchair, and (b) an electrically-propelled wheelchair

Reading and hearing aids

For those elderly people with arthritis of the fingers or wrist, help is available in the form of page turners and writing aids. Those with sight problems can obtain reading glasses or computers which have large letters so that partial-sighted people can read. Talking books and large print books are also available.

Safety and care of assistive equipment

All equipment must be serviced regularly according to the manufacturer's recommendations. Any loose screws, damage or other worries you may have about a piece of equipment should be reported to your supervisor.

Lifts and hoists should only be used according to the instructions. These will indicate where the equipment should be used, in a bathroom or bedroom for example. The instructions will also explain the maximum weight that the equipment will bear. Very heavy weights will need special equipment to move. Lifting a person who is too heavy could either break the equipment or unbalance it causing serious injury to both the carer and client.

Maintaining independence using assistive equipment

'I was a very fit person until I fell down the stairs and broke my hip. I was in bed for some time and now have great difficulty in walking. At first as I was not able to get about to the pub and football, I felt that life was not worth living. I could not enjoy my life or see my friends.

I felt very silly having things done for me – personal things such as washing. I asked the social worker if she could do anything and she said that when I got a bit stronger she would ask the occupational therapist to see me.

The OT talked to me and asked me to do things, like trying to walk, dress myself and wash. We discussed what I wanted to do and I explained that I wanted to see my friends at the pub and go to football matches. She let me try lots of different walking aids. One type of walking stick helped me to steady myself and walk very slowly. I can now go to the pub and see my friends. I feel great and I am looking forward to going to football in a few months when I get stronger and more secure.'

It's a fact
- Over a third of people over 65 live alone and about the same percentage live with their spouses (husbands or wives) who are also elderly.
- As women live longer than men, it is women who are more likely to live alone. About 45 per cent of women live alone, compared to approximately 17 per cent of men. However, it is women who are more likely to suffer from chronic (long-term) illness.
- Nearly one in ten elderly people are unable to leave their homes and walk down the road on their own.
- About the same number cannot manage stairs or steps on their own.
- For those over 85 years, the percentage increases dramatically. Half of people over 85 years of age are unable to walk down the road on their own and about 33 per cent (a third) cannot manage stairs or steps.

Many elderly people have difficulty with self-care, such as cutting toenails, bathing, showering or washing all over, feeding, brushing hair or shaving.

Many of those over retirement age who have mobility problems receive help from various sources with assistive equipment. Where do they get this support from?

What are the main sources of assistive equipment?

There are four main sources from which clients or their families or carers can obtain aids to daily living and adaptations to make it safer and easier in their own homes.

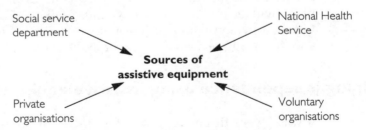

Where can a client get information?
There are centres where people can go to see aids and adaptations and try them out. These centres are provided by:
- some social service departments
- some of the larger chemist chains
- voluntary organisations such as the Spastics Society, Red Cross or Help the Aged.

The DSS also provides a leaflet (reference no. HB 2) which gives information about centres and where people can get help.

Activity 8.14

Find out if your local social services department or any other local organisation provides a service which allows people with disabilities to see aids and try them out.

If such a service exists, make arrangements to visit it.

On a national level, the Disabled Living Foundation (380–384 Harrow Road, London W9 2HU) runs a free information service for clients, their families or carers. They will either give helpful information or refer you to someone who can advise. They also have a permanent exhibition of aids and other equipment which can be tried out.

Social services departments

Since 1948 local authorities have had a responsibility to provide aids to daily living for people living in their own homes.

> **It's a fact**
> A survey carried out in the mid-1960s found that then over 3 000 000 people were disabled and more than half of these were over 65 years of age. Many of those who were very severely handicapped were found to be living alone and most were elderly people.

The increasing demand for support for those with a disability living in the community led to the Chronically Sick and Disabled Persons Act 1971. This stated that local authorities had a duty to find out the number of disabled people living in their area and their needs. The Act also stated that public buildings must have access for disabled people. Televisions and telephones could also be provided by social services departments.

Activity 8.15

Of the 3 000 000 people who were found to be disabled in the mid-1960s, how many were over 65 years of age?

Social services departments now also have the responsibility for providing non-medical aids and equipment to help with everyday life.

Many aids are provided free by the social services department, but in more and more cases there may be a charge. Wheelchairs may be loaned as well as the more personal non-medical aids such as cutlery, eating aids, hoists, commodes and walking aids.

If you ask the local social services department for help, they will usually ask someone such as an occupational therapist to visit and discuss the suitability of the various aids available.

The social services departments can also alter a client's home or put in some specialist equipment which can make life easier for them. They can:

- install hand rails in bathrooms, hallways and stairs
- provide stair lifts
- provide ramps for wheelchair access
- widen doors
- build specially-designed bathrooms or toilets.

Clients usually make a financial contribution towards the costs of alterations or large adaptations.

The National Health Service
- The district nursing service can provide aids to help with home nursing, such as commodes, incontinence pads and bed aids.
- A GP can prescribe a number of medical aids, such as wheelchairs.
- A hospital can also provide aids, such as support collars, callipers, wheelchairs, walking aids, hearing aids and low vision aids.

Voluntary and private organisations
If clients experience difficulty in getting appropriate aids, they can be obtained from either a voluntary organisation or bought from large chemist shops. Some voluntary organisations, such as the Red Cross, provide equipment and aids on short- or long-term loan. They can supply wheelchairs, commodes, bed rests, feeding cups, etc.

Support groups to help elderly people with dependent needs
The voluntary organisations play an important role in the provision of care for elderly, dependent people. They can be very flexible in the services they provide and how they provide them. They are not bound by rules and regulations which hinder statutory services. (See Chapter 3 to remind yourself about statutory organisations.)

Voluntary organisations and self-help groups can be of great help to elderly people, particularly those who are housebound. They can:
- provide information about services available and help people get appropriate support
- provide information about assistive equipment
- visit and provide support.

Age Concern, for example, provides a wide range of services for elderly people:
- visiting service for elderly people offering companionship
- good neighbour scheme, provision of visiting, shopping, gardening and other household tasks
- holidays
- a telephone link – volunteers contact the housebound elderly person at pre-arranged time each day to check they are OK and also to offer support
- day centres
- coffee shops and luncheon clubs
- free transport.

Activity 8.16

Find out what other services are provided by voluntary agencies in your local area.

Self-help groups such as pensioners organisations provide support and representation for elderly people. Other groups such as the Association of Stroke Clubs provide self-help and information to members.

Cross-roads is a voluntary scheme which provides a support system for people in their own homes by offering temporary or regular care relief. This provides support and a rest for the carer by allowing the volunteer to attend to the personal needs of the client.

About six million people are involved in providing voluntary service. The day-to-day work that the volunteers do is varied. They offer an informal system of caring which bridges the gap between the elderly client and the statutory services.

Activity 8.17

a As a group or class, obtain the local directory of Voluntary Care Agencies. Make a list of the organisations which provide services to elderly people living in their own homes.

b Each member of the group should choose one agency and find out as much as they can about its services.

c As a group, bring together all your research to produce a booklet to explain to local elderly people what services these agencies provide.

Test yourself

1 What do you understand by the term 'daily living activities'?

2 List four degenerative diseases and describe them.

3 List eight services which are available to elderly dependent clients.

4 What rules apply when lifting a client?

5 List six ways that you can empower clients.

6 What do you understand by the term 'body language'?

7 What does the term 'confidentiality' mean?

8 Where can clients go to ask for assistive equipment?

9 What services may be provided by voluntary organisations?

10 What is the Cross-roads scheme?

Assignment A8.1
The provision of physical assistance

In this assignment, you will be expected to investigate and identify physical assistance for two elderly clients. You will need to indicate the physical assistance needed with daily living activities and safe lifting techniques, remembering that at all times you must maintain the client's independence and dignity.

Your tasks

1 a List the three ways of identifying whether someone needs physical assistance.

b Give three examples of each of the three methods.

Case study: Mrs Delaney

'I worked in a shop since my 14th birthday. It was a wonderful feeling working. I can remember how proud I felt. I have already tried to keep active and work. I don't understand the young ones today who don't want to work and lie about all day. I think doing things is important, it helps to keep your mind active. I used to read a lot and go out three evenings a week to see my friends at the local club. I liked playing cards.

A few years ago, after my retirement, I got arthritis in my hands and pains in my legs. I began to have great difficulty in putting on my stockings and shoes and also doing up my buttons. I get very angry with myself. I feel that people should be able to do things for themselves. I do have a friend who helps me dress in the mornings and also cuts my food up although I still have difficulty getting it off the plate because it slips about the table or tray. I feel embarrassed at having to get someone to adjust my clothes when I want to go to the bathroom. I feel like a baby.'

2 Read the case study about Mrs Delaney.

   a Describe the difficulties that you think that Mrs Delaney has with her mobility.

   b List and describe the assistive equipment which she could obtain to help her with her daily living activities. Be sure you describe assistive equipment which might help her with feeding and dressing. Make drawings of the aids.

3 a Describe how Mrs Delaney is feeling as a result of her loss of mobility. Why you think she is feeling so? Remember that she has always been a very independent person.

   b What situations might be contributing to Mrs Dalaney's loss of dignity, and why?

   c What steps would you take to restore Mrs Delaney's dignity?

Case study: Mr Jackson

❝I live by myself and have done so for a number of years. My home is a usual two-storey, three-bedroom semi with living room, dining room and kitchen on the ground floor. The bathroom and toilet is on the first floor.

I had a serious car accident some months ago. As a result of my injuries I must live in a wheelchair for the rest of my life. As soon as my home has been adapted to my new needs, I can leave hospital and go home.❞

4 Read the case study about Mr Jackson.

   a List the statutory, voluntary and private agencies that might be involved in supporting Mr Jackson in his own home.

   b Describe the services each agency might offer.

5 a List the adaptations which it might be necessary to carry out to Mr Jackson's house to allow him to live an independent life.

   b Describe the assistive equipment which Mr Jackson will need to be able to perform daily personal tasks.

6 a Describe the procedures you should carry out before lifting a load.

   b List the special difficulties that might arise when lifting people.

   c What equipment would you use to lift Mr Jackson?

Assignment A8.2
The use of aids to physical care

In this assignment you will be asked to describe:
- how items of assistive equipment can meet client needs
- how each piece of equipment is operated
- the health and safety factors involved and the constraints on each piece of equipment.

Your tasks

1 **a** What needs would a wheelchair meet for a client with severe mobility problems?

   b What needs would a mobile hoist meet for a client who has severe mobility problems?

2 Visit your local assistive equipment centre or talk to an occupational therapist or visit a client who uses any of the two pieces of equipment named in Task 1. Find out how each of the two pieces of equipment is operated. Make notes of what you have found out.

3 Find out what health and safety factors you should apply to each piece of equipment. Write them down.

4 Find out what limitations there are to the use of each piece of equipment. Write down what they are.

Assignment A8.3
Maintaining independence

In this assignment, you will be expected to investigate two clients needing different pieces of equipment. You will need to:
- describe the main source of equipment
- describe the support networks available to each client
- discuss how the equipment helps the clients maintain independence.

Your tasks

Case study: Mrs White
❝I have been having difficulty with my hearing for the past few years. I have been using a hearing aid for some time now.**❞**

1 Find out what types of hearing aids are at present available from the statutory and private sectors.

2 **a** Mrs White has difficulty with her hearing. What support groups are available to help her?

b List the groups and the services they provide.

3 Explain how the use of a hearing aid helps Mrs White retain her independence.

> **Case study: Mr Jones**
> Mr Jones has been having difficulties with arthritis of the knee joints. He uses a zimmer frame to move about the house and a stocking gutter to put on his socks.

4 Find out what types of aid to help with walking are at present available from the statutory and private sectors.

5 **a** What support groups are available to help Mr Jones?

b List the groups and the services they provide.

6 Explain how the use of a walking aid helps Mr Jones retain his independence.

Key words

After reading this chapter you should be able to understand the following words and phrases. If you do not, go back through the chapter and find out, or look them up in the Glossary.

Daily living activities

Degenerative disease

Day centre

Moving and handling techniques

Empower

Body language

Confidentiality

Assistive equipment

CHAPTER 9

Investigating Health and Social Care Provision

What is covered in this chapter

- The organisation of health and social care services
- Access to health and social care services
- Communicating information in health and social care

These are the resources that you will need for your Health and Social Care Provision portfolio:
- leaflets you have collected about local services
- copies of patient's charters
- your written answers to the activities in this chapter
- your written answers to the Test Yourself questions at the end of this chapter
- your completed assignments: A9.1, A9.2, A9.3.

Introduction

This book has been about the health and social care services. But we have not yet discussed the services and their different roles in detail. It is important to recognise the four aspects of health and social care:
- nationally organised health care
- locally organised health care
- nationally organised social care
- locally organised social care.

Clearly, although they work together in many ways, the health services and social services are very different. It is also important to realise that the services can have both a local and national focus.

The organisation of the health and social care services

The 1990s will have seen one of the biggest changes in the organisation of the health and social care services. To understand what is happening, it is important to know something of the history and historical structure of these services. For this we can break the discussion into four sections:
- the NATIONAL HEALTH SERVICE (NHS)
- the local authority SOCIAL SERVICES
- the VOLUNTARY SECTOR services
- the PRIVATE SECTOR health and social care services.

The National Health Service and the social services (together with the Probation Service) form the **statutory** sector of the health and social care services. They are so-called because they were set up by Acts of Parliament and are funded by public money.

The diagram on page 270 shows the network through which these services are

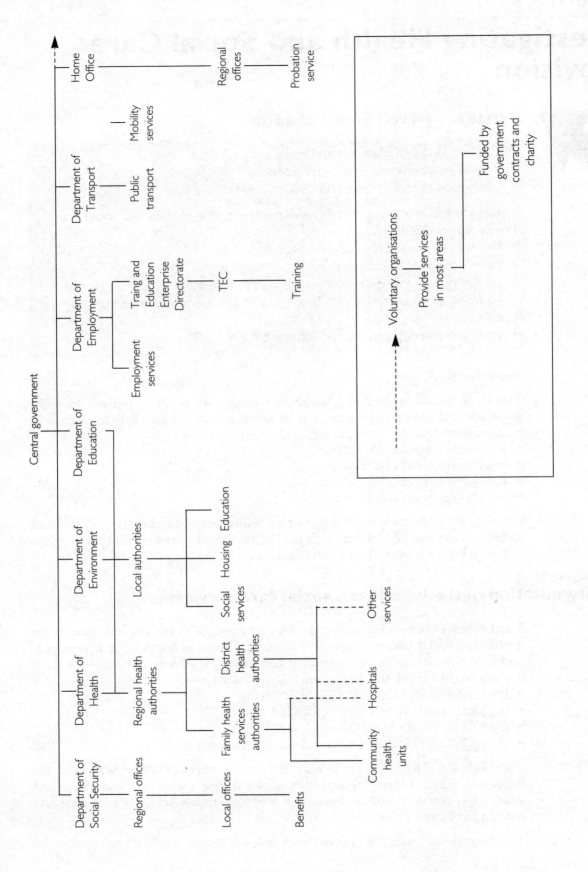

The organisations involved in health and social care

controlled in England and Wales. You will see that many government departments have an influence on health and social care.

The National Health Service

The structure of the health services is based around the National Health Service (NHS) which was formed in 1948 by the National Health Service Act. The Act brought the health services, and in particular the hospitals, under the control of the Ministry of Health.

Before the Act, most of the hospitals had been controlled by charities or voluntary organisations. The idea behind the setting up of the NHS was to provide health care for all that did not involve charging patients directly. The money was to come from:

- general taxation
- national insurance contributions
- charges made to private patients.

It was thought that there was a fixed amount of illness in the community. The introduction of the health service was expected to reduce the amount of illness and so reduce the costs. The reality has been that health care costs have increased and so the expected savings have not happened.

The organisation of the NHS has changed over the years until the current structure (shown in the diagram below) was established. This structure has developed since the 1990 NHS and Community Care Act began to be implemented.

The diagram below shows the basic structure in England and Wales. There is, however, a distinctly regional flavour to the structure of the health services:

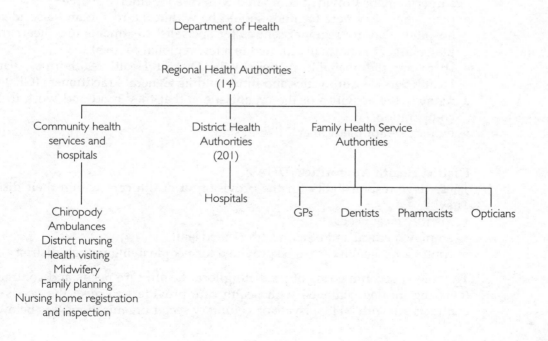

The current structure of the NHS

- In **England** there are eight Regional Health Authorities which are responsible for the District Health Authorities and Family Health Service Authorities in their region. We will describe these in more detail later (page 273).
- **Wales** is rather like England except that the whole of the country can be considered as one regional health authority run by the Welsh Office. Within Wales there are nine District Health Authorities.
- **Northern Ireland** has four Health and Social Services Boards that provide both health and personal social services.
- **Scotland** is like Wales. The whole of Scotland is organised like a regional health authority run by the Scottish Office. Within Scotland there are 15 Health Boards that combine the roles of District Health Authorities and Family Health Service Authorities.

Activity 9.1

a   Find out the name and address for the Regional Health Authority that is responsible for your local area.

b   What is the name and address of your District Health Authority?

(If you live in Northern Ireland find similar information for your Health and Social Services Board.)

Regional Health Authorities (RHAs)

These authorities are responsible for regional planning and sharing out resources. They:
- identify the regional needs and priorities, such as how much specialist surgery will be provided compared with care for elderly people
- plan where any new facilities should be within the region and also identify hospitals that are regional centres for specialist treatments (e.g. heart transplant surgery is normally located in a few regional centres)
- share out the available money to the District Health Authorities, Family Health Service Authorities and fund-holding General Practitioners (GPs)
- monitor the activities of the organisations that they fund and work to help co-operation
- employ senior medical and dental staff.

District Health Authorities (DHAs)

These have responsibility for the provision of health care within their district. They:
- identify local needs
- employ medical and other health-related staff
- contract for health care to be provided for people living in their district.

The role is becoming one of predicting local health care needs and contracting (entering into agreements) with health care providers to meet the needs. The contracts are with NHS, private or voluntary sector organisations (see below).

Family Health Service Authorities (FHSAs)

These are responsible for the provision of **primary care services**. These are the services provided by:

- general practitioners (GPs). There are over 31 000 in the UK.
- dentists – many now work exclusively in the private sector and are not funded by the FHSAs
- opticians – who test eyesight and prescribe lenses to correct vision defects
- pharmacists – who are responsible for providing medicines prescribed by doctors.

NHS TRUSTS

A careful study of the diagram on page 271 will show that there are also NHS trusts involved in care delivery. The NHS and Community Care Act made it possible for units (individual hospitals, community health services or services such as the ambulance service) to opt for trust status.

Trusts have responsibility for managing their own money. They employ their own staff. They compete for the contracts to provide health care alongside private and voluntary sector providers (see pages 274–6). It is expected that this competition for money will increase the value-for-money of the health care provided.

Purchasers and providers

These terms were introduced by the 1990 NHS and Community Care Act. You will often come across them in relation to health and social care. Their meanings are quite clear: a **purchaser** buys (or purchases) health or social care from a **provider** of that care.

In the health services, when a purchasing organisation (an RHA, DHA, FSHAs and fund-holding GP) identifies a need for care, any care-providing organisation (NHS, voluntary or private) can bid to provide that care. The organisation that wins the bid enters into a **contract** with the purchaser – that is, an agreement to provide the care. The purchaser has to try to get the best care possible for the money available.

So NHS patients, for example, may receive treatment in private establishments. A person needing an operation may be sent to a private hospital and the bill will be paid by the NHS. This would be because the private hospital had won the contract to provide the operation. The patient would still be receiving care from the NHS, but the care would be provided by a non-NHS organisation.

This purchaser and provider system also exists in social care.

Social services

The origins of the social services are not as clearly defined as those of the NHS. Laws relating to social service-type provision go back to the nineteenth century. In fact, some of the organisations are still controlled by laws that were introduced in the early part of this century.

The organisation of local authority social services has changed several times. The latest changes have come about as a result of the NHS and Community

> ### The setting up of the social services
> 1968   Social work departments established in Scotland and the Probation Service incorporated into them.
> 1970   Local Authority Social Services Act set up local authority social services departments in England and Wales.
> 1972   Health and Personal Social Services (NI) Order established the four Health and Social Services Boards in Northern Ireland (see page 272).
>
> The aim was to form an effective, family-oriented, community-based service that was available to all who needed it.

Care Act. As with the health services (see above), this Act established a division between:

- the parts of the social services that **purchased** the care needed
- the parts that **provided** the care.

The purchaser half could contract with the private and voluntary sectors as well as their own 'provider' half. The different roles will be further explained when you look in more detail at local provision.

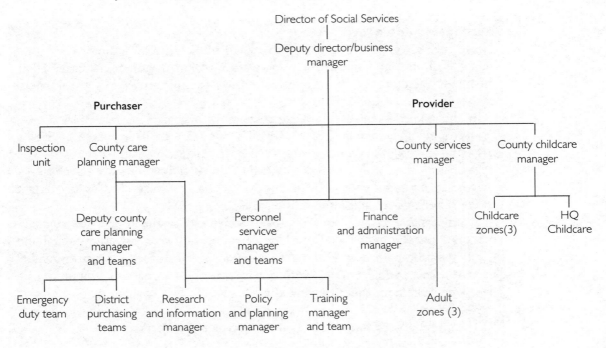

The structure of a typical social services department in England and Wales

The voluntary sector

The term 'voluntary sector' refers to all non-statutory organisations which contribute to social care. That is, the majority are not set up by government and many are charities.

The formation of the charitable organisations in the nineteenth century was the start of social care and social work in an organised way. Many charities act as a focus for fund-raising to provide for people with specific needs. The funds are then used to purchase the equipment or care required. Others, such as Anchor, provide specific residential or sheltered accommodation for older people around the country.

The traditional image of charities is of well-meaning amateurs. This image is no longer true. While some charities work with unpaid volunteers, most are staffed almost totally by salaried staff. The term 'voluntary' refers to the status of the organisation and not to the status of the workers.

The NSPCC

One example of voluntary sector organisation is the National Society for the Prevention of Cruelty to Children (NSPCC). It has the authority to take legal action on behalf of a child and has access to records such as the register of children at risk.

To carry out its work, it employs qualified social workers and works closely with the social services departments and the police. A child may be referred to the NSPCC who investigate the case and work with the family. If there is a need for the child to be taken into care, the case may be taken to court by the NSPCC or passed over to the local authority social services.

The emphasis of the organisation is working with families and seeking to prevent their break up.

Organisations within the voluntary sector can be very large, like the NSPCC, or very small local groups that are dealing with a specific need. Voluntary sector organisations work alongside the statutory sector providing care. They are one of the provider groups that can be contracted to provide care. This means that the organisation can be paid by the NHS or the local authority to provide the care. Clearly to do this the organisations need to be run as efficient businesses.

The Council for Voluntary Services

The voluntary sector is co-ordinated by the Council for Voluntary Services (CVS). It brings together the broad range of organisations and provides a focus for discussion with government (and the European Union).

While the CVS is nationally-based, it has local offices throughout the country. It brings together the various voluntary organisations to attempt to reduce the duplication of provision. It also acts as a pressure group for the member organisations. The local CVS often speaks for the voluntary sector when working with the local authority. On a national level, the CVS speaks to the government.

Activity 9.2

Find out if you have a local office of the CVS.

Try to arrange for someone from the CVS to talk to your group about voluntary sector organisations in your area.

The private sector

There are many organisations involved in health and social care that charge for their services with the intention of making money. These organisations are part of the private sector. The private sector provides services from complete hospitals and residential homes to individuals working as private nurses, physiotherapists or care assistants.

Private organisations may bid to provide care, such as residential care for elderly people. The local authority can purchase places in a home for those people in need of the care. In this case the person needing care is often required to pay part of some of the fees.

Private health care

When the NHS was formed in 1948, many health professionals in particular doctors, were unhappy at the thought of giving up their private practices. They wanted to retain their freedom to charge for services outside the NHS. It was agreed that doctors would be allowed to work both within the NHS and in private practice.

Private health care is available:
- within NHS-owned institutions, with the patient paying for the services
- within totally separate private health care facilities.

Services provided by health and social care services

Again we need to look at the health and social care sectors separately:
- community-based health care services
- hospital-based health care services
- residential social care services
- community-based social care services

Community-based health care services

Doctors' surgeries

The focus of health care within the community is the General Practitioner (GP) or family doctor. GPs are qualified doctors who have undergone further training. Everyone permanently resident or working in the UK may be registered with a GP. They may select their own GP when they are over 16 years old from the list of GPs kept by the Family Health Service Authority.

The first port of call for most people requiring health care is the doctor's surgery. As an individual, the GP provides limited care. He or she:
- diagnoses what is wrong with an individual.
- prescribes treatment, wherever possible, such as medicines which are then obtained from a pharmacist.

GPs are specialists in general diagnosis. They have a good knowledge of a broad range of types of ill-health. When they do not have the facilities or skills to diagnose or treat a patient, they refer the patient to a specialist doctor based in a hospital.

Some doctors' surgeries dispense the medicines that the doctors prescribe. This usually occurs in areas where it is difficult for patients to get to a pharmacist, such as in rural or remote areas.

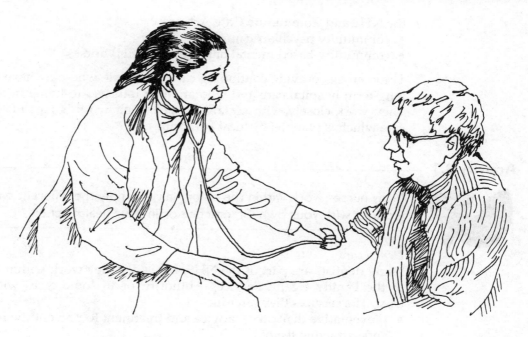

It is now common for a group of GPs to work together. Each of the doctors will have the general diagnostic skills, but each will also have a specialist interest or skill to contribute to the practice. The move towards group practices started in the 1960s. It is now very common for a practice to be based in a health centre.

Health centres
In a health centre you will find:
- GPs
- receptionists, a practice manager and clerical staff
- a practice nurse
- services provided by the Community Health Unit, such as:
  - midwives, who work with pregnant women, assist the mother to give birth and support the mother and child in the following few weeks
  - health visitors, who take over the support of children from midwives. They have a responsibility until the child is five.
  - community nurses (formerly district nurses), who work with people recovering from illness who require health support in their homes. They may be involved in changing dressings on wounds or monitoring recovery from illness.

There may also be other services, such as:
- the school nursing service
- speech therapists
- occupational therapists
- physiotherapists
- dentists.

Those staff who not employed by the GPs in a particular health centre provide support for the whole community and work with all GPs in the area. They also work in co-operation with hospitals. The services they provide are part of the **Community Health Service**. This is often an NHS trust.

Also based in the community, and developing a more important role following

the NHS and Community Care Act, are:
- community psychiatric nurses
- community-based mental handicap (RNMH) nurses.

These nurses provide continuing care for people who may have been receiving long-term hospital care and who are now returned to living in the community. They work closely with social workers. Their work is part of the community care which is planned by local authorities.

Activity 9.3

Many nurses work within the community. Identify the different types of nurse working with your own GP practice or in your health centre.

Dental care

Many dentists are part of the NHS. Like GPs, they work within the framework of the Family Health Services Authority, or in some cases within a hospital trust. The services they offer include:
- preventative dentistry – advice and treatment to prevent the need for fillings and extracting teeth
- dental treatment – including fillings and extractions
- remedial treatment – including corrective work to ensure teeth grow in appropriate positions and the provision of crowns.

A large part of a NHS dentist's income is in the form of payment for treatment. In recent years, people have been taking better care of their teeth and payments have been reduced. So, in some cases, dentists have moved outside the NHS and work in the private sector. By working in the private sector, dentists can maintain their income by undertaking preventative and remedial work that is poorly funded by the NHS.

Some dentists work within the Schools' Dental Service. This service provides for the tooth checks and treatment for school children, although many children visit their own dentist.

There are some dentists who work in hospitals. These may be dental hospitals where dental students also learn their skills. Dentists also work alongside doctors in providing dental treatment for people with facial injuries that have occurred as a result of an accident or because of illness and bone decay.

Hospital-based health care services

Hospitals are traditionally seen as places where people, who are too ill to be cared for at home, are taken for treatment. They are also the places where people go for operations or for help from a specialist on an out-patient basis. They are staffed by specialist doctors who each concentrate on a small area of medicine.

Patients are normally referred to a specialist by their GP who provides details of the initial diagnosis. Most people are seen first as an out-patient following referral. This means that they attend hospital at an appointed time, when the specialist reviews the situation, attempts a diagnosis and plans a course of action. This can involve:
- referral for further specialist information (such as an X-ray)
- admission to hospital for treatment

- treatment at home
- planned admission and treatment on a day basis (day care).

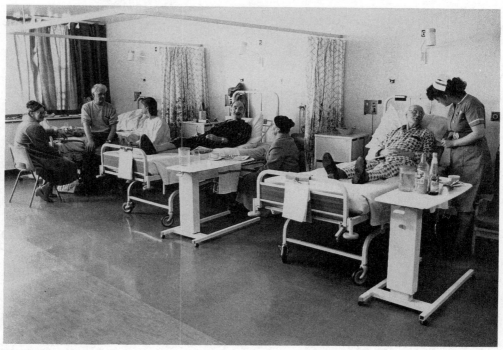

A hospital ward

Hospitals have a range of specialist equipment and staff. These help to diagnose and treat patients' illnesses. The staff involved include:

- **Nurses** The main role of nurses is to carry out the care plan that has been developed by the doctors. Within nursing there are several specialisms: nursing sick children, mental health and mental disability.
- **Health care assistants** These people work closely with nurses in delivering practical care.
- **Radiographers** have two important roles:
  – they use X-rays and ultrasound to produce pictures of internal structures
  – they use X-rays in the treatment of, for example, some cancers.
- **Physiotherapists** help people to improve their ability to move, often helping a patient to develop full movement after breaking a bone. They are also assist with breathing and treatment routines to help people with cystic fibrosis to clear their lungs.
- **Occupational therapists** (OTs) work to treat illness, both mental and physical, with activity. They work on a one-to-one basis, with groups and with recreational activities. Many OTs work in the community.
- **Speech therapists** work with people with speech disorders. These range from children with delayed speech development to older people recovering from strokes. Speech therapists work throughout the health service, often going into schools.

Residential social care

There are times when people are unable to be cared for in their own homes. These people may include:

- elders

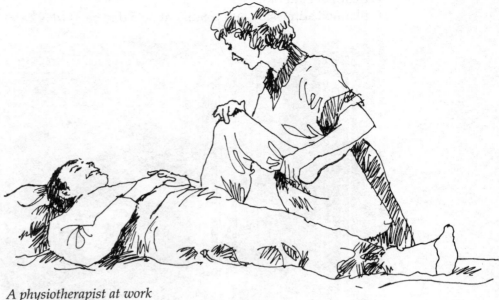

A physiotherapist at work

- children
- people with disabilities.

Residential care for elders

The largest group of people requiring residential care are elders. The reasons for entering residential care vary:

- They may be unable to care for themselves.
- They may simply wish to live with other people while still maintaining their independence.
- They may be recovering from an illness.
- It may be to give their families or carers a break.

Because the needs of people vary, the types of residential care also vary. Residential care includes:

- **Nursing homes** which provide care for people needing the support and skills of a nurse. These people may be recovering from illness or in need of regular nursing treatment.
- **Residential homes** which provide all the necessities for daily living. People in residential homes can be almost self-supporting or need support for almost all activities.
- **Sheltered accommodation** is a form of residential care where individuals take a lot of responsibility for themselves, and may be almost totally independent. What it does provide is the support of other people and, in particular, the support of the organisation providing the accommodation. There may be a warden or wardens who live on site. Food, cleaning and laundry services may be provided depending upon the type of sheltered accommodation.

Residential care for children

At one time many children who were not being looked after by their parents were cared for in children's homes. These varied in size, but they all provided for the needs of children and were staffed by resident and non-resident workers.

Many local authorities have moved away from children's homes and now place children in **foster care**. In this situation, a child or children lives with foster parent(s) as part of their family. The foster care can be for a short time, such as when a natural parent is in hospital. It can also be longer term when the child's own family structure has broken down because of abuse, for example.

In some cases the care offered for children may need to be one in which they become a permanent part of a new family. This process is called **adoption**. Many people think of adoption as involving young babies who are not wanted by their parents. In fact, most adoptions are of older children. More adoptions now also involve maintaining strong links with the natural family. As such, adoption is a form of residential care that gives children a stability while not denying their links with their families.

Residential care for people with disabilities

There are many people who need specific support because of a disability. This includes people with both mental and physical disabilities.

The purpose of the residential care is to provide the support necessary to enable the individuals to become as independent of the help as possible. For example, many people who are registered blind spend some time in residential care. There they learn the skills necessary to live safely and with confidence in a society of mostly sighted people.

For some people the disability may be so great that they would find it difficult to cope outside their residential care. Their care is planned to enable them to be as independent as possible. In some instances, the residential care may be in a therapeutic community. In these communities, individuals are supported and enabled to fulfil their full potential.

In the past, people who were termed 'mentally handicapped' or 'mentally subnormal' were placed in 'mental hospitals'. These terms are no longer used and the hospitals are closing down. The residents are, in many cases, moving into community-based care and sheltered accommodation. This is a recognition of their rights to be treated as members of society and not shut away from it.

Community-based social care

The aim of a lot of social care is to support a person living in their own home. The range of support is vast. It includes:

- Home visits by a social worker to support a child and family in conflict. This may prevent the later need for the child to move into foster care.
- Domiciliary support for people unable to do everything for themselves. This includes 'home help' support for elderly people which involves housework and shopping. But most important of all, it provides regular company and conversation.
- Day care. Many people who can be supported at home benefit from the opportunity of being with others by regularly attending a day-care centre. The day care may be to provide the home-based carer with time to themselves. It may enable the home-based carer to go to work. Day nurseries and child-minders are included in this.
- Sheltered workshops provide a halfway stage for some people with disabilities. They provide an opportunity to learn and develop skills. These may be the skills of daily living or they may be skills associated with employment. Employment in sheltered workshops provides both an income and builds self-confidence in the people working there.

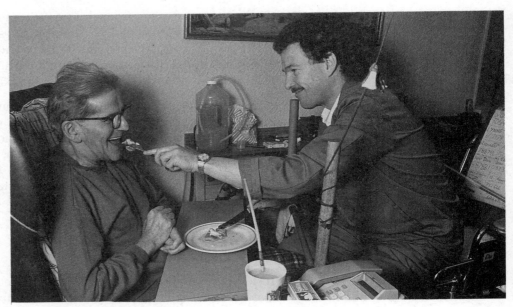

A home carer with a client

Voluntary groups and support groups

This covers a range of organisations from major voluntary sector organisations, such as the WRVS, to neighbourhood groups that are formed to support an individual in need of care. Support groups can also be for people who have had a specific crisis, such as victim support groups and rape crisis centres.

The case study on page 283 gives an example of a small support group forming to meet a specific need. It is often the case that a group of people, or even an individual, identifies a care need and does something about it. From this small development, many national voluntary organisations have been formed. For example, Oxfam started in 1942 as the Oxford Committee for Famine Relief with the aim of helping hungry civilians in Nazi-occupied Greece. It is now the UK's largest overseas development agency.

So far we have discussed health and social care provision on a national scale. It is important to know what is available in your local area. Assignment A9.1 on page 295 will help you to do this.

> **Case study**
>
> James had suffered a serious injury and was having to relearn how to move about. Part of his therapy involved being encouraged to move his legs. To do this required one person to work with him for half an hour at a time.
>
> James's parents were able to do this, but they were worried that they would have to give up work and that their other children would suffer. People from the local community heard about the problem and arranged a rota of volunteers to come in each day to work with James.
>
> To make sure that they knew what was necessary, the physiotherapist working with James arranged for all the volunteers to be trained to give the specific support James needed. As a result, James received the therapy necessary. The stress on his family was reduced and, as James improved, his family life could return to normal.

The WRVS is a voluntary organisation that provides a vast range of services, including working in hospitals and prisons, and working with families and elderly people

Who pays for health and social care?

Care is not free. Even when it is a friend or unpaid volunteer providing the care, they are paying with their time.

Paying for health care

In the UK much of the statutory health care is not charged for at the point of delivery (that is, when it is delivered). It is paid for through general taxation and National Insurance contributions.

However, not all services are free at the point of delivery. There are some services for which a client still has to pay all or part of the costs. The payments may be affected by the clients's age or ability to pay. If you are under eighteen, for example, you may not have had to pay yet. Generally people over the national retirement age do not have to pay for basic services.

Common NHS services that require contributions to the costs from the clients include:
- prescriptions for medicines
- prescriptions for appliances, such as surgical corsets
- dental checks
- dental treatment
- eyesight tests
- glasses and contact lenses
- transport to and from hospital (in some cases)
- the costs of transport and treatment following a road accident*
- some medical checks and vaccinations for business purposes.

* The Road Traffic Act makes the vehicle owner responsible for the costs. Car insurance normally covers this.

Paying for social care
Local authority social care often requires some payment to be made. Generally payment levels are assessed on the basis of income. Here age is not a factor and so elders with savings are not exempt from the payments.

Social care services that normally require some contribution from the client include:
- day nurseries
- residential care (although not for children)
- day care
- domiciliary care (home helps).

Paying for care in the private sector
Private sector care requires payment. This payment can be:
- by the client
- by an insurance company
- by the statutory services (where the care has been purchased by the statutory sector)

Private sector health care is often paid for by insurance companies where the client pays regular contributions to the company to insure against treatment costs.

Residential and nursing homes
As we have already mentioned, there are very many residential and nursing homes in the private sector. Until recently, the fees for residents who could not pay for their care were often met by the Department of Social Security (DSS). However, the increasing number of people requiring residential care means that the money available does not meet the needs. People are now being advised to take out insurance to pay for residential care. This is because it is unlikely that the statutory sector will be able to provide sufficient care for those who cannot pay in the future.

Access to health and care services

It is easy to describe the different services but, in order to use them, people need know about them and also make contact with them. In this section we will help you to understand how people can be referred to different care services. But first, it is important to recognise that people have different requirements for care. Individuals may have different requirements from the same care service. Needs include:

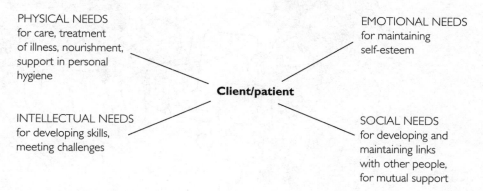

PHYSICAL NEEDS
for care, treatment
of illness, nourishment,
support in personal
hygiene

EMOTIONAL NEEDS
for maintaining
self-esteem

Client/patient

INTELLECTUAL NEEDS
for developing skills,
meeting challenges

SOCIAL NEEDS
for developing and
maintaining links
with other people,
for mutual support

All four areas affect both physical and psychological health. It is essential that any care planned meets the individual's needs.

How do we gain access to services?

It is important to look at how people can make use of the services offered. There are three ways that a person can be referred to the care services. These are:
- SELF-REFERRAL – where people seek help themselves. This may involve support from family members.
- REFERRAL THROUGH A PROFESSIONAL – in this case a doctor, social worker, nurse, teacher or other professional may assist the person to request care.
- COMPULSORY REFERRAL.

Self-referral
This is often the first route for most people receiving health and social care. Within the health service, this may be by simply turning up at the GP's or dentist's surgery. Within social care, referral may be to an area office, or direct to a care facility, such as a day-care centre or a nursery.

In all cases, the person requiring care (or a friend or relative) makes the first contact. For example, a mother of a child would enquire about a place in a day nursery.

Referral through a professional
Planned access to hospital care is usually by referral a GP. Where a GP suspects ill-health that requires specialist treatment, the patient is referred to an out-patient clinic or, in more urgent cases, direct admission to a ward may be arranged.

In social care, an example of referral by professionals would be when a teacher in a school suspects child abuse and refers the case to the duty social worker in

the social services department. Under the 1989 Children Act, all schools should have a named person who makes this type of referral. Another example would be when the police have given a 'warning' to a child who has committed an offence and they feel he or she should be referred to social services.

Activity 9.4

As a group, discuss different scenarios that might lead to people seeking care. Identify the people who might assist them.

Compulsory referral

There are some cases where a person can be compulsorily referred into care. This may involve either a doctor or a social worker who identifies a person unable to make a decision for themselves. This may be because the person is too young, or unable to make a decision because of mental ill-health

Activity 9.5

Read the case study opposite.

a What type of referral was John's referral to the doctor?

b What type of referral was John's referral to hospital?

c What type of referral was Alice's to residential care?

d From the local services identify where John and Alice might have received their care.

Case study

Alice had been a teacher. Soon after she retired, her family noticed that her behaviour had altered. She was forgetting things that had just happened. She was able to talk about her teaching as if it was still happening. Her GP noticed a little increase in her confusion, but he always asked basic questions requiring only yes or no answers.

Eventually Alice became so confused that her husband, John, was becoming very concerned. He spent a lot of time looking after her and could not easily approach social services in the nearest town which was seven miles away.

The situation changed when John developed a chest infection. The doctor wanted to refer John to hospital but was surprised when he was asked, 'Who will look after Alice?' This was the first time that the GP had realised that Alice was becoming seriously ill with Alzheimer's disease.

The doctor contacted the hospital to arrange for John to be admitted. At the same time, he contacted social services to arrange for Alice to move temporarily into residential care.

e   What voluntary organisation might have provided John with specific help because Alice had Alzheimer's disease?

f   Where in your locality would he have contacted the voluntary organisation?

What stops people from receiving care?

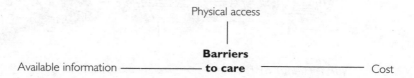

Available information

The first barrier to receiving care is lack of knowledge. If you do not know what is available or how to ask for support, your chances of meeting your needs are low.

To ensure that people know what is available, the health and social services provide publicity about what they do. This is available in a wide variety of places that are regularly visited by the public, including:
- health centres
- doctor's surgeries
- libraries
- colleges and schools
- Citizens Advice Bureaux
- post offices
- council information offices
- Thomson directories, *Yellow Pages* and the *Phone Book*.

Not all sources contain all the information, but most can guide people as to where more information is available.

For more about communicating information about health and social care services, see pages 290–4.

Physical access

Have you ever considered why new buildings are allowed to have steps up to the main entrance? A major difficulty of gaining access to buildings can be the steps at the front door. If all new buildings had to have ramps instead of steps then the access problem would be solved!

Caring services are aware of the difficulties that people have in walking into buildings. It is not only people with physical disabilities that have problems. Parents with children in prams or buggies can also find physical access difficult.

Worries about theft or loss can provide barriers to access

Cost

There are two aspects to this:

- If the client has to pay for care, can he or she afford it?
- Do the services have enough money to provide the care needed by everyone?

Can the client afford the care?

Where a service has to be paid for by a client, there are often times when the cost is difficult to meet. For people who receive social security benefits, there may be no charges. People with low wages may find the costs too great.

Activity 9.6 ——————————————————————————————————————

Read the case study opposite. We do not expect you to solve Tom's problems. In your group, discuss how you might feel in Tom's position. Suggest who Tom might go to for advice in your local area.

Case study

Tom is a pensioner. He and his wife have, until now, been able to live at home quite comfortably on the money from their two pensions. His wife's pension is much higher than his.

However, Tom's wife has recently had a stroke and become paralysed down her left side. After she left hospital, Tom tried to look after her at home but found it very difficult. Eventually he decided that he needed to consider residential care for her.

When Tom asked about the care, he found out that for his wife to go into a nearby nursing home they would have to pay part of the cost. If they did this, then Tom would not have enough money to pay all the household bills and provide for himself. He has a problem. He cannot look after his wife. He cannot afford for her to go into the local nursing home.

Sometimes the cost of prescriptions has to be balanced against other things

Has the service enough money to provide all the care needed?

When the NHS was established it was thought that health would improve and the costs of the service would drop. They didn't. There is always a demand for caring services that cannot be met immediately. There are also problems about deciding who is first in the queue for the available money.

There are more older people in the UK than ever before. The number of people who pay national insurance and income tax is not going to be sufficient to pay for all the services that are needed. The people who manage the caring services have to make decisions about the amount of care available. They also have to decide which care is most important.

When the decisions are made there are bound to be some people who do not get the care they need.

Activity 9.7

Imagine that your group has to make a decision about care funding. You have enough money for just one of the following:
- an incubator that will help to keep premature babies alive
- a kidney transplant that will keep a teenager alive
- physiotherapy to help five accident victims walk and work normally again.

In your group, think about the things that the manager might take into consideration. Is it easy to choose how to spend the money?

The problem of funding care is recognised by the NHS and Community Care Act. The Act states that people can expect to have their care needs assessed but that they have no right for the needs to be met. For example, a person may have been assessed as needing a home help every day, but may be offered help on just two days a week.

Communicating information in health and social care

You have already looked at where information about your local health and social care services is available. It may be in:
- health centres
- doctor's surgeries
- libraries
- colleges and schools
- Citizens Advice Bureaux
- post offices
- council information offices
- Thomson directories, *Yellow Pages* and the *Phone Book*.

In general this information will be in the form of printed leaflets, possibly illustrated with diagrams to make them look more interesting. Their aim is to tell you about the services available. Other information about health and social care frequently appears in newspapers. For example, there are annual reports of how different services are meeting charter standards (see below).

There are two other major sources of information about services. These are:
- the people who work in a particular service
- people who have already used a particular service.

It is often the first source of information that is the most difficult to find. But once a client has gained access to care, he or she has access to a network of information about caring services. The first source can very often be someone who has already received care or the carers themselves. When a person makes use of a health or care service, the people delivering the care are able to pass on information about other services available.

Charters

Since 1990 caring organisations have produced charters, such as the Patient's Charter, to explain the standards of service that a client can expect. The individual services also publish figures to show how well they are meeting the

charter standards. The statistics can be used by clients and care professionals to help them to choose which organisation to use.

Activity 9.8

Dr John Smith is a GP who is trying to work out where to refer one of his patients. There are two local NHS trust hospitals. He has the following information from each:

Hospital A

Waiting time for an appointment	= 8 weeks
Proportion of patients treated within 6 months	= 85%
Average length of stay in hospital	= 5 days
Daily cost of patient care	= £220

Hospital B

Waiting time for an appointment	= 50 days
Proportion of patients treated within 6 months	= 1 in 10
Average length of stay in hospital	= 4 days
Daily cost of patient care	= £250

a Which hospital:
  • has the longest wait for an appointment?
  • is more likely to treat the patient within 6 months?
  • will cost the most for the stay in hospital?

b What advice would you give to Dr Smith about the hospital trust to use?

Activity 9.9

a Ask a health or social care service of your choice whether they have a charter. Obtain a copy of it, if you can.

b Find out what information the service publishes about how it meets the charter standards.

Some trusts produce newsletters to inform people in the area about existing, new and improved services

Adapting communication to meet client needs

Most of the information that you have found about services available will have been written down. What did you find that was written in a language other than English? How do you think a person with little or no sight would be able to find out about services available?

Most caring services recognise that they need to adapt communication to meet the needs of different groups of people. Most leaflets are available in the major languages spoken by people living in the area. Where people do not speak English well, many services employ people to act as translators.

Sometimes interpreters are needed to assist communication

There are two other languages that are important in providing care information:
• Braille
• sign language.

Braille
Some visually-handicapped people are able to read words written as a code of raised dots. This language is called Braille. Many leaflets are translated into Braille so that information is available. Often information about these leaflets is broadcast on the radio during programmes such as 'In Touch'.

Written information for visually impaired people who have some vision is also available in large print.

Sign language
People with hearing difficulties are normally able to read information leaflets. When it comes to receiving care, it is important to ensure that the person involved understands as much as possible. In many cases, communication can involve using a standard sign language such as the British Sign Language.

Other adaptations are available to hearing-impaired people once they are in contact with the services. These includes an electronic 'phonic ear' hearing aid linked to a microphone that is worn by the carer.

Location of publicity

Sometimes it might be necessary to place posters and leaflets in specific places in order to reach particular groups of people. For example, it might be more effective to place a poster advertising a new clinic for drug users in a place where they are likely go.

Different styles or designs of leaflets or posters may also be found to be effective with different groups of people.

Activity 9.10

If you have the opportunity to talk to a health or care service provider (such as a visiting speaker to your class), ask how communication is adapted to meet client needs.

The Patient's Charter is available (free of charge) in 12 languages, and also in braille, in large print, as an audio cassette and as a sign language video

Test yourself

1 What are the three major sectors involved in health and social care?

2 What are the main services provided by your GP?

3 What are the main services provided by social services departments?

4 Which groups of people do not need to pay for NHS prescribed medicines?

5 What type of referral is it when a person goes to a GP?

6 How would a person normally be referred to a hospital specialist, and what type of referral is it?

7 Where could you find information about immunisation for a baby?

8 How might information about social services be given to a blind person?

9 What social service provision might help a young child who was being abused by his or her parents?

10 What voluntary sector organisation might help a child being abused by his or her parents?

Assignment A9.1
Local health and social care services

For this assignment you will investigate the health and social care services available in your local area. You will have to:
- describe their purpose
- identify who pays for the service
- explain how they are organised.

You will also need to identify how the national health and social care services are organised.

You will probably find it easier to carry out this assignment as a group activity in order to collect all the information you will need. This will also provide evidence for Optional Unit 4 if you are studying it. The information in Chapter 4 will help you to organise yourselves for this assignment.

Your tasks

1 As a group, decide who is going to investigate the different services. You could break it down as follows:
- **Health care**
  Hospitals, GP's surgeries, health centres, dentists, community health units/trusts
- **Social care**
  Residential care, community care
- **Voluntary groups**
  (including support groups)

2 Carry out your individual research. See page 290 for ideas for sources of information.

For example, if you have chosen to investigate the local hospitals:
a Make a list of all the hospitals in the area.

b For each hospital, decide:
- What is its purpose?
- Is it private or NHS?
- Does the client have to pay for the care?

> - How is it organised?

This preliminary research will also be used for Assignment A9.3 so keep a note of where you found information.

3 Write up your research as a short report covering all the points in Task 2.

4 As a group, combine your separate reports into a guide to local health and social care services.

Include some simple 'family tree' diagrams to show how the national health and social care services are organised and show where your local services fit on the diagrams.

To provide evidence for the core skills Information Technology and Application of Number:
- You could write your reports using word processors or other software packages.
- You could also illustrate them with appropriate charts, diagrams and tables (also created on computer, if possible). Use illustrations wherever possible to make the reports interesting.
- You could also mark all the local services on a map of the area, and create a key to identify hospitals, residential homes, etc.

Assignment A9.2
Access to services

For this assignment you will identify two local clients with different needs and investigate how they gained access to health and social care services. You will need to:
- identify the referral methods used
- identify the barriers to access experienced
- suggest how access could be improved.

Your tasks

1 Identify two clients with different needs using the same service.

These might be real people whom you have met on work placement. If so, ask their permission first and arrange to talk to them about their experiences of health and social care services.

Alternatively, you might make up two imaginary clients.

For example, if you choose to look at maternity services, consider how easy access would be for a pregnant woman who is physically fit and a one who uses a wheelchair.

You will need to consider:
- how they were each referred to the service (in this example, it would

probably be self-referral)
- where the antenatal classes are held
- where the maternity hospital/wards are
- what the car parking facilities are like for the pregnant women
- what public transport is available, and what areas are not served by it
- what transport can be provided by the service (ambulance?)
- how easy it is to physically get into the building:
  - Are there ramps, lifts, steps?
  - Are the doors easy to open?
  - Are there areas to rest before a journey home?
  - Is there easy access to toilets?
  - Is the lighting near the entrance appropriate?
  - Are there areas where a person might feel vulnerable to being approached by strangers?

2   Write a short report about what you have found out and suggest how you could improve access to the service.

3   When you have considered your chosen service, compare your conclusions with the rest of your group. Produce some guidelines you would give to people wishing to improve access to services.

When you are planning the guidelines, consider how you could provide evidence of the core skills. See Assignment A9.1.

Assignment A9.3
Communicating information in health and social care

In Assignment A9.1 you researched information about the local health and social care services. In this assignment you are going to use that information again.

This is a group activity. The outcome will be an individual investigation of two local services:
- the main sources of information for each
- the ways of publicising and communicating the information
- how the communication has been adapted to meet different client needs.

Your tasks

1   a As a group, decide who is going to investigate which services.

   b Look at the information you collected for Assignment A9.1. Is any more research necessary for the services you have chosen? Discuss other possible sources of information.

b Collect any further information you need from each source and clearly label where it came from.

Collect as many different versions of the same leaflet as you can find. They may be printed in different languages, available on cassette tape or in Braille, for example.

If you find that there is only one leaflet left, **do not take it**. Tell the person in charge that there is only one leaflet. If you did take the leaflet, it might mean that someone in need of the service would be unable to find out about it.

2   Individually, sort out the information you now have on your two chosen services. Prepare a short report or display including the following:
   • the main sources of information for each service (and give examples)
   • the ways of publicising used (for example, the media, the service itself, health and care workers)
   • the methods of communication used (oral, written, graphical, statistical)
   • examples of how the communication has been adapted to meet clients' needs.

3   As a group, prepare a short leaflet to advise people as to what types of information are available from each of the sources you have used.

Key words

After reading this chapter you should be able to understand the following words and phrases. If you do not, go back through the chapter and find out, or look them up in the Glossary.

National Health Service (NHS)	*Physical needs*
Social services	*Intellectual needs*
Private sector	*Emotional needs*
Voluntary sector	*Social needs*
NHS trusts	*Self-referral*
Compulsory referral	*Referral through a professional*

APPENDIX A:

Glossary

Adolescence The period of life between the onset of puberty at about 11 to the beginning of adult life at 18

Advertisement A public notice to sell something, in this case to tell people that a vacancy for a job exists

Allergic condition A reaction to a substance, such as pollen, smoke, animals, foods. May take the form of breathing problems (asthma), a rash, vomiting or sneezing

Application form A form supplied by an employer for an applicant to complete with details about him or herself

Assistive equipment Equipment that allows a person to live as independent a life as possible in their own home

Balanced diet A diet that provides you with enough of the various types of nutrient to meet your needs, with neither too much nor too little of anything

Basic health needs Physical (food, water, warmth, etc.), social (for relationships), emotional (to be valued, respected, etc.), intellectual (learning, problem-solving)

Body language Communication with or without speaking, involving facial expressions, eye contact, posture, gestures

Brainstorming An intensive discussion to solve problems or generate ideas

Carbohydrate A macronutrient in two forms: digestible starch (potatoes and grains) and indigestible cellulose, one of the things that makes up dietary fibre, *see also* **Fibre** and **Macronutrients**

Compulsory referral Access to health or social care in which either a doctor or a social worker identifies a person unable to make a decision for themselves

Confidentiality The practice of keeping to yourself what a client has told you in confidence

Constructive feedback Responding, verbally and non-verbally, to what someone has said or done in a fair and positive way, without criticism

Covering letter A letter to accompany a CV or application form

Curriculum vitae (CV) A summary written by a job applicant of the relevant information that an employer needs to know

Daily living activities Things we do every day, such as eating, walking, hearing or seeing

Day centre A service provided by the social services and by some voluntary organisations for elderly or disabled people to socialise and have a meal

Degenerative disease A disease which gradually worsens over time, such as atheroma (of arteries supplying the brain or the heart), osteo-arthritis, Alzheimer's disease, cancer

Diet The food and drink that a person regularly consumes

Diploma in Social Work The new professional qualification for all social workers

Directed thinking The ability to concentrate on one task and finish it

Empower To offer a person choice and so give them a sense of dignity and worth

Fat A macronutrient. A group of chemicals, some of which are essential in the diet. An energy source found in animal and plant products, but excess fat is stored under the skin, *see also* **Macronutrients**

Fibre Indigestable form of carbohydrate, mainly from plants (vegetables and grains), *see also* **Carbohydrate**

First aider A person trained in first aid and who has gained a first aid certificate. The certificate has to be renewed every three years

Health care support worker Someone who assists health care professionals with practical tasks in hospitals, clinics and community nursing

Health plan A plan to improve or maintain health and well-being

Identity The things about you that make you different to everyone else

Intellectual recreational activities Activities which involve learning or problem-solving, such as reading and chess

Intelligence The ability to understand

Interpersonal communication Communication between two or more people, verbal or non-verbal

Language The organised system of sounds and symbols which humans use to communicate and establish relationships with one another

Life expectancy The number of years a person can expect to live

Macronutrients Nutrients that we need in large amounts, *see also* **Carbohydrate**, **Fat** and **Protein**

Major life changes A death, moving house, marriage, divorce, changing school, unemployment/redundancy

Mandatory A mandatory sign indicates something you must do (blue circle)

Menopause A series of changes in hormones which begins at any time after 40 and which eventually means the end of a woman's ability to have children. Also known as 'the change of life'

Micronutrients Nutrients that we need in very small amounts, *see also* **Vitamins** and **Minerals**

Microbes Living organisms, or micro-organisms, so small that we need a microscope to see them: bacteria, viruses, fungi, protozoa

Minerals Micronutrients – calcium, chlorine, cobalt, fluorine, iodine, iron, magnesium, phosphorus, potassium, sodium, zinc, *see also* **Micronutrients**

Monitoring a person's ability To keep a continuous check on a person's skill in particular tasks

Monogamy The custom of one woman having one husband, or one man having one wife

Moving and handling techniques Ways to moving and handling clients that are safe both for the client and the person doing the lifting

Mutual exchange The giving and receiving of information between two or more people

National Health Service (NHS) The statutory health care service, set up by an Act of Parliament and funded by public money

National Vocational Qualifications (NVQs) Qualifications which recognise the skills of previously untrained, unqualified staff. NVQs measure what you can do, as well as how much you know and understand about the job

NHS trusts A unit (such as a hospital or an ambulance service) that has opted for trust status. They manage their own money, employ their own staff and tender for contracts to provide care

Note-taking Making notes of important points you wish to remember

Nutrients The components of food *see also* **Macronutrients** and **Micronutrients**

Oestrogen The hormone that produces female characteristics in girls during puberty

Passive smoking Tobacco smoke inhaled by non-smokers in the vicinity of smokers

Personality The things about you that make you different to everyone else

Physical recreational activities Activities which involve physical exercise such as sport, walking, jogging and dancing

Plasma Colourless fluid in blood

Polyandry The custom of one woman having several husbands

Polygamy The custom of one husband having several wives

Pre-school child A child between the ages of 3 and 5

Private sector Health and social care services provided by private organisations

Prohibition A prohibition sign indicates something you must not do (red circle and red cross bar)

Project 2000 The new three-year training programme for nurses

Protein A macronutrient and source of amino acids, used to make proteins in the body, *see also* **Macronutrients**

Psycho-social Something which is both psychological and social

Puberty The time (starting at about the age of 11) when physical changes occur as a result of increased production of sex hormones: oestrogen in girls and testosterone in boys

Recording Making notes, writing reports, making audio or video recordings to be used as evidence of what you have done, both as a team and individually

Recruitment The process of finding someone to fill a vacancy

Reference nutrient intake (RNI) The amount of a nutrient that will meet the needs of 95 per cent of people (similar to the recommended daily allowance quoted in some books, but normally higher)

Referral through a professional Access to health or social care where a doctor, social worker, nurse, teacher or other professional may assist an individual to obtain care

Registered General Nurse (RGN) A nurse who works in a hospital, carrying out practical tasks, such as giving injections, dressing wounds, administering drugs, washing and feeding patients

Risks to health Poor diet, lack of exercise, poor personal hygiene, drug abuse (including alcohol and tobacco), unsafe sexual practices

Safe condition A safe condition sign indicates a safe way of doing something (green rectangle)

Safety hazards Situations in which a person's safety may be affected

Self-esteem How you feel about yourself. When you have self-esteem, you value yourself and feel confident because you know you have the esteem of others

Self-referral Access to health or social care where an individual seeks help themselves

Signs of shock Anxiety, pale skin, cold, sweating, restlessness, shallow breathing, rapid pulse, pain, great thirst

Social recreational activities Activities which involve interaction with other people, such as parties, family outings and gatherings of people with similar interests

Social services The statutory social care service run by local authorities, set up by an Act of Parliament and funded by public money

Socialisation A process that continues throughout life. It means to become part of society by learning the 'rules' of how to behave

Stereotyping A standard image of a group of people held by another group of people, for example 'Young people today don't respect their elders'

Team action plan A plan that records all the tasks to be carried out by a team, who will do each task, and the date by which it should be done

Testosterone The hormone that produces male characteristics in boys during puberty

Time management How fit all the tasks you have to do into the time available

Toxic effects Harmful effects caused by poisonous substances

Vegetarian Someone who eats no meat or fish, but who does eat eggs, milk and milk products. Someone who eats no animal products is called a vegan

Vitamins Micronutrients – vitamins A, B_1, B_2, B_5, B_6, B_{12}, C, D, E, K, *see also* **Micronutrients**

Voluntary sector Health and social care services provided by voluntary organisations, such as charities and self-help groups

Warning A warning sign indicates a risk of danger (yellow triangle with black outline)

APPENDIX B:

Bibliography

Chapter 1: Understanding Health and Well-being
Anderson, J., *Health Skills for Life* (Nelson, 1994)
Mackean, D, and Jones, A., *Human and Social Biology* (John Murray, 1992, 2nd edition)
Mansfield, P., *The Good Health Handbook* (Grafton Books, 1988)
Taylor, D., *Human Physical Health* (Cambridge University Press, 1989)

Chapter 2: Understanding Personal Development and Relationships
Adams, R., *Skilled Work with People* (Collins Educational, 1994)
Penny, S., *Examining Relationships* (Heinemann, 1993)
Trobe, K., *Understanding Race Relations* (Stanley Thornes, 1991)
Parents and Teenagers (The Open University/Harper & Row, 1982)

Chapter 3: Investigating Working in Health and Social Care
Collins, H., *Human Resource Management* (Hodder & Stoughton, 1993)
Irving, J., Munday, S. and Rowlands, A., *Pathways into Caring* (Stanley Thornes, 1993)
Tossell, D. and Webb, R., *Inside the Caring Services* (Edward Arnold, 1994)

Chapter 4: Contributing to a Team Activity
Armitage, A., *Do it yourself* (Edward Arnold, 1981)
Hutchings, S., Comins, J. and Offiler, J., *The Social Skills Handbook* (Winslow Presss, 1991)
Owler, P., *Investigating the Media* (Collins Educational, 1992)

Chapter 5: Investigating Common Health Emergencies
Happs, I. and Penny, S., *Examining Health* (Heinemann, 1993)
St John Ambulance/St Andrew's Ambulance Association/British Red Cross, *First Aid Manual* (Dorling Kindersley, 1992)
Essentials of Health and Safety at Work (Health & Safety Executive, 1992)
HSE publications are obtainable from: Health & Safety Executive, Library and Information Services, Baynards House, 1 Chepstow Place, Westbourne Grove, London W2 4TF (0171 2210870).

Chapter 6: Planning Diets
Madden, D., *Food and Nutrition* (Gill & Macmillan, 1980)
Secretary of State for Health, *The Health of the Nation: A Strategy for Health in England* (HMSO,1992)
Tables showing the composition of foods (and other useful tables) can be found in:
Bender, A.E. and Bender, D.A., *Food Tables* (Oxford University Press, 1986)
MAFF, *Manual of Nutrition*, 10th edition (HMSO, 1995)

Chapter 7: Exploring Health and Recreational Activities
Beashel, P. and Taylor, J., *Sport Examined* (Nelson, 1992, 2nd edition)
Finkelstein, V., *et al.*, *Disabling Barriers: Enabling Environments* (Sage, 1993)

Chapter 8: Exploring Physical Care
Smyth, T., *Caring for Older People* (Macmillan, 1992)
Stoyle, J., *Caring for Older People* (Stanley Thornes, 1991)
Windmill, V., *Ageing Today* (Edward Arnold, 1990)

Chapter 9: Investigating Health and Care Service Provision
Family Welfare Association, *Guide to the Social Services*
Family Welfare Association, *Charities Digest*
Tossell, D. and Webb, R., *Inside the Caring Services* (Edward Arnold, 1994)

APPENDIX C:

Answers to Test Yourself questions

Chapter 1, page 32

1. Recreation, diet and exercise
2. Answers include: improved physical, mental and social well-being, reduced risk of disease, improved self-esteem, increased mobility
3. Answers include: lung cancer, emphysema, chest and throat infections, bronchitis, heart disease
4. The unborn baby, passive smokers
5. Gives a person something to aim for
6. Physical, social, emotional, intellectual
7. Basic health needs change as a child gains more independence and more opportunity to make choices for itself. Different levels of achievement will affect levels of need.
8. 4 units; no units
9. Predictable: moving school, moving house, starting work Unpredictable: sudden illness, death in family, unemployment
10. Answers include: depression, increased levels of stress, effects of changes in diet

Chapter 2, page 69

1. At birth
2. 3.5 kg
3. A child between 3 and 5 years
4. At about 11 years of age
5. At any time after the age of 40
6. To make social, to become part of society, to observe the behaviours, values and rules of society
7. Mental and emotional distress
8. A group of people who are about the same age, share similar interests and value each other's opinions
9. The need for food, drink, sleep, sensory pleasure, maternal behaviour and sexual desire
10. Confidentiality establishes a relationship of trust between a client and carer.

Chapter 3, page 106

1. Nurses, physiotherapists, occupational therapists, radiographers and social workers
2. Project 2000
3. Childcare, provision and regulation of residential accommodation, welfare services for old people and statutory powers under the various Mental Health Acts
4. Diploma in Social Work
5. Diploma in Nursery Nursing, BTEC National Diploma or Certificate in Nursery Nursing
6. Job centres, the careers service, local press, employment agencies, Community Care, Nursing Times and the British Medical Journal
7. The skills, knowledge, education, experience and qualifications necessary for the job.
8. A written summary of your personal details, education, qualifications and experience.
9. The date, place, time and length of the interview, who to report to and when you will be told of the outcome
10. A form sent out by an employer asking an applicant for personal details, education details and details of work experience

Chapter 4, page 136

1. For security, to help others, to get things done

2 A group of people share and write down individual contributions concerning a particular problem or task
3 Planning an activity within the time allocated
4 Who do you need to contact, how you will contact them, what you want them to do
5 To provide an accurate, written record
6 A plan to co-ordinate what each member will do, setting targets, standards and deadlines for action
7 Different: ethnic backgrounds, social class, cultural or religious beliefs, social values, sex
8 Looking back at what you have done, deciding what needs to be done in the future
9 Telling people what you are doing, explain things to people, responding to their conversation
10 Body language

Chapter 5, page 172
1 One where matters of safety, hygiene, welfare, comfort and cleanliness are applied
2 It must be carried out or adhered to
3 The inhalation of other people's tobacco smoke
4 A trained person who has a valid first aid certificate
5 Not moving or handling a person or a load in proper manner
6 Anxious expression; pale skin; restlessness; cold skin, yet soaked in sweat; rapid and shallow breathing; rapid and feeble pulse; pain and thirst
7 Sit the casualty up in a comfortable position. Loosen their clothing. Lean them slightly forward. Ensure there is plenty of fresh air. Call a doctor or ambulance. Help them to use inhaler if they have one. Give lots of reassurance.
8 Open airway. Try to remove the obstruction with finger. If cannot, give sharp blows with the heal of the hand between the shoulder-blades to dislodge it. Ensure the casualty's head is lower than their chest. If cannot clear obstruction, give abdominal thrusts. If this fails, get the person to hospital as soon as possible. If a baby or child is choking, hold it upside down by ankles and smack back to dislodge obstruction. Only use abdominal thrusts on children over 5.
9 Open fracture – the broken bone penetrates the skin; closed fracture – no open wound; greenstick fracture – a partial break, common in children.
10 A – Airway; B – Breathing; C – Circulation

Chapter 6, page 206
1 Proteins, fats, carbohydrates, vitamins, minerals, fibre, water
2 a   Proteins, fats, carbohydrates (including fibre)
  b   Vitamins, minerals
3 Growth and repair
4 Vitamin C
5 Reduces the risk of cancer of the colon, increases speed of passage of food through digestive system
6 Because of the child's size and its rate of growth
7 Vegetables and fruit
8 Anything from an animal
9 Muslims, Jews
10 Strain on the heart, strain on the joints

Chapter 7, page 236
1 Social, physical and intellectual
2 Intellectual (chess also social)
3 Social and physical
4 Answers include: dancing, attendance at any club, team sports, quiz nights, etc.
5 Attitudes, costs, physical access, availability

6 Cost, stereotyping by adults
7 Poor self-esteem, attitudes of others
8 Social, physical and intellectual stimulation and well-being; improved health
9 Answers include: walking, swimming, golf, dancing
10 Danger of broken bones, lack of joint suppleness, risks associated with less efficient breathing and circulation

Chapter 8, pages 263-4
1 Activities such as eating, walking, hearing and seeing.
2 Atheroma: The build-up of fatty deposits on the walls of the arteries giving rise to coronary heart disease and strokes. Osteo-arthritis: Changes in the joints giving rise to pain and loss of mobility. Brain degeneration: Caused by either Alzheimer's disease (excessive degeneration of the nerve cells) or atheroma of arteries supplying the brain. Both can lead to gradual loss of intellectual power and ability. Cancer: There is an increase in the incidence of many cancers with advancing age.
3 Transport, wheelchairs, aids to daily living, home helps, nursing aids, vehicles, recreation and house adaptations
4 Wear flat comfortable shoes. Remove rings and watches. Explain to the client what you are going to do. Clear the area. If two lifters, co-operate to lift together. Do not rush. Do not drag the client. Apply all the general rules of lifting.
5 Be sensitive to their needs. Listen to what they are saying. Do not to 'talk down' to them. Do not to label those elderly people with disabilities. Negotiate with the client, carer and any other professionals. Give appropriate support as necessary.
6 Body language is a way of communicating with people, in addition to speaking - by the way we use our face, the way we stand, sit or gesture.
7 Not to pass information told to you in confidence by a client to anyone else.
8 Social services department, National Health Service, the private sector or voluntary organisations
9 Information about services and assistive equipment available and help to get people appropriate support, visit people and provide support
10 A voluntary support scheme for people in their own homes, offering temporary or regular care relief, providing support and a rest for the carer by allowing the volunteer to attend to the personal needs of the client

Chapter 9, page 294
1 Statutory, voluntary, private
2 Diagnosis of illness, treatment of illness or referral to a specialist doctor, special clinics for children, expectant mothers, etc. Find out more from your own GP.
3 Support and care for children in need, elders, families, people with different abilities
4 Answers will probably include people in receipt of certain benefits and those with specific illnesses. You will need to check what is the most up-to-date information.
5 Self-referral
6 By a GP; referral by a professional
7 Health centre, GP, health visitor
8 By talking to them, using Braille or by audio-tape
9 Foster care or family care
10 NSPCC

Index

ABC rule 153
access to services 285–90
Access to Personal Files Act 68
accident book 140
activities of daily living 66
administrators 88
adolescence 44–7, 62, 195, 216, 220
adults 47–50, 62–3, 195–6
ageing 49
AIDS 25, 26
airway 153, 154
alcohol 21–2, 190, 191
Alzheimer's disease 19, 242, 287
anaemia 16, 188, 196
application form 99, 102, 103
applying for a job 99–102
artificial respiration 155–6, 164, 171
assessment 64–6, 68
assistive equipment 255–9
asthma 158–9
atheroma 242

balanced diet 183–93
balancing diets 193–204
bandaging methods 164
basic human needs 11–13, 38, 55, 64–6, 67, 285
bleeding 164
blood and body fluids 152
body language 133–4, 250–2
brain degeneration 242
brainstorming 114
broken bones 167–9
burns 162–3

calcium 16, 189, 196
cancer 242
carbohydrate 178, 182–3, 190, 191, 202, 203
cardio-pulmonary resuscitation (CPR) 156–7
care assistant 90–3, 282
career paths 90
chemical burn 162

chest massage 156–7, 164
children 39–44, 60–2, 194–5, 213, 216, 217–19, 280–1
Children Act 1989 84
choking 166–7
Chronically Sick and Disabled Persons Act 1971 261
cleanliness 139
clerical jobs 88
client rights 68–9
closed fracture 167–8
comfort 139
communicating information 290–4
community-based health care services 276–8
community–based social services 276, 282
community care plan 243
Community Health Service 277
community nurses 277
compulsory referral 285, 286
concussion 160–1
conditions of employment 98
confidentiality 67–9, 254–5
Control of Substances Hazardous to Health Regulations 1988 (COSHH) 142–3
covering letter 99, 101
culture 200–1, 215
cultural needs 64
curriculum vitae (CV) 99–100
cuts 152, 164–5

daily living activities 239
day centre 234, 247, 263
degenerative diseases 242
dementia 19
Department of Social Security (DSS) 261
dentists 83–4, 277, 278
diabetes 202–3
diet 3, 14–16, 31, 59, 177–209
dignity 239, 249–55
disinfecting 152

District Health Authorities (DHAs) 272
district nurses 79–80, 262, 277
doctors 76–8
domestic staff 88
drug abuse 22–3, 24

education 55
elders 50–3, 196, 214, 216, 220–1, 234–5, 280
electric shock 163–4
emotional development 40–1, 43, 44, 46
emotional needs 11, 12, 13, 38, 64, 285
emotional support 243
employment 95–106
empower 249
energy 187, 193, 201–2
epilepsy 159–60
European Community Manual Handling Regulations 1993 148, 247
exercise 3–9, 16–17, 31

family 52–3, 53–4, 55, 216, 221
Family Health Service Authority (FHSA) 77, 273, 276
fat 178, 181–2, 190–1
feedback 118, 133–5
fibre 182–3, 187–8, 191, 203
fire fighting 146
fire hazards 144–7
Fire Precautions Act 1971 144
fire rules 145
first aid 153
first aid box 147
first aider 147, 153
first aid regulations 147–8
fitness 214
foreign bodies 164
foster care 281
fractures 167–9

general practitioners (GPs) 77–8, 243, 262, 276–7

greenstick fracture 167–8
grief 28
group membership 57–8, 62, 112

handling and lifting 137, 148–51, 247–9
hazard warning signs 142, 143
head injuries 160–1
health and safety 125, 131, 233–4
Health & Safety at Work Act 1974 138
Health & Safety Executive 147
Health & Safety (First Aid) Regulations 1981 147
health and safety officer 141
health and well-being 1–35
health care support workers/assistants (HCA) 83, 279
health centres 277
health plan 11
health visitors 77, 80, 277
heart attack 169–70
HIV 25, 26
hoists 256–7
home care staff 85–6
homelessness 19
hospital-based health care services 276, 278–9
hospital doctors 76–7
hospitals 76, 262, 278–9
housing 56, 57, 60
hygiene and welfare 139

identity 44, 60, 254
independence 239, 249–55, 259–63
information 287–8, 290–4
illegal drugs 24
individual action plan 120, 126–8
infectious disease 151–2
intellectual activities 211, 223
intellectual development 40–1, 42, 43, 46–7
intellectual needs 11, 12, 13, 55, 64, 285
interpersonal communication 124
interpersonal skills 133

interview 102, 104–6
iron 16, 188–9, 196

job advertisements 49, 96–7
job description 98
job specification 102

language 55, 61–2
learning 52, 61
leisure 59
levels of consciousness 154
life stage 49
lifting 148–51, 247–9
lifting equipment 256–7
listening 253

macronutrients 177, 178, 179–83
maintenance staff 88
major changes 27–31
managers 88
mandatory signs 139
Maslow's theory of human needs 12, 64–6
meals-on-wheels 86
Medical Records Act 68
meeting clients' needs 66–7
memory 51–2
Mental Health Act 68
menopause 16, 49, 51, 189, 196
microbes 151
micronutrients 177, 178–9, 180
midwives 77, 80, 277
minerals 177, 180, 188–90
mobile hoists 148–9
mobility 239, 258–9
mouth-to-mouth resuscitation 155–7
moving and handling techniques 247–9

National Advisory Committee on Nutrition Education (NACNE) 190–2
National Assistance Act 1948 84
National Health Service (NHS) 75–84, 260, 262, 269, 271–3, 284
National Vocational Qualifications (NVQs) 88
needs of clients 64–7

NHS and Community Care Act 1990 271, 273, 278
NHS trusts 273
nicotine 20
non-verbal communication 133–4, 250–2
note-taking 118–19
numeracy 55
nursery nurses 86, 93–5
nurses 78–80, 277–8, 279
nutrients 177–83

occupational first aider 147
occupational therapists 82–3, 243, 261, 277, 279
oestrogen 45
old age 50, 241–2
open fracture 167–8
opticians 84
osteo-arthritis 242
osteoporosis 16, 189

passive smoking 144
Patient's Charter 68, 290–1, 294
peer groups 58, 62
personal care 256
personal development 37–60
personal hygiene 17–18, 31
personality 51, 60
personal relationships 43, 60–3, 63–9
personal support 245
physical access 226–8, 288
physical activities 211, 222–3
physical aids 245–6, 247
physical care 239–65
physical development 40–1, 42, 43, 45–6
physical disabilities 231–2
physical needs 11, 12, 13, 38, 64, 285
physiotherapists 81, 243, 277, 279
planning diets 204–6
planning a team activity 111–25
poisoning 170–1
poverty line 20, 59
power 63, 249
practice nurses 79, 277
primary groups 58

private sector services 75, 89, 260, 262, 269, 275–6, 284
prohibition signs 129
Project 2000 78
prone position 154
protein 178, 179–81, 190, 191, 203–4
puberty 44–5

radiographers 80–1, 279
receptionists 88
recording 123–4
recovery position 154–5, 160, 161, 164, 170, 171
recreational activities 9, 211–38
recruitment 95–6
redundancy 49
referral through a professional 285–6
reference nutrient intake (RNI) 184, 185, 193, 201, 204–5
Regional Health Authorities (RHAs) 272
Registered General Nurses (RGNs) 78
Registered Homes Act 1984 85
Registered Mental Nurses (RMNs) 78
Registered Nurses for the Mentally Handicapped (RNMHs) 78
relationships 23, 43, 60–3, 63–9
relaxation 9–11, 31
religion 200–1

residential social care 276, 279–81
restricted mobility 244–7
resuscitation 155–7, 170
retirement 49, 52
reviewing 125–6, 128–35
rickets 189
risks to health 11–31

safe condition signs 139
safe use of chemicals 166
safety needs 65
safety policy 138
salt 191
scalds 162–3
school nurses 80, 277
secondary groups 58
self-actualisation needs 66
self-esteem 11, 62, 66, 233
self-fulfilment needs 66
self-image 3, 44
self-referral 285
sexual practice 23, 25
sexual relationships 48
sexually transmitted disease 25, 26
skeletal growth 47
sheltered housing 57, 280
shock 158, 165
sleep 9–11
smoking 20–1, 144, 145
social activities 211, 224
social development 40–1, 43, 46
socialisation 55, 56, 60–1, 214

social needs 11, 12, 13, 64, 65, 285
social services 75, 84–7, 260, 261–2, 269, 273–4, 284
social services committee 84–5
social worker 85, 243
special diets 201–4
speech therapists 83, 277, 279
stereotyping 56, 214
stress 27, 28, 29, 30, 137
support groups 262, 282

team action plan 120–3
team activity 111–136
testosterone 45
theory of human needs 12, 64–6
time management 115–16
toxic effects of chemicals 143

undertaking a role in a team activity 126–8

vegan diet 203
vegetarian diet 188, 203–4
vitamin D 16, 189, 195, 201
vitamins 178–9, 188–90
voluntary sector services 75, 89, 260, 262, 269, 274–5, 282

W position 170
warning signs 139
weight-reduction diets 201–2
Women's Royal Voluntary Service (WRVS) 89